THE OTHER AMERICAN DRAMA

MARC ROBINSON

THE JOHNS HOPKINS UNIVERSITY PRESS
BALTIMORE AND LONDON

Printed in the United States of America on acid-free paper

Originally published in a hardcover edition by Cambridge University Press, 1994
Johns Hopkins Paperbacks edition, 1997
06 05 04 03 02 01 00 99 98 97 5 4 3 2 1

The Johns Hopkins University Press
2715 North Charles Street
Baltimore, Maryland 21218-4319
The Johns Hopkins Press Ltd., London

Library of Congress Cataloging-in-Publication Data

Robinson, Marc, 1962–
The other American drama / Marc Robinson.
p. cm.
Originally published: Cambridge : Cambridge University Press, 1994.
Includes bibliographical references and index.
ISBN 0-8018-5630-2 (pbk. : alk. paper)
1. American drama—20th century—History and criticism. 2. Experimental drama, American—History and criticism. I. Title.
PS350.R63 1997
812´.5409—dc21 96-53224
CIP

A catalog record for this book is available from the British Library.

THE OTHER AMERICAN DRAMA

PAJ BOOKS

Bonnie Marranca and Gautam Dasgupta
Series Editors

For April Bernard

CONTENTS

Ladies' Voices by Gertrude Stein. Presented by the Living Theater, New York, 1951. *Left to right:* Judith Malina and Helen Jacobs. Photograph by Carl Van Vechten.

Four Saints in Three Acts by Gertrude Stein. Directed by John Houseman at the Wadsworth Athenaeum, Hartford, 1934. Photograph by White Studio.

Doctor Faustus Lights the Lights by Gertrude Stein. Directed by Robert Wilson at the Hebbel Theater, Berlin, 1992. Photograph by Archie Kent.

Four Saints in Three Acts by Gertrude Stein and Virgil Thomson. Directed by Robert Wilson at the Houston Grand Opera and the New York State Theater, 1996. *Foreground, left to right:* Suzanna Guzman (St. Theresa II) and Ashley Putnam (St. Theresa I). Photograph by Ken Howard.

Suddenly Last Summer by Tennessee Williams. Directed by JoAnne Akalaitis at Hartford Stage, 1994. *Left to right:* Mark Deakins (Dr. Cukrowicz) and Anita Gillette (Mrs. Venable). Photograph by T. Charles Erickson.

Cowboy Mouth by Sam Shepard. Directed by Bob Glaudini at the American Place Theatre, New York, 1971. *Left to right:* Sam Shepard (Slim) and Patti Smith (Cavale). Photograph by Gerard Malanga.

Buried Child by Sam Shepard. Directed by Marcus Stern at the American Repertory Theatre, Cambridge, 1996. *Left to right:* Jeremy Geidt (Dodge), Charles Levin (Bradley), Jack Willis (Tilden). Photograph by Richard Feldman.

Fefu and Her Friends by Maria Irene Fornes. Directed by Lisa Peterson at the Yale Repertory Theatre, New Haven, 1992. *Left to right:* Julianna Margulies (Emma), Tonia Rowe (Paula), Mary Magdalena Hernández (Sue). Photograph by Gerry Goodstein.

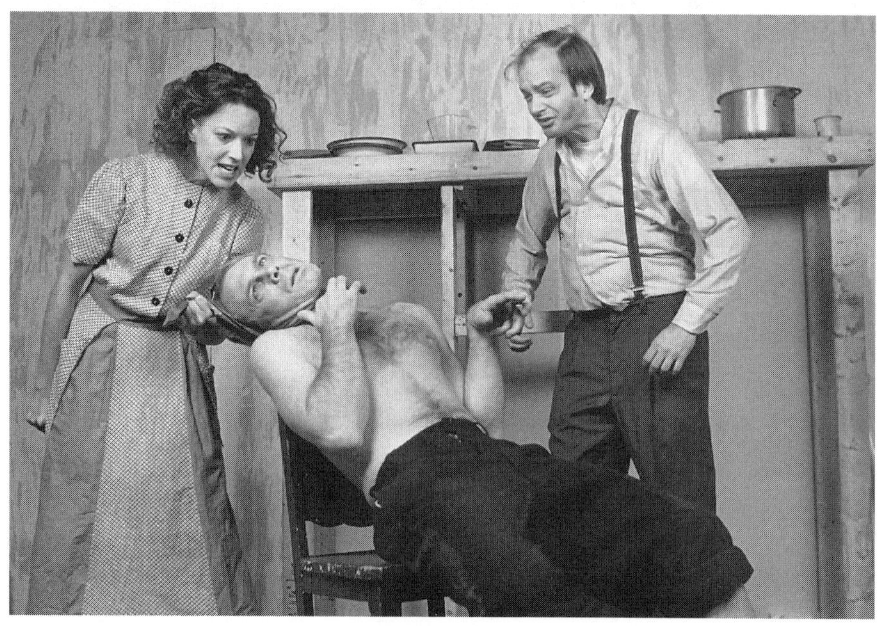

Mud by Maria Irene Fornes. Directed by Maria Irene Fornes at Theatre for the New City, New York, 1983. Photograph by Carol Halebian.

The Danube by Maria Irene Fornes. Directed by Maria Irene Fornes at the American Place Theatre, New York, 1982. *Left to right:* Kate Collins (Eve), Richard Sale (Paul), Thomas Kopache (Mr. Sandor). Photograph by Martha Holmes.

The Ohio State Murders by Adrienne Kennedy. Directed by Gerald Freedman at Great Lakes Theater Festival, Cleveland, 1991. *Pictured:* Ruby Dee (Suzanne). Photograph by Roger Mastroianni.

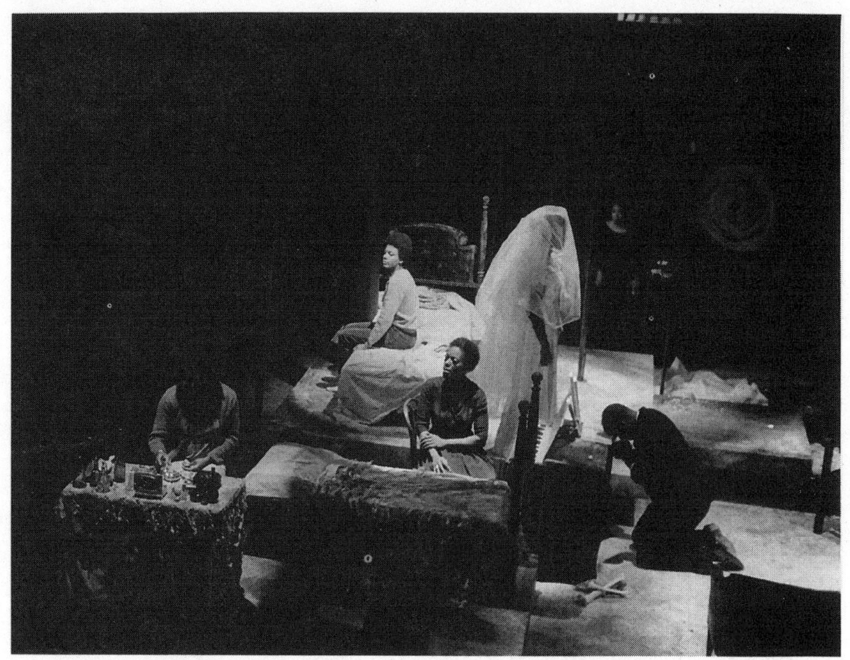

A Beast Story by Adrienne Kennedy. Directed by Gerald Freedman at the New York Shakespeare Festival, 1969. Photograph by George E. Joseph.

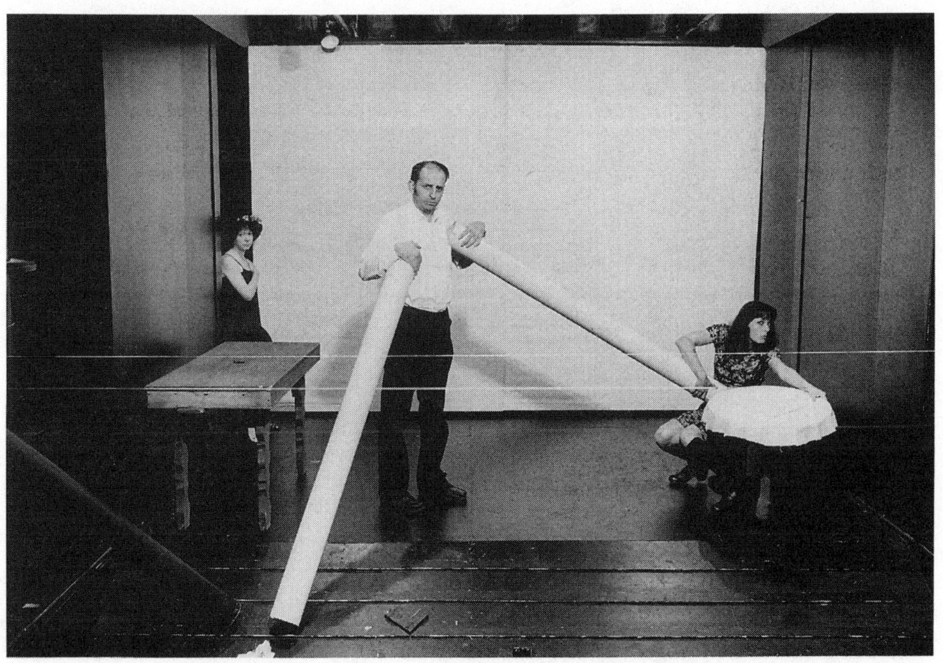

Rhoda in Potatoland by Richard Foreman. Directed by Richard Foreman at the Ontological-Hysteric Theater, New York, 1975. *Left to right:* Rena Gill (Sophia), Bob Fleischner (Max), Kate Manheim (Rhoda). Photograph by Babette Mangolte.

What Did He See? by Richard Foreman. Directed by Richard Foreman at the New York Shakespeare Festival, 1988. *Left to right:* Will Patton and Rocco Sisto. Photograph by Martha Swope.

Aunt Dan and Lemon by Wallace Shawn. Directed by Max Stafford-Clark at the New York Shakespeare Festival, 1985. *Left to right:* Kathryn Pogson (Lemon) and Linda Hunt (Aunt Dan). Photograph by Martha Swope.

2 Samuel 11, Etc. by David Greenspan. Directed by David Greenspan at Home for Contemporary Theatre and Art, New York, 1990. *Pictured:* Ron Bagden (Character 1).

The America Play by Suzan-Lori Parks. Directed by Liz Diamond at the Yale Repertory Theatre and the New York Shakespeare Festival, 1994. *Foreground, left to right:* Gail Grate (Lucy), Reggie Montgomery (The Foundling Father, on television), Michael Potts (Brazil). Photograph by T. Charles Erickson.

Murder of Crows by Mac Wellman. Directed by Jim Simpson at Primary Stages, New York, 1992. *Foreground, left to right:* Lauren Hamilton (Georgia), Stephen Mellor (Raymond), Annie O'Sullivan (Nella), William Mesnick (Howard). Photograph by Marvin Einhorn.

ACKNOWLEDGMENTS

I WOULD NOT HAVE BEEN ABLE to begin work on this book without the generosity of the MacDowell Colony, the Edward Albee Foundation, the Edna St. Vincent Millay Colony, and the Ragdale Foundation. Each of these colonies provided priceless time and a protective environment in which to write – as well as the friendship of fellow writers, several of whom were helpful readers of these essays.

Many critics have written well about the drama discussed here – in some cases, championing the playwrights when the rest of the theater community was looking the other way. In fact, I had read *about* Maria Irene Fornes, Richard Foreman, and Suzan-Lori Parks before ever seeing one of their plays. When finally I did attend performances of *Fefu and Her Friends* and *The Cure* and *The America Play,* I went with the sympathies and perceptions of their best critics echoing in my mind. I owe a particular debt to the work of several predecessors: Kate Davy on Richard Foreman, Elinor Fuchs on Adrienne Kennedy, Richard Gilman on Sam Shepard and Tennessee Williams, Bonnie Marranca on Shepard, Foreman, and Maria Irene Fornes, Gordon Rogoff on Williams, Alisa Solomon on Suzan-Lori Parks, and Ross Wetzsteon on Fornes, Shepard, and Wallace Shawn. No less illuminating, of course, have been the words of the playwrights themselves in essays, interviews, lectures, and program notes.

Three critics read this book in its earliest form and offered invaluable responses. Gordon Rogoff and Richard Gilman were sounding boards when I had only a few inchoate ideas about American drama. They allowed me to talk through my first readings of plays, pointed out much that I had overlooked, and steered me to related writing that powerfully influenced my thinking. Stanley Kauffmann read the finished manuscript with care and enthusiasm, as thoughtful in his responses to the smallest matters of style as he was to large matters of critical approach.

A number of other people generously consented to read all or part of the manuscript; I hope that the finished book well reflects their comments. I am especially thankful to Robert Brustein, Valerie Cornell, Gautam Dasgupta, Elana Greenfield, Laura Kauffmann, Jennifer Krauss, Herb Leibowitz, Bonnie Marranca, Sigrid Nunez, and Ross Wetzsteon. Frank Lentricchia of the *South Atlantic Quarterly* and Erika Munk of *Theater* magazine enabled me to try out two of these essays in somewhat different form in their journals, and they enhanced the final versions with their editorial advice.

Various other kinds of help – from putting me up for a week of writing, to sending me an unpublished script, to offering thoughts on these plays from a director's perspective – have come from Carol Bellini-Sharp, Stephanie Coen, Paula Court, Scott Cummings, Clark Dougan, Suzanne Palmer Dougan, Cheryl Faver, David Feiner, Seth Goldstein, David Herskovits, Pam Jordan, Leon Katz, Douglas Langworthy, Gloria Loomis, Donna Moy, Steve Oxman, Janice Paran, Gillian Richards, Irene Rothberg, Steve Samuels, Glen Seator, and Marcus Stern. My parents have been reliable supporters all along, inspiring harder work by their steady interest.

At Cambridge University Press, T. Susan Chang, Michael Gnat, Julie Greenblatt, and Janet Polata ably guided this book through the editing and production processes. They were more patient than they needed to be with my many questions and qualms.

Finally, my wife, April Bernard, regularly took time away from her own writing to read multiple drafts of these chapters, and enriched them with her editorial suggestions and fresh thinking. She was also unstinting in her encouragement, instinctively ready with more when it was most needed. For that, for her infectious interest in drama, and for her love, this book is dedicated to her.

INTRODUCTION

What shall I love if not the enigma?
GIORGIO DE CHIRICO

THIS BOOK WAS BORN of a student's disenchantment. In the standard-issue anthologies and textbooks that I read in school, twentieth-century American drama always seemed sluggish, bloated, mechanical. The writers admitted to our pantheon paled when set alongside the more robust experiments of non-American artists, and collapsed outright when considered after the pioneering work of the nineteenth-century modern tradition. Like most students, I learned that modern American drama began with Eugene O'Neill. His ambition to limn all manner of suffering – and to dramatize how the accursed ones beat back guilt, loss of faith, and the burden of genealogy – set the scale of value for writers to come. Equally ambitious (if not as searching) writers lined up smartly behind O'Neill, becoming his heirs – among them, Clifford Odets, Arthur Miller, Lillian Hellman, and, in recent years, August Wilson. Situated nearby were landmarks by other, only slightly less celebrated writers: wet nostalgia like William Saroyan's *The Time of Your Life* and William Inge's *Come Back, Little Sheba;* a brigade of stirring, point-making social dramas by Sidney Kingsley and Robert Sherwood; overheated historical verse plays; drawing-room doodles with champagne chitchat; and the odd genre-snubbing effort like Mary Chase's *Harvey*.

Many of these works were edifying in their way, occasionally (as in a few plays by O'Neill) even profound; but taken as a whole, the making of American drama, as it was being told, had an overwhelming predictability to it. For all the seriousness and intelligence of these writers, and despite the debt even the best of future artists owe them, few of their plays repaid added readings. After a while, the plays stopped giving. The one canonized writer who seemed most original, Tennessee Williams, was often discussed only as a naturalist, as though he were just like the others – his groundbreaking ideas of character and his poet's sense of language and image not nearly as interesting to these critics as were his bittersweet narratives.

If one believed the loudest historians, all good American drama in the first half of this century was essentially plot-based, built on the trusty model passed down by the melodramatists, in which a successful play begins with an exposition, leads inexorably to a conflict among characters (or between characters and their fates), and drives on to a climax and denouement. Stories are told. Crises ensue and resolve. Characters change. We identify.

Surely something had been left out. Couldn't there have been other kinds of drama unfolding at the same time? American art-history books don't discuss only Thomas Hart Benton and Maxfield Parrish; there is ample room for Marcel Duchamp and Man Ray, Marsden Hartley and Arthur Dove, each of whom gets his due. Music history isn't so besotted with George Gershwin that it ignores John Cage; literary critics nod to Carl Sandburg and Sinclair Lewis, but spend most of their time with T. S. Eliot, Ezra Pound, and William Faulkner. Historians of American theater seemed to have their priorities wrong.

Looking for the alternative in drama, I finally came across the plays of Gertrude Stein. She wasn't easy to find. Her theater has long been overlooked by critics and teachers; most people, I suspect, aren't even aware she wrote plays. Only a handful of her more than seventy dramatic works are still in print, and her famous pieces, *Four Saints in Three Acts* and *The Mother of Us All*, are known more for Virgil Thomson's music (or by reputation) than for their theatrical inventiveness.

After one has read the overearnest plays of the O'Neill tradition and withstood their makers' anxiety about "authenticity" and "depth," Stein's plays feel invigorating. Alone among her contemporaries, it seems, Stein was proposing that playwrights think longer and more self-consciously about the formal choices they make, and that they call into question the doctrines of figurative loyalty and narrative cogency inherited from the nineteenth century. Stein laughed off the superstition that demanded a plot in every play. "What's the use of telling a story," she once wrote, "since there are so many and everyone knows so many and tells so many."[1] She preferred instead to build a play using other elements, all the things that often fell away when a narrative whisked readers from station to station.

Stein was the first American dramatist to infuse the basic materials of dramatic art with independent life, making them noteworthy in themselves. She reanimated language, letting it be heard for its own sensual qualities, no longer just serving stories but now aspiring to the same radiance as, say, a wash of paint on an abstract-expressionist canvas. She rethought the use of gesture in the theater, devising a poetics of movement, wherein simple actions have a beauty and significance apart from their functions. The rhythms of dialogue, the syntax of sentences, and the physical relationships among characters became as important as what they said. Stein made abstractions like time seem tangible, easily manipulated; and she found in prosaic matters, like stage space and the human body, new dimensions of lyricism. Stein took nothing about theater for granted; everything received a fresh, skeptical look, and the plays she left us still have the power to upset assumptions and open up new possibilities for dramatic art.

After one has read just a few of Stein's plays, one looks at other theater differently. For the first time, perhaps, one notices formal qualities along with aspects of narrative or character; and one finds thematic significances in places that before seemed mere structural necessity. Suddenly, something as simple as a body movement or the sound of a recurring phrase has genuine emotional value and a beauty that was missed when plots commanded all of one's attention. Plays now look sculpted, scored, or built, whereas before they seemed merely spilt onto the page or stage.

This study reflects this change of outlook, and attempts to tell the story of American drama in a new way, with the acute sensitivity to form that Stein encouraged. The five other playwrights I discuss may seem like a hodgepodge. What could Tennessee Williams have in common with Stein? He's so emotional, she's so cool. Maria Irene Fornes's quiet grace sounds like a rebuke to Sam Shepard's loud machismo. Adrienne Kennedy's small, anguished plays shrink and look sentimental when set alongside Richard Foreman's rigorous stagings of his philosophy. Foreman is the only one of these writers deliberately to make use of Stein's theories (and to acknowledge doing so); but as one looks closer at his plays, Stein's model fades away, and Foreman's work defines a clear reaction to it.

The differences among these six writers are substantial, and it's not my aim to erase those idiosyncrasies and define a school. In general, I'm suspicious of blanket terms (of which the most notorious is Theater of the Absurd), believing that the yoking of writers to a trend dissolves what makes them most compelling: their very distance from trends. This book describes a loose cluster or set of affinities rather than something so dogmatic as a tradition, and aims to demonstrate a way of looking at drama more than a way of classifying it. Yet once Stein is acknowledged as a major figure in American drama's adolescence and is set alongside O'Neill in importance, an entire world of drama comes into clearer focus. Much of the most penetrating recent work acquires a history, a context, whereas before it was considered merely a digression from the mainstream – something abnormal.

In their own highly individual ways, each of the writers discussed here turns his or her attention away from plots, reducing their importance or eliminating them altogether, and rediscovers the essential elements of dramatic form – language, gesture, presence. Tennessee Williams puts a character, not a story, at the center of his dramas, and directs our attention to her inner life. His characters appear worlds unto themselves, spectacles on their own; and Williams lets us contemplate them for such a sustained period of time that subtleties of behavior surface, subtleties that wouldn't turn up were Williams hurrying to a climax or looking over his characters' shoulders at a resolution. The endings of Williams's plays are often shattering, and throw the preceding action into high relief, but they're no more important than any other moment in the play: Something is always happening on Williams's stage, there to be detected and reflected on – a psychological equivalent to Stein's "continuous present." Moreover, Williams's characters attract most attention when they speak: Their language has a lyric splendor because it doesn't always have to report events.

Sam Shepard and Maria Irene Fornes also exploit the idea of language that Stein left behind, and they relish the same sense of liberation. Shepard allows his characters to stop in their tracks, just as a story works up steam, and step outside the context of a scene to deliver roaring, intoxicated speeches, cascades of language. Fornes achieves the same disruption with an opposite approach. She'll let a character speak only a single sentence – and then close the scene down with darkness – but the emotion behind the speaking is sharper than it would be in an effortless dialogue: It lingers on in the darkness. Fornes does the same with movement, isolating the smallest quiver, asking for precision in order to affirm the significance of sheer presence, an aspect of performance often assumed rather than carefully achieved. Shepard worries about presence too, but, as one might expect, he establishes it with harsher, brighter bursts of activity. The gesture rarely clarifies a narrative, but it invariably releases a more powerful dramatic energy running under the text – complicated emotional states inaccessible with words.

Adrienne Kennedy and Richard Foreman move readers and spectators even deeper into inner, psychological realms. Kennedy experiments with stasis and the emotional qualities of incantatory, repetitive dialogue – a variation on Stein's insistent speech patterns. Her characters go over the same experience searching for its secrets, its implications; the outside world nearly vanishes. Foreman is just as obsessive, using theater to retreat from the everyday world and reach into his consciousness, a broader, wilder place. Both artists are absorbed with the process of writing, tireless about plumbing its mysteries even as they venture into other subjects.

The way Stein makes readers acutely sensitive to form recalls a famous comment by Samuel Beckett: "I am interested in the shape of ideas even if I do not believe in them."[2] Beckett knew that there are meanings other than those declared or demonstrated; but the thinking behind his comment has often been distorted by new discoverers of formal pleasures. It's possible to leap from Beckett's interest in the meaning of shape to the mistaken conclusion that ideas, and the problem of "belief," are old hat – and that substance doesn't matter as much as style or structure.

It's easy not to ask for much more than rebelliousness from writers stationed outside the mainstream. Many of the so-called conventional writers work so gracelessly and didactically to persuade their readers of ideologies, moral systems, and political temperaments that when writers like Stein offer a chance to look at aesthetics, it's tempting never to think again about the "real" world. This new writing feels so bracing that one commends it simply for being *different*. The force of its reaction sets the terms for the discussion of its merits; only later, if at all, do we measure the qualities of the work itself, on its own, apart from its fierce relationship to tradition. Too often, it seems, we limit our discussion of alternative writing to questions of form (as though it could be isolated), and rarely venture into those foggier zones where one must reflect on how form embodies thought. Terms like "experimental" only enforce this sense of detachment, connoting a kind of irresponsibility or work that's so chameleonlike that any interpretation is impossible.

Each of the following essays reflects frustration with this protocol of cool regard. And the book as a whole attempts to discover how six very different writers answer a perennial challenge: How does one represent emotion without slipping into sentimentality? In some quarters, just the mention of "emotion" in criticism is a sign of naïveté. But why should it be? Why can't we demand emotional pleasure from a drama that is also ingenious about structure? Why should we have to go to nineteenth-century naturalist novels, Hollywood movies, or grand opera for compelling depictions of basic human experiences: longing, pain, ecstasy, loneliness, wonder, love? Couldn't a formally inventive piece also conduct a searing intellectual adventure, or even execute a warm, all-consuming seduction? I think such a play could do just that, but much of our dominant critical discourse doesn't look beyond the art's artifice.

Since most of the playwrights discussed here do not tell stories, I have looked for the emotion of their work in unorthodox places. For instance, as one rolls up and down the cadences of Gertrude Stein's language, one can come to a new understanding of sensual abandon or of a kind of manic neediness. After getting winded by the explosive gestures of Shepard's characters, one can think about notions of identity, freedom, home, or the frustrations of attachment. Similar meditations about emotion are possible as one settles into the stillness between Fornes's luminous sentences, or becomes entranced by the digressions of Foreman's dialogue, or compares the multiple variations on a single litany in a scene by Kennedy.

These plays are so exciting precisely because of such large, numerous resonances: Gestures, rhythms of speech, tones, designs of stage space, and even lengths of scenes have spiritual, moral, even political meanings. Only by looking for them do we avoid the sterility Robert Lowell warned against in *Notebook:* "Unrealism can degenerate into meaningless clinical hallucination or rhetorical machinery, but the true unreal is about something, and eats from the abundance of reality."[3]

In order to locate these layers of meaning, it is necessary to redirect our natural urges to identify with characters and get involved with stories. For in much of this work, the most compelling character is the playwright: In plays without stories (or with minimal importance accorded them), we often can enter the story of the writer and of the writing. We can watch a saga in which an individual – the playwright – confronts a world of experience, tries to understand it, contain it, draw lessons from it, and finally, through writing, finds a way to accommodate it in his or her life. The title of a play by Gertrude Stein, *Listen to Me,* could be spoken by all of these writers: Frustrated by the boxy, uncongenial, formulaic dramatic structures they've inherited, they all hope to create a dramatic world in which their peculiar way of speaking can best be heard. This book is also a challenge to their readers – asking that we go beyond merely hearing the melody of their work, and really listen to the words, closely attend to the matter within their mode.

In writing *The Other American Drama,* I've gradually learned what kind of critic I am – someone still in thrall to ideas of aesthetic mystery, spirituality, beauty, and humanism. This is a deliberately old-fashioned book, for it was conceived not to demonstrate a theory about drama; nor does it make use of a single method. Rather, *The Other American Drama* is a collection of enthusiasms, in which I've tried to offer a response to Roland Barthes's quandary, first mentioned in his essay on the romantic song: "Once again I realize how difficult it is to talk about what one loves. What is there to say about what one loves except: *I love it,* and to keep on saying it?"[4]

The personal nature of this enterprise accounts for its gaps. *The Other American Drama* is meant neither as a survey of twentieth-century American dramatists nor even as a comprehensive account of one strain of that history. These six writers are, however, representative of what I think are the most exciting theatrical energies in circulation during this century. Several other distinguished playwrights share or extend some of their attitudes about theater. At times, Thornton Wilder took bold distance from his realism-bound contemporaries and expanded our sense of theatrical time and space with Stein-like eagerness. Jane Bowles's *In the Summer House* (1953) and e. e. cummings's *Him* (1927) are major documents of the American avant-garde, meriting renewed attention for the wit with which they upset orderly dramaturgy. Sophie Treadwell's forays into the grim, stark realities of domestic life, and her keen sense of composition, still have the capacity to startle. Not incidentally, her writing (especially *Machinal,* from 1928) echoes in the work of Maria Irene Fornes. Lee Breuer, David Mamet, Charles Ludlam, and a range of other writers have all, at one time or another, produced challenging, stirring work; their absence here is less an indication of their quality than of limited space. (Given that this book is a study of playwriting, and not theater in general, I've also omitted important American artists like Robert Wilson and Meredith Monk because their work, for all its marvels, is not primarily written.)

One way to go beyond Barthes's impasse, where one can only say "I love it," is to describe "it" as rigorously as one can, in the hope that a close transcription will reveal secrets hitherto unseen. Reveal, but not decode. In his most eloquent statement on the critical act, the long story "The Figure in the Carpet," Henry James shows how elusive the object of criticism is and how fanciful the strategies of the critic. A young admirer persistently asks a famous novelist, Vereker, to show him the "very passion of his passion," the key to the mystery of his writing – the figure in the carpet. But Vereker keeps foiling him and eventually tells the would-be critic to give up, that the "secret" is the most obvious thing about his novels and the most difficult to grasp. It's not a matter of substance or style, he says, but "the very organ of life."

Vereker's coyness aside, the story deserves rereading in an age like ours, where "zealots of explanation" (in Denis Donoghue's felicitous phrase) threaten not only to provide a wan symbolic equivalent for Vereker's "figure," but to unravel the entire carpet. James teaches fine lessons in discretion, and I've tried to hold on to them as I've made my way through the works of these playwrights. At a scholarly conference, I once heard a critic introduce himself by saying "I *do* Beckett," and later refer to "*my* writers" – comments indicative of the kind of sweeping presumption and intrusiveness that seem to prevent the careful mingling these plays invite. I'm hardly advocating a critical stance of utter passivity and gaping dumbness – that would be to adopt the very detachment I lamented earlier – but in these essays I have tried to preserve some of the allure and mystery at the core of all extraordinary theater.

I have also tried to recreate the sense of astonishment one is likely to experience on first encountering these plays. Ideally, the moment of viewing a play blinds you to all other works, erasing for a spell the memory of other artistic encounters. That astonishment is no less a part of the theatrical experience than the words and images populating the stage, and any critical response that leaves it out risks seeming bloodless, perfunctory, boilerplate. The critic Arthur Danto has described what he calls the "transformative impact" of certain painting and sculpture, and has decried any critical theory that proposes to deny its importance. Too many art historians, he writes, "have neglected these powers, and in consequence there are entire empires of art to which the formalistic and iconographic modes of analysis they (and most art critics) favor have no application. They do not touch that which in images verges on their presumed magical and moral force."[5]

"Magic" is another word likely to trip up the self-serious – perhaps because it suggests a troubling openness to ambiguity. Richard Foreman, in a recent play called *Symphony of Rats,* celebrates ambiguity, and proposes that only those people comfortable with the continually fluctuating parameters of experience are able to live fully. Once we try to parcel out and cram the unruly mélange of events, sensations, and individuals into tidy categories, he suggests, real significances are lost. Foreman's play offers useful guidance for critics, I believe, and in these essays I've steered clear of categories, of "isms," of forced comparisons between writers, and of overgeneralized meditations on genre. Instead, I've preferred to approach each artist on his or her own terms, and trust that the correspondences with contemporaries and the clues to the writer's proper place in an evolving tradition of writing will emerge on their own. As a consequence, many of these essays indulge in biographical reflections and speculations – not in order to read the work only through the lens of the life, nor (in the manner of the crassest psychological criticism) to use details of the life *against* the writer, but only to discuss the making of the play as much as the play itself, to depict an entire artistic temperament as much as the art, and to recall that this drama has its origins in lived lives – often inconsistent lives, vulnerable to chance and whim – not in formulas or image machines.

Finally, the preponderance of references to other arts in these essays may strike some readers as reckless. But since so many of these plays articulate their makers' rejection of other drama, it simply made sense to approach the work from untheatrical perspectives: to read Stein while thinking about dance or cinema, to read Shepard with an understanding of action painting and rock music, to think about Kennedy for a moment in terms of the Psalms or Beethoven's quartets, to sort out Foreman with the help of Rilke or Valéry. These varied approaches aren't meant to suggest that the work of any of these playwrights is somehow undramatic or not of the theater. Far from it: In the hands of these artists the ways in which we define and experience drama have never been more various, never more lively. Yet, in American culture, drama has been set apart from the rest of the arts, banished to a dark corner, perhaps because it's too disruptive, too unwieldy, or just too slow to catch up with the advances in the other arts. Few serious students of music, literature, or painting take an interest in drama; few cultural forums find room for spirited debate about theatrical concerns. Part of the problem, of course, is temporality. Performances disappear; productions close after only a few people see them; only a fraction of dramatic literature is part of the living repertoire – even the best contemporary writers see just a few of their plays performed more than once. Plays are rarely considered literature by anyone outside the academy, and so, despite their existence as texts, are never read. It's one of this book's aims to challenge that prejudice. Reading a play has its own pleasures quite apart from those available in a theater.

Introduction

Theater critics sometimes have a bathetic air, for they live in perpetual bereavement, watching the objects of their affection slip away into obscurity as the lights on stage go down. Writing about plays, then, becomes genuinely restorative, in a double sense: invigorating, as exercise might be; but, more important, life restoring, setting the plays before all of our minds once again and allowing a longer look. *The Other American Drama* tries to make a handful of compelling plays keep us company longer than they have in the theater.

1

GERTRUDE STEIN

WHILE GERTRUDE STEIN was quietly bringing out her first plays with an obscure Boston publisher in 1922, *The Hairy Ape* began performances in New York, establishing Eugene O'Neill as the nation's most serious, "difficult" playwright. A year later, Elmer Rice would announce his own reputation with *The Adding Machine.* Both plays were anxious efforts by authors fearless about exposing each character's aggrieved interior – the "soul" that this particular variety of American drama would quickly make its province. Stein traveled much the same region in *Geography and Plays,* the title of that first collection, but her voice was quieter, the temper bemused rather than raucous, and her approach to her characters a desultory appraisal instead of the earnest lunge that distinguished O'Neill and Rice. If these qualities weren't enough to isolate Stein from other playwrights of the day and their audiences, certainly the small number of copies printed and the absence of producers willing to stage her plays made her entrance into American drama wholly forgettable even for her admirers.

Stein wandered into a theater that was just beginning to move out of the nineteenth-century melodramas and into the grittier, but no less mechanical, realism that would dominate playwriting until Tennessee Williams rediscovered the lyric. Stein loved melodrama more than did most contemporary writers, zealously attending performances of *Uncle Tom's Cabin, Secret Service,* and their ilk while growing up in San Francisco. And, by moving to Paris in 1903, she skirted the rush into sobriety that swept up many writers after melodrama faded. Out of step with her peers and, living abroad, out of reach, Stein had to construct a community to accommodate herself, a place attuned to her own variety of lyricism. That process, slow, unplanned, constantly obstructed, was more than her vocation: It entered her plays and became their most prominent concern.

It's strange to think of Gertrude Stein as a solitary figure. The biographies we have and, more seductive, the myth of her life leave her rarely alone. There she is, always glowing wisely among other artists, protégés, and groupies – and, when the salon at Rue de Fleurus emptied out at last, with the unobtrusive, worrying Alice B. Toklas. Her later celebrity, fueled by the soldiers who kept up a constant vigil at her home during World War II and her barnstorming American lecture tour, refined an image of Stein as compulsively social, genuinely interested in even the humblest visitor. Indeed she was interested. But most of those whose lives attracted her attention, and attended to her, rarely read her prose and, save the successful *Four Saints in Three Acts* and *Yes Is for a Very Young Man*, never really cared about her plays. Easily gregarious, she was nonetheless artistically marooned. Like the other expatriates, Stein stowed a cluster of true colleagues onto a cramped island and with them created a parallel American culture, one free of native assumptions and paralyzing traditions when it wanted to be, yet also deprived of a larger sustaining community of readers and spectators flexible enough to grow with the artists.

The exigencies of exile hurried Stein through the customary rites of all developing writers. Unimpeded by the protocol of American literary circles, she easily rejected worn approaches to writing and, out of necessity, initiated an urgent reinvention of her native language, now distant and inaccessible. Stein started over as a writer in Paris, leaving behind her some scientific papers from her years as a medical student and some miscellaneous creative efforts, including her first play, *Snatched from Death, or the Sundered Sisters,* written when she was eight. In *The Autobiography of Alice B. Toklas,* Stein specifies what she rejected: She once tried to write a Shakespearean comedy, but got only as far as a single stage direction: "The courtiers make witty remarks." She couldn't think of any, though, so she gave up. She also shed the baggage that most playwrights haul about – the orthodox structure, predictable rhythms of dialogue, and purposeful narrative of standard successful plays. In this lighter, unfettered condition, Stein was free to find her own method. And she started by considering only what remained after everything inessential had been discarded: words, unmoored to a story or even to conversation, and people on stage, not necessarily doing anything, but surely present.

Stein wrote more than seventy plays, and while many correspond, at least at moments, to familiar brands of drama, all are dazzlingly unpredictable. Some are exercises in sheer whimsy, tiny in length and scope; others, grand, stirring operas like *The Mother of Us All.* There are also comedies of manners and, almost as a refreshment after the earlier work, a handful of moral tales and psychological studies. (With some, we have to take Stein's word for it that they *are* plays.) Even at their most conventional – necessarily a relative term with this artist – Stein's plays always bear the marks of her determination to reinvigorate those elements of theater that others take for granted. Each play also forms part of what would be a rigorous lifelong search for the essence of drama – the qualities without which plays really would be indistinguishable from poetry or prose. It is for this, and for the lesson in artistic freedom, that Stein's contribution as a playwright is so important. Long valued for her prose, Stein as dramatist has yet to find a place in our standard theater histories, our courses in modern drama. But without her, our understanding of the evolution of an American dramatic language remains incomplete.

There was about that language more athleticism, Stein felt, than most writers gave space to; and so sentences should show the sweaty history of how a writer considered some words and excluded others, tried out a series of phrases, adjusted the tension holding them together, pushed and pulled until communication surged through freely. Stein's favorite language was one in which "words have the liveliness of being constantly chosen."[1] The English of the Elizabethans, who refreshed a tired discourse, was for Stein a good example; American speech, once weaned from colonial influence, an even better one. While she disdained those who merely invented new words at this late date, Stein tried to carry the Elizabethan and American brio into her own writing, not just dutifully setting down on paper the words a character must speak, but luxuriating in the language others used without thinking. "I caressed completely caressed and addressed a noun," she once wrote.[2] This is the source of Gertrude Stein's sensuality – a heat that pervades all the plays, even those that seem intransigent and remote.

"Vocabulary in itself can be interesting," she said,[3] and if she could somehow detach words from things, she thought, and start them moving through the page on their own, unharnessed, a play might finally take shape, active and animated as plays by definition should be, distinct from other kinds of more grounded writing. "I like anything that a word can do," she once remarked, making it clear that, for her, language was a collection of forces rather than a supine *thing*.[4] Sometimes her plays seem too full of words, each peculiar in its context, as though plucked at random from different sentences, none making sense set next to another in this new arrangement. Yet that very variety was but another attempt to resurrect the odd exuberance she loved about newborn languages. If everything in a play changed, if she kept the language mutating so vigorously that it never froze and readers never got used to it, then her drama would lift off and she would fully inhabit a language in which others feel indentured or only temporarily welcome.

As Stein was refurbishing her language, she was also learning that a playwright's central purpose is not merely to display characters or even to reenact events. Setting aside the obligation to make "resemblances," as she called them, she allied herself with the painters gathered about her; like

Picasso and Braque, she worked to bring out a new awareness of art as the work of imagination, not merely the record of disciplined observation. "An oil painting is an oil painting," she wrote, anticipating ideas about representation and the integrity of the canvas surface that would still preoccupy painters fifty years later.[5] Likewise, she reasoned that a play should be a play – not a re-creation of something else, studied only to detect the accuracy of the reproduction. It should be "just there," Stein would say, announcing its playness at every juncture. Sometimes it did so with bald declarations like "here is scene two," "there is no Act Five," or with lengthy disquisitions, as in *Byron,* which is so caught up with the effort to be a play that it never reaches its supposed subject.

Stein's first mature play, in fact, did begin with observation, but what she did with the accumulated evidence and conclusions bore only tangential relationship to the occasion. After attending a party in 1913, so the legend goes, Stein returned home eager to make a play out of the evening's proceedings. But *What Happened: A Play,* as it came to be called, would not recount the anecdotes and gossip, the varied amusements and consternations and minor hurts that fill most such evenings. "What is the use of telling a story," she later wrote, "since there are so many and everybody knows so many and tells so many." *What Happened: A Play* would "tell what could be told if one did not tell anything." "In short," it would prove to be "the essence of what happened."[6]

Naturally, nothing happens in *What Happened,* at least according to criteria followed in most theaters of the day, where activity earned the name only when it corresponded to behavior seen outside the auditorium. But much happens dramatically; a kind of theatrical movement – with its mechanics determined inside the play, and affecting the writing more than the subject – supplants merely imitative movement.

What Happened consists of five acts filling, in the 1922 edition, five pages. The characters, if there are characters, haven't names, unless a series of numbers in parentheses is meant to signify presence. Otherwise, the voices are devoid of descriptive elements that would determine identity. It's not clear whether the play's words are meant to be spoken or if they simply provide descriptions of a condition, a setting, or an obscure occurrence. Perhaps both. There's no obvious feeling of engagement among the speakers; one talks of a sound or a sensation, another follows with a list of objects, the next asks an unanswered, unanswerable question: "What is length when silence is so windowful."[7] Nothing resolves; the play seems to go nowhere; little stays in the memory after it's over.

What Happened is incoherent in the purest, least pejorative sense: None of its pieces hold together. But in exchange for unity, Stein achieves a refined kind of clarity. Each utterance sounds livelier; and each picture stands alone, with equal status, more vivid than it would be as a link in a chain of associations or a participant in the relay race of ordinary dramatic banter and bustle. In this play, and in so many of the others that fill these early years, Stein concerns herself with the deceptively simple task of defining phenomena. By making deft use of only the staples of dramatic structure she is able to bracket experiences, and further break them down into their constituent elements, making distinctions as she goes. "Acts" and "scenes" function like frames around paintings, directing and focusing our attention on discrete sections of the perceived world. "A cut is not a slice." "A blanket, what is a blanket." "Is it really an oleander."[8] *What Happened* is speckled with questions and exclamations and hypotheses like these, all aspects of Stein's broad interrogation of a befogged encounter. (In a later play she will extend this technique: She fills each act [and there are 145] of *Counting Her Dresses* with just one utterance, and so makes the separate parts of a conversation equally important, demanding the same amount of sustained listening. A voice speaking literally becomes an act.)

"A series of photographs and also . . . a treacherous sculpture," someone says at the end of Act I of *What Happened.*[9] The phrase offers little to readers intent on locating the story of *What Happened,* but it says much about the play as a whole. Each of its inscrutable subjects and temporary themes occupies a space to itself; each has been captured and exposed to view, like a photograph, or shaped into presence, like a sculpture. Stein's first action as a playwright is to summon the materials of her recreation before her – the gestures, voices, things, and bodies – to establish their "being" before their "doing." The movement follows, to be sure, for the static pictures form a rapid series, as Stein notes, and sculpture hides an unpredictable element of treachery, as though loathe to rest too long and turn familiar. What happens in *What Happened* is looking itself, a living process, the act of perceiving made as visible as the thing perceived. Stein is delighted to roam, take in the things that cross her path, and register both their astonishing presence and the eye's own movement with a language that sounds like a discovery itself.

"Theater resides in a certain way of furnishing and animating the air of the stage," wrote Stein's contemporary (but probably not acquaintance) Antonin Artaud.[10] As Stein set about marking the arrival of her dramatic material, she also began considering arrangements. Objects and people were now indisputably in her theater – her continual naming of them ensured that – but how would they share the stage? In the long series of plays that followed *What Happened,* most of which she gathered and published herself in *Operas and Plays,* Stein's sense of the particular, and the miniature, unassuming beauties of things seen alone, evolved into a feeling for totalities and the grandeur that accompanies them. Her word for these larger pictures was *landscapes;* and her most celebrated work, *Four Saints in Three Acts,* is also her finest landscape play.

The title alone announces themes of placement, but its usefulness proves limited once the reader notices that the opera really contains four acts, and that the saints have been proliferating rapidly after the first four have had their say. Stein enjoyed upsetting expectations like these: By doing so she could direct attention to what really mattered, the world of the play seen as a play, considered apart from questions of narrative, the rigid theatrical logic that demands beginnings, middles, and ends – and readers eager to count acts instead of beholding them.

Like all the landscape plays, *Four Saints* feels static; but just as a stunning vista commands attention with what seems like inexhaustible subtleties, so too does the complicated terrain of Stein's play. For all its tranquillity and the self-possession associated with both saints and stable landscapes, *Four Saints* is a remarkably busy work. As acts and saints accumulate so do the spectator's perceptions of the play's world. Stein takes the spectator across the same terrain over and over, and with each circuit a new detail emerges for the watchful visitor. She reintroduces a saint briefly mentioned in the first act and now clarifies his position; the distance between two others she helps us more accurately measure. Pascal wrote that "a town or a landscape from far off is a town or a landscape, but as one approaches it becomes houses, trees, tiles, leaves, grass, ants, ants' legs, and so on, ad infinitum. All that is comprehended in the word 'landscape.'" In the same way, the world of *Four Saints* expands in richness and complexity as Stein charts its hills and thickets, and with workmanlike precision populates its plains. In arranging the inhabitants of her play almost before our eyes, perceiving and altering proximities, she gives the play its peculiar theatricality, its shivering life.

The procedure led Stein to deliver, years later, a lecture called "Composition as Explanation." It helped answer all those bewildered readers who enjoyed the pretty decor and tunefulness of the saints' patter, but still couldn't help wondering what it all meant. Stein redirected their attention: Meanings weren't invisible or obscure, something to be dug out from the granite of a play; there was no submerged significance that dogged philosophical inquiry would retrieve. The "meanings" were obvious to all who were patient enough to see what lay before them. The long passages in *Four Saints* that chronicle the gradual settling of Saint Therese into her seat, and subsequent ones that mark the way other saints array themselves around her, establish a condition more than a story; but it is a condition that, like the best stories, contains a compelling tone and mood. Just as a Renaissance painting asks one to understand sentiment in terms of perspective, Stein makes her commentary simply by choosing to see things one way instead of another, to look at her landscape from a specific promontory – say, a place that keeps

Saint Therese in the foreground, closest to her, and others receding, or only partially visible. If Stein had been "standing" in another place, looking from a different angle, the contents of her picture and their relationships would change – and so change the meaning.

This is perhaps clearest in another play, *Civilization,* in which, after a busy passage with much activity and talk of many characters, Stein makes of a single sentence an entire scene – "She chews gently at her food."[11] That picture, perceived and arranged independently, and placed far from the other parts of the play, conveys a feeling of deprivation, or perhaps of proud independence, that only a dispassionate eye for the geometry of a play can achieve. Stein's restraint, her understanding that the subtlest choices release the largest dramatic consequences, charges her landscape plays with considerable tension. They become places that compel neurotic fascination; that contain barely suppressed delirium; that suggest, at least in the verbal zone, incipient ecstasy.

Delirium and ecstasy seem unlikely qualities in plays so fiercely disciplined, where the discussion of structure prevents outbursts or arias or impassioned contretemps. But it would be a mistake (and a loss) to think of Stein's plays only as ingenious exercises or formal experiments, devoid of content. e. e. cummings wrote that Stein "subordinates the meaning of the words to the beauty of the words themselves," and Roger Fry explained to us that formal design matters more than subject matter in her work.[12] Both attitudes keep engagement with her work only superficial, an amusement more than a communion. All her plays start from and return to feeling: It is the site for our keenest understanding, she advised, and for her own creation. "By written I mean made," she once said to an interviewer, "and by made I mean felt."[13]

At the center of the best plays – and running through all her dramatic work – is unadorned, appealingly clumsy emotion, free of the coyness and inscrutability that, to the impatient eye, characterize her theater's surface. Because the plays contain little sentimentality, and because Stein doesn't insist on pulling audiences into characters' lives and ordeals, her enthusiasm for detecting relationships can seem merely a mildly diverting pastime or a clever experiment carried out with odd devotion, neither requiring anything more than exactitude. Yet the plays can surprise with a psychological force greater for being unannounced. Instead of manipulating emotion, Stein simply shows it, as clearly as she shows Therese rising or fruit hanging on a tree in *Four Saints*.

For Stein, the display of emotion always had a purpose: Her theater's pervasive formalism, the worry over presence and placement and proximity, emerged out of her personal needs – in these plays, the need to comprehend the differences among people, and to feel the possibility and pleasure of genuine attachments. The plays helped her to organize those desires. Stein's attention to the integrity of objects and utterances never signaled mere fetishism. Although she always had a good word for avarice, her accumulation of phenomena in the plays really served a humane cause and expressed a generous spirit. Stein directed her fascination most fervidly toward individuals, and that larger purpose, embracing plays from all stages of her career, expressed an abiding desire to understand identity. Stein always kept alert to what surrounded her, the lay of her stage and the obstacles filling it, but she felt most urgently about discovering *who* surrounded her. Each of her plays helped her learn whether or not she could ever know another human being. That passionate project – writing her way toward people – kept her art from becoming the thinnest, most desiccated kind of abstraction.

Such a process required more than merely naming the figures accompanying her into a play. And Stein's curiosity was not satisfied simply with tracing and reporting the outward traits of her characters, or even with exposing their personalities. Like plot, which she banished from *What Happened* because it crowds out the real interest in drama, personalities proliferate at a dizzying pace in the social world and the drama meant to reflect it, there for everyone to see, broadcast, underscored so continuously that they cease to be reliable (or even interesting) indicators of character. Stein probed more deeply, certain that beneath each public persona, camouflaged by the behavior that comprises visible human nature, there lay a truer self, what she called the "intensity of anybody's existence."[14] If she could locate that, and then somehow release it into her art, she felt sure the problem of character in drama – and identity in her own life – would resolve.

Stein's quest for identity began during the writing of *The Making of Americans*, a 1,000-page novel that chronicles the history of the Herslands, a family clearly based on Stein's own. It is a work of almost devotional power, in which she marshals enormous faith in the ability of sheer description to embrace the world, "every kind of human being that ever was or is or would be living."[15] That same faith gives the plays their disarming poise, as though Stein were thinking, *if I only say what I see, what I see will live before you.* Her understanding of description is particularly rigorous, however, consisting not simply of reportage, but also of attention and excavation, moving about the subject and reassessing it from different times and in different conditions. In a sense, her passion recalls her days in medical school; indeed, when she speaks of hoping to classify "every kind of human being," the scientist in Stein threatens to loom larger than the artist. But her project never leaves the personal realm, and her work steadily grows more lyrical as her abiding humanism returns her always from taxonomies to individuals. Realizing that external appearance does not mark identity with sufficient accuracy, she begins to question what passes for psychological insight in the art around her. Her fascination with internals, the force that turns types into genuine characters, deepens and expands as she perceives the complexities of an endlessly dilating identity. "Of course I am interested in anyone . . . . I must find out what is moving inside them that makes them them."[16]

In the plays, Stein's methods of locating identity are in fact thoroughly unscientific, with all the vitality and idiosyncrasy of any spontaneous, pressing interest. She wants to find the "rhythm of anybody's personality" and so allows time and space for that quality to be heard.[17] The stillness that settles over so many of her plays is perhaps the crucial condition in which to perceive identity. In most theater, a plot, or a complicated series of conversations, distracts the spectator's attention from the participants. Stein dismantles that scaffolding and works to coax reluctant characters, rarely so unsupported by activity or "ideas," into a drama they alone define. Her spectators can then finally see the small gestures or hear the faint inflections that make one person different from the next.

In a late work, *A Play Called Not and Now,* conventional definitions of character are so suspect that Stein names her characters only as "A Man Who Looks Like Dashiell Hammett" or "A Woman Who Looks Like Anita Loos." But if likeness doesn't indicate identity (just as resemblance never represents the natural world to modern painters), something less obvious might. Stein subjects one person's inadvertent sigh near the end of *Not and Now* to exhaustive scrutiny, until she, and we, are clear about who sighed, when and where it happened, and what the consequences were. The sigh establishes presence more forcefully than could any speech or stage business.

That passage in *Not and Now* is tiring to read, as Stein brings us back to the sound over and over, obsessively repeating her perceptions and thoughts about it, fixing it in the fabric of the play. (This brand of repetition would become the most notorious characteristic of Stein's writing, subject to parodies that themselves grew wearily repetitive.) Disregarding the possible frustration of the reader accustomed to progress of a more invigorating sort, Stein uses repetition as a kind of bulldozer, clearing away the inessential by addressing only the parts of character in which she sees the most vivid life, then tricking out elusive identity wearied of the scrutiny. In fact, because this approach makes such an attack on her subject, Stein prefers to call it "insistence": A repetition changes nothing, she notes, but insistence keeps pushing at different parts of obdurate surfaces, each push having a changed emphasis and speed and direction. In many of the plays, Stein keeps up a constant interrogation of her characters, allowing them to press for more information about one another, and more specificity to the information, piecing together a presence out of the answers.

A character's name is often the first topic of an interrogation. "Mr. and Mrs. Leland Paul. Do you know that name," someone asks in *Mexico*. "How do you pronounce my name," Don Nicholai wonders earlier in the same play.[18] Names are everywhere in Stein – many so sonorous that they suggest demeanors on their own, as names from the novels of Henry James or Virginia Woolf do. And, as in Woolf's fiction, the talk in Stein's plays is constant, with all the musicality of a crowded parlor or patio – voices melding stylishly, peculiarities and propensities on stunning display. The dialogue always has the sound of overheard conversation – most explicitly in a play called, appropriately enough, *Ladies' Voices.*

But neither names nor the cadences of voices revealed the internal self Stein kept hunting. Nor, perhaps, is there any reason to think Stein thought she could find it. Her accumulations, her portraits in gesture and sound, her insistent questioning of bodies, may ultimately dramatize the need to know more than they dramatize the object of inquiry itself. That object remains forever remote and impenetrable.

Such quiet desperation, the longing for more certainty, gives Stein's theater a strangely spiritual aspect. *Four Saints* openly inhabits a religious setting, but in many of the other plays the same mysticism arises from their placid surface, and is heard in the sound that hums through them, the fever of insistence resembling a litany. There is also a feeling of devout belief in the resilience of Stein's characters. They admit no discouragement in what is really a doomed attempt to understand others. Like disciples of a hidden savior, they faithfully speak over and over the words necessary to secure genuine attachments.

Only in terms of these linkages – welcomed, forced, or failed – can Stein's characters be fully understood. They are fixed in space, usually a landscape, or at least a stage, a forum for perception; and they are also fixed in time, as the hero of *Yes Is for a Very Young Man* painfully learns, wedged as he is in a confusing adolescence, "when your food card gives you the right to have cigarettes *and* chocolate."[19] Beyond this temporal and spatial placement, however, Stein's individuals feel the presence of others acutely; and the weave of the social fabric focuses most of their attention and absorbs the bulk of their neuroses. Her investigation into human exchange lacks the dry, cool manner that readers familiar with her "still-life" writing, like the prose collection *Tender Buttons,* might expect. At their most confident, her plays radiate the pleasure of companionship achieved and sustained – or else the complementary dread of bereavement.

How striking it is, after pages of Stein's fanciful wordplay in *The Five Georges,* to hear a voice say "Love me." The plea is but one of many that erupt precisely at moments when the writing has grown most hypnotic, rupturing the tranquillity and organizing the entire play around a poignant core. "Do be pleasantly with me," says Cora in *They Must. Be Wedded. To Their Wife.* Someone in *Saints and Singing* suddenly says "Do please please please please me."[20] Read in the context of these central exclamations, even the most innocuous chatter appears part of their speakers' quest for connection, engagement of any sort, even that of sheer talking and listening. *Listen to Me,* calls out the title of a late play, by which time the desire for contact needs little disguise. *Look at Me Now and Here I Am,* declares the title of a collection of prose, a phrase in which Stein seeks out attention and then announces her presence in space and time. It is in moments like these that Stein seems most vulnerable, her voice raw, uncovered by the customary melody of her writing.

Stein's love of company, the comings and going at Fleurus, and even the travails of life with Alice work their way into the plays, buoying them and allowing a personal warmth to pervade their structure. Because the plays always reflect her desire to rejuvenate dramatic art and exercise her skills of perception, it's easy to exchange the characters with Stein herself; but the prudent reader uses caution when inferring that the needs are identical for both. Stein herself is responsible for the confusion. Most of the plays are like ingeniously coded telegraphic reports about her private life and the emotional climate surrounding her. Many sequences in the plays can be traced to incidents from Stein's days in Paris or Belley, her country retreat. The nicknames that Alice and Gertrude called each other often float into the dialogue, and some plays even portray the couple fairly frankly – as in *A Lyrical Opera Made by Two,* an adorable paean to love that opens with a pair sitting in a room that closely resembles the Paris salon. So much of Stein's work contributes to an ongoing, swelling memoir, of which *The Autobiography of Alice B. Toklas* and *Everybody's Autobiography* are only the most explicit chapters.

It's not for the gossip, however, that Stein's plays command attention. The plays explore the dimensions of human contact so thoroughly and voice a faith in fellowship so persuasively that no biography is needed to feel their peculiar force. Their impact would be the same even if the personal references weren't there to be unearthed. *Four Saints* is the most eloquent about attachment, as it is about so many other things. The constant return of the word "with" obliquely expresses Stein's sense of relationships; she pushes to clarify the connections with questions like "Who separated saints at one time" or "Can two saints be one," and, after much experiment, declares her vision of human combinations outright. "There is a distance in between in between others," says one figure, and soon the scene settles into resignation: "It is very easy to love alone."[21]

The anguish beneath these words spreads throughout the play, as Stein shows how, in some instances, detachment all too predictably succeeds attachment and, in others, independence gives way to dependence. Individuals are always negotiating their places in groups; all her characters shuttle back and forth between solitude and sociability. *They Must. Be Wedded. To Their Wife.* enacts that transit most wittily. The theme, of course, is marriage, but attachments are complicated by dramatic structure. The periods between the actions in the title correspond to the gulfs between the characters, and add more obstacles to the joining. Stein interrupts the attraction to analyze the mechanics of exchange. She won't allow the movement of figures toward each other to proceed fluidly. Without making bald statements, she clarifies how an essential loneliness never fully dissipates, even in the most crowded room or most intimate encounter.

Formal experiment led Stein to emotional engagement, ensuring that her plays would never be mere exercises. In turn, her understanding of emotion brought her closer to perceiving unacknowledged qualities of dramatic form. In what is still the clearest explication of her art, her own essay "Plays," she describes how as a young theatergoer – and her youth was the only period in her life that she *did* go to the theater – she was always irritated because the pace at which her emotions unrolled never matched the tempo of the play. She was either ahead of the stage, numbly waiting for inevitable resolutions, or lagging behind, reflecting on something interesting that went by too quickly or reassessing an early image that only made sense later on. At no time was she fully engaged in the experience as it unfolded before her – and because of that disjunction theater always made her feel "nervous." Also a bit cheated: She wasn't allowed the emotional bath she wanted from art.

Stein set out to enhance her emotional involvement by repairing theater's sense of the present. "The business of art is to live in the actual present," she asserted, "to completely express that complete actual present."[22] Of all the arts, theater should be closest to the here and now; but the drill-sergeant logic of narrative, with its teleological imperative, and the arduous task of "getting acquainted" with characters and situations, prevents theater from directly communicating anything. So many plays, it seems, can only be understood in recollection.

Stein's first initiative was her simplest, but also the most effective: The language in the plays almost never deviates from the present tense. This change gives the blandest speech an air of breathlessness; every character sounds importunate – while whole passages in the plays take on the feeling of eyewitness reports. Then, by repeating sentences charged with the excitement of the present tense, or by modifying them only slightly over several pages, Stein completes her entrapment of her listeners. They must hold fast to each word, look for the subtlest change, remain attentive to each declaration, if they hope to enter into the play.

Stein learned her technique from the cinema, then in its fledgling days and for her the most intoxicating development in art. A film's collection of frames – so many nearly identical, yet crucially different – is the clearest expression of the present tense in performance. Each frame announces the situation, the composition, the characters anew; the "story" starts over each time; only when the parts are taken together and followed sequentially does the film move and seem to breathe. When Stein starts a play over an exhausting number of times – *Civilization* has 44 first acts – she's working to bring theater in line with cinema: "I was making a continuous succession of the statement of what [a] person was until I had not many things but one thing."[23] She uses the same technique – insistence – to make the events of her play live now, not *then;* here, not *there.* And if a play never moves beyond Act I, then there's no past or future, no enslavement to memory, no nervousness about what's next.

Stein succeeds in getting an elusive abstraction – time – into her plays, making it as vivid a presence as Saint Ignatius or a hilltop in Mexico. We attend to time's fluctuations, its manner of spreading through space, even its temperament (sometimes sluggish, sometimes ebullient) as much as we monitor the behavior of characters. Stein doesn't merely *portray* time, however. She sinks her plays into it, as though certain that if plays occupy time fully they won't be burdened with having to run along beside it: They will *define* time, so the anxiety produced by the conventional theatrical clock will easily dissipate. "You have to denude yourself of time so that writing time does not exist," she advised fellow artists. The work, she went on, should have an "existence suspended in time" rather than merely "a sense of time."[24]

Why then do so many of Stein's plays feel like melodramas? Melodrama, after all, is the ultimate time-bound form, built on the rhythms of escalating expectation and startling fulfillments. The resemblance is superficial: Stein revises the familiar suspense structure by withholding the denouement, or by humorously deflating its importance. In *Four Saints* the endless preparation for an unnamed something gives a simple occurrence – "Saint Therese advancing" – unusual importance.[25] This way, spectators pay more attention to the increments of activity, the moments before them, and are unable to detect where the play is going. They don't bide time until a more "significant" event happens. Stein's fidelity to the continuous present makes everything significant: It takes the mechanical predictability out of melodrama, while retaining, and perfecting, its ability to excite and ensnare the spectator.

Given such a loving relationship with popular theater, and after deliberate effort to align the spectator's sense of time with the play's, Stein's drama should warmly welcome the innocent first-time visitor. But it rarely does. No matter how well we detect the concerns and trace the pattern of a Stein play, something forever remains inaccessible, holding more mystery than is usually comfortable in a work of art, continually repelling our approach. The simplest act of reading her sentences and putting their elements together proves so challenging that all sense of the larger work vanishes. Her writing alternately broods and exults, at times putting obstacles in the reader's path, making progress choppy at best; at other times, allowing unimpeded reading, great bursts of energy and velocity. It's important, when the reading gets most strenuous, to recall the love of play, of fun and surprise, at the base of Stein's theater. The musicality of the writing and the horseplay with homonyms, the devious punning and rhyming jags, are but the clearest reminders of a hedonism and spiritedness at the heart of even her soberest plays.

The difficulties in understanding that afflict even her most valiant readers actually mirror Stein's own predicament. She once spoke of how she "groped" through her writing, feeling her way haphazardly toward the right expression or composition of experience. This makes for the obsessiveness of all Stein's drama. She would write a dozen plays on the same premise – arrivals, attachments, departures – until she perfected the techniques needed to represent them. Only then would her art move on into undiscovered terrain. This rigor displays anxiety and self-reliance more than it does clerklike predictability: Her method bespeaks a yen for total control, a desire to map the scene around her so that it can't overwhelm her. Perhaps that's why she seems never to want to let a play end, tirelessly extending a series of variations beyond any "reasonable" point. Her plays stop rather than end, for to end a play means to surrender to convention and, worse, to presume that one has mastered one's subject. Such arrogance, she implies, is unseemly.

There are some plays in which Stein welcomes the abundant world, warmly and generously. There are others in which she closes herself off in a tiny, insulated sphere, deaf to the imprecations and importunities outside her door. There are those plays in which she enters into other personalities and those in which she clarifies only her own. Her brother, Leo, once said that you had to know Gertrude personally – her habits, proclivities, and aversions – to understand her work. Her plays may contain all the detritus of the external world – everything is recognizable, taken on its own – but invariably those elements are put to idiosyncratic use, combined in peculiar ways, infused with secret significance. In one of her autobiographies, Stein marks this progression from outside in. Writing of her experience of World War I, she asks, "Do you remember it was the fifth of September we heard of asphyxiating gases. Do you remember that on the same day we heard that permission had been withheld. Do you remember that we couldn't know how many h's there are in withheld."[26] Stein's world, and the world of most of her plays, contracts until it houses only the writer herself. "I write for myself and strangers," she writes in *The Making of Americans*.[27] Why are friends left out? Carl Van Vechten reports that she later closed the door on strangers, too.

Stein spent much of her career pushing her sensibility into the shadowy interiors of lost lives and recondite experiences. The final stages of her life as a playwright relieved this hermeticism. In her last plays, composed between 1938 and her death in 1946, Stein brought herself back into the public arena.

"My writing is clear as mud, but mud settles and clear streams run on," she said.[28] The writing streamed into the world of history, politics, and the impressive cultural inheritance her readers once shared with her. With the change of scene, the style altered as well. There's more air in these final works, an ease even the blithest small early pieces couldn't achieve. Generous amounts of open space surround her characters: room for them to be unsupervised or pensive, places where the pace of the play slows down to a leisurely gait, the dance of language rests for an instant, and we see how a private moment fits together with a crowded world.

Doctor Faustus Lights the Lights, from 1938, is Stein's most charming and most alluring play – perhaps because many of her favored concerns echo the still mysterious themes familiar to us from mythology. Stein strips away all but the essentials of the myth, then intensifies the encounters that remain. *Doctor Faustus* presents a tetchy Faustus whose only retort to Mephisto is "go to hell," and who is helpless before the enchanting presence of "Marguerite Ida and Helena Annabel," a hybrid, of course, of the two foils in the original *Faust.* The urgent curiosity propelling all of Stein's writing here returns to its source: Faustus becomes something of an Ur-Stein, confronting the consequences of such willful investigations for her. The story that Stein borrows also allows her to further her experimentation with relationships. In this, her darkest portrait of attachment, Faustus's vulnerability to temptation leads him toward others as forcefully as his scruples will later drive him away. The tension grows almost unbearable as first Mephisto, then Marguerite Ida and Helena Annabel, orbit Faustus, drawing the circle closer around him. The whole play, taut with anticipation, seems to sit on the edge of a precipice. Stein dramatizes fear for the first time – using the steady escalation available through repetition to create an atmosphere of foreboding. Perhaps because we know the dangers in advance, the nature of our engagement changes. When placement carries such risk, we look at the arrangements more warily. Stein rejuvenates another abused aspect of melodrama: menace.

The integrity of identity is never at more risk than in *Doctor Faustus,* Stein having built up an understanding of self, feature by feature, in each of the plays that precedes it. Its value is never more significant – perhaps because, instead of scrutinizing other people's identities, she is at last assessing her own. In *Everybody's Autobiography* Stein describes how sudden celebrity has forced her to reassess the gulf between her public persona and her real self, and how it has changed her identity as an artist: "I am I because my little dog knows me. But was I I when I had no written word inside me."[29]

That worried question spurs Faustus's own "How can I be I again."[30] Other questions follow. Marguerite Ida and Helena Annabel join in, asking if they are one person or two, or nothing but phantoms. The bigger mysteries loom over these. Will the quest for understanding exact the price of Faustus's identity? What of himself will he sacrifice for knowledge of others?

Something that had always been a matter of strictly psychological interest in Stein's theater, originating with emotion, here becomes a troubling philosophical, theological question. And, as important, what had become an overfamiliar archetypal encounter – the Faust story, with only its broad strokes remembered – receives in Stein's hands a diagraming explicit about the inexorability of the seduction and its peril.

Stein's *Doctor Faustus* showed to the most skeptical spectator what her theater could be, what startling visions it could conjure. Her understanding of heavily traveled territory – the psyche – and her sensitivity to how it is buffeted by social and metaphysical winds made this play the sleekest expression of her dramatic art, and arguably the finest achievement in American drama before World War II. The plays that followed the war, and that marked her farewell to the theater, must have astounded even her least critical acolytes. In a sense, *Yes Is for a Very Young Man* and the second opera she wrote with Virgil Thomson, *The Mother of Us All,* are pieces simpler than anything Stein had written before. *Yes* is her most conventional work, and, apart from the operas, the only one of her plays to be staged in her lifetime. In its story – and it *is* a story – of a family's moral struggles in occupied France, Stein sacrifices none of her obsessions: Characters still fret over their place in a group, work to cultivate viable identities, and plunge into doomed relationships. But the narrative encasing them gives political, historical weight to what is dramatized.

The Mother of Us All also bears the weight of history, as befits a play about Susan B. Anthony's struggle for women's suffrage, but it is also one of Stein's most personal, and most exposing, works. The historical figure actually brings more of Stein onto the stage than her anonymous characters do. (There is a Gertrude Stein figure that flickers in and out, but Susan B., as she's called, carries in her the real Stein.) The play buzzes with famous personages, politicians caught up in rallies, friends from Stein's Paris ("Virgil T." makes an appearance); yet none of that seems so compelling as the picture of one of Stein's earliest interests – a solitary figure, here Susan B., thinking about how to furnish the solitude.

Aloneness in such a public world gives aloneness a political value, and in *The Mother of Us All* the politics are sexual. A woman's isolation means something different from a man's, though relieving that isolation has consequences just as various. What changes a woman into a wife? When Stein resumes her favorite pastime of making distinctions, she is stumbling toward questions like this one, not just enjoying the pleasure of her perceptiveness. "I am John Adams, there is Constance Fletcher."[31] John's assertion would be just another clarification of arrangements in an early play; here it suggests one frustrated individual struggling to assert his identity against another's determination to maintain her own. When a pair of newlyweds, Jo the Loiterer and Indiana Elliot, skirmish over changing names, it might sound strangely like the fountains of naming in Stein's other plays; here, though, with the rights of women on her characters' minds and sexual identity at stake, keeping your name in marriage and defiantly declaring it over and over has more than musical significance.

Susan B. paces the perimeter of her own detachment, despite the reliable presence of the Alice-like Anne, and the laudatory offerings of the women rallying around her. Susan B. echoes the plaintiveness of other Stein figures when she's irked by the fitfulness of the attentions of her audience, a group sometimes unheedful of this latest variation on the cry *listen to me*. But she is also determined to turn what is the inevitable condition of her celebrity – isolation – into an asset. She skillfully turns out the strength within the solitude. Susan B. is no object in space, or floating figure reflecting all of our ingenious interpretations but absorbing none; she's a more unequivocal, declarative display of self-reliance, self-sufficiency, and even embattled pride than any Stein character preceding her.

Preoccupied as it is with contesting ideologies, *The Mother of Us All* never sounds didactic; there is no smug conclusiveness to its arguments. In fact, nothing concludes. Even in this last play, so firmly, unapologetically rooted in the social world, Stein maintains her loathing of a dramatic structure built on beginnings and endings. But, as with the examination of aloneness and attachment, this choice now acquires political necessity. "Do I want what we have got," asks Susan B. at the end, "Has it not gone, what made it live, has it not gone because now it is had."[32] As wisely as any activist, Susan B. understands that, in projects for social change, the doing is always more crucial than the having; achievement risks inducing complacency; each conclusion should only spark a fresh beginning, energy directed toward a new end. The fervor of preparation in Stein's other work, the anticipation that shakes her versions of melodrama, are here too, but with an explanation. The imperative of continual movement is still an aesthetic issue, a necessity for lively, enlivening theater; it's now also a lesson in conducting a life. "My long life, my long life," Susan B. murmurs just before the curtain: It's the only time she allows herself to contain and set aside what has been an anxious gust of dramatic energy, looking at herself in tranquillity, just as it's the only place where the play itself relaxes.[33] Yet the perception remains active even then: Susan B.'s eye and mind still move when all else in her and in her world slowly, wearily settles.

"Has it not gone, what made it live." The question comes back as one looks over the whole of Stein's dramatic writing. Are these late, "accessible" plays something of a compromise, a concession to fidgeting audiences? Not really. Surely they will remain her most popular, read, like *Three Lives* and *The Autobiography of Alice B. Toklas,* by those who never venture into the other, more strenuous work. There's nothing wrong with this, of course, for in each of the crowd pleasers there are plentiful traces and reminders of what fills the neglected work, and they can act just as powerfully on the receptive reader. What would be regrettable, however, would be for us to draw conclusions about Stein only from these last plays. Perhaps any conclusion remains suspect, or at least flimsy. Stein knew that constant movement is just as essential to an artistic career as to a political one: The doing takes precedence over what's done; the course of one's art making is often more interesting than the monuments left in its wake. Gertrude Stein's theater resists all attempts to fix it with a label, to anchor it with an "ism," to make it demonstrate a theory or subscribe to an influence. It asks to be taken (in the critic Richard Bridgman's phrase) "in pieces," viewed as it moves, by spectators also on the run, just as the elements of her paragraphs do. *The Mother of Us All* is no more the quintessential Stein than *What Happened* is: Her best readers are those prepared to plod, or at least to coast, through each station of her dramatic passion, not those who hope only to generalize afterward. Like all good artists, she never proceeded in ways easy to chronicle.

Stein kept tearing open the fancy stitching of orthodox drama – returning to a writer's innocence, in a way, with each play, testing and refuting all assumptions about the craft, never resting in one manner if others were available. Restless, but not reckless – smart about the best ways to destroy ossified forms, but also guileless – she cried out that "writing should go on."[34] And after jettisoning most of the punctuation that would impede its progress, and letting her novels run to rude length, she started lining up a self-perpetuating series of plays, each bizarre and droll, each refusing to correspond to examples we had, yet also partaking of a logic she slowly formed to encompass her work, her work alone.

Her project was to probe and show and interpret all manner of human behavior. This never varied. Such a huge task, though, required her strategies always to change, with old ones tossed aside after their usefulness, in one or two plays, was exhausted. Why has she never made it into the textbooks? She clearly presented an artistic temperament, but for all her easily parodied turns, she refused to define a "style": The very word suggests too much rigidity and complacency, too much settled too early, for a writer who worried if it had not "gone because now it is had." Stein's theater preserves the image of that chronic dissatisfaction; and her impatience became a model for the acts of inspired vandalism (and later, energetic renovation) that occupied the writers who followed her into her drama and then emerged into their own.

Stein herself was the mother of us all, many of those followers have declared; but she was also the rambunctious child – teasing, reproaching us with her ingenuousness, shouting her immaturity in order to pester a gouty culture. Alone with her paper and pen, she traced shapes of experiences that others "wiser" and more "sophisticated" dismissed as doodles. Emotions in her work lay on the surface, like a child's, exposed to wounds and others' indifference, simple in their clarity and sincerity but never simpleminded. Again, many readers given over to other, more sonorous drama of the day, complained that there was nothing to "get" from Gertrude Stein, and what was there was incomprehensible, or sounded ugly, silly. "I speak as loudly as I can," Susan B. insists. "They deny that they listen to me, but let them deny it, all the same they do they do listen to me."[35] As Susan B. fades away, she carefully allows long, languid silences to cushion her last words and enforce time for our own alert listening. That time may be Stein's greatest gift to her audiences – that, and the daring to make a noise.

2

TENNESSEE WILLIAMS

TENNESSEE WILLIAMS SPENT a lifetime trying to escape clichés, those about his theater and those about the people his theater portrays, but the clichés still cling to him. They simplify his evolution as a writer and, what is perhaps worse, they persistently attract readers eager to diagnose his characters rather than listen to them. "Lonely outcasts," "sadly maimed," "torn by the passion of life" – the same phrases returned to herald each play, no matter how much richer it was than the last one, no matter how complicated and tentative its conjuring of emotion. To read Williams now, decades away from his period of greatest celebrity and after his subsequent notoriety has subsided, requires one first to weed out those epithets and clear a generous approach to his art. We think we know his world, so familiar does the summary of each play sound, but in fact we know only the accolades, or only the tone of the put-down. We're sure that our theater has moved on from the kind of writing Williams did, as perhaps it has, but after reading the writers who succeeded him in our devotion, his plays astonish us anew: They set a standard for emotional truthfulness that most playwrights still fail to match. What irritated our sensibilities twenty years ago is now refreshing, and what we passed over in the search for confirmation of the clichés now shines out, making those plays enthralling again, for different reasons, and their creator an ineffably moving figure once more.

In *Purification,* an early one-act, a judge speaks of the "stammered cry" of vulnerable people, a sound that "gives more of truth than the hand could put on passionless paper."[1] Williams always wrote in such halting rhythms (even his most fluent characters never lose their edge of panic), and set against the eloquence of his critics, they show how misleading the old familiar descriptions really are. Dime-store terms like "lonely" and "longing" aren't nearly as raw and shambling as the lives they mean to describe. Nor do his characters "have emotions," regardless of how much he is praised for expressing them. Such a conception of his theater suggests that each character totes about a well-ordered set of feelings – "sorrow," "frustration," "love," "jealousy," "grief" – which he confidently exhibits as the action unfolds. Rather, Williams deals in great washes of affect, only vaguely understood though viscerally felt, that sweep up his characters and surge through his plays. The size of feeling, unwieldy and impossible to measure, concerns Williams as much as the feeling itself. In fact, if his characters could name their conditions as deftly as many spectators have, they wouldn't suffer from them so.

Such opulent poignancy seems old-fashioned from our perspective. Williams himself saw this emotional accessibility going out of style even as he was writing toward it. "So successfully have we disguised from ourselves the intensity of our own feelings, the sensibility of our own hearts," he wrote in the preface to *The Rose Tattoo*, "that plays in the tragic tradition have begun to seem untrue."[2] Perhaps this is why some of his last plays sound so clumsy, with garrulous characters who never fully convince spectators that their sentiment is anything more than an exaggeration of the subtle feeling warming the early work. The stammered cry encountered in these plays sounds only like a rude, tuneless wail. And, at his theater's most strained, the awkwardness that Williams hoped to reveal really only reflects his own desperation. Too often Williams lets people speak when silence would be more affecting; he ruthlessly yanks them out of chiaroscuro when their half-hidden faces suggest deeper currents of feeling. In his *Memoirs* he declares his youthful admiration for Chekhov, but complains that "now I find that he holds too much in reserve."[3] If only Williams had been a better student of Chekhov, a reader might think, he wouldn't have had to grab at our sympathies so frantically and his plays would have easily coaxed readers into them.

And yet – it's hard not to feel sympathetic even to his disasters. His embarrassing gush was once liberating, a rare instance of sincerity and honesty in the relatively puritan culture of the forties and fifties. Something of that courage shows through all his work – especially the failures, where it is all the more indispensable. The years since *The Glass Menagerie* have taught playwrights to beware of sentimentality; and that restraint ensures theatrical force, that formal precision is more aesthetically pleasing than unbuckled psychological sprawl. We have grown accustomed to cooler, more decorous drama. How could such a simple approach – exposing all, saying everything – ever succeed? Didn't he know the usefulness of detachment? Thankfully, he did not. A Puccini in a world crowding with Philip Glasses, Williams shouldn't interest "serious" writers and readers any more, we're told – but now his steady faith in feeling dazzles because for so long it has been refused by others. Reading one of his plays now is exhilarating as it can be only in a culture hushed with minimalist pieties. Even his missteps, most written in the sixties and seventies, look strangely noble, if still not skillful – remarkable for holding themselves upright amid a theater community with which they had less and less in common.

Williams never really fell in with prevailing tastes, even in his golden age. He learned early in his career that "outsiderhood" was the source of his peculiar strength, what enabled him to make his special contribution as a writer. Part of no community for long, he could wholeheartedly enter others' lives, his sympathy for them wide open and unrestrained by provincial biases. His first adult years set the pattern for the wandering that would fill his future. His was a "lifetime of rented rooms," he once wrote, and it began even before his earliest success. In the years leading up to *The Glass Menagerie,* Williams lived briefly in Columbus, St. Louis, and Iowa City; in Los Angeles, New Mexico, and Provincetown; in New Orleans and Georgia. When he received a $100 prize for three one-acts submitted to a contest held by The Group Theater, he used the money not to go to New York, as any playwright eager to "make it" would have done. Instead, he and a friend rented bicycles and traveled down to Tijuana.

Only someone who never stayed long enough in one place to learn and abide by its standards of what was "appropriate" and "decent" would have risked as much as he did. The biggest risk was aesthetic. In 1964 Susan Sontag wrote a piece in which she dismissed claims for what other critics were calling Williams's radical inventiveness.[4] Only those writers who significantly alter our theater's sense of *form* can rightly be called radical, she argued; Williams really only retrieved for theater a harvest of long-avoided topics – sex the most prominent of them. But Sontag underestimated the degree to which such a choice of subject matter would in fact change one's idea of form. Williams made room in his plays for a startling frankness about erotic attraction: He allowed scenes to follow the course of sexual approach and retreat, the strategies of seduction. Characters no longer had only an intellectual life: They had bodies as well, and a need of a dramatic structure that wouldn't cramp them. Gore Vidal wrote that, with *A Streetcar Named Desire,* Williams introduced the idea of masculine sex appeal to the theater. Until then, Vidal argued, an actor was only a cardboard figure in a suit.[5] Williams allowed women the same freedom: When Serafina in *The Rose Tattoo* meets her would-be suitor, Williams lets her glance below the man's belt freely, unselfconsciously. Blanche in *Streetcar,* Maxine in *The Night of the Iguana,* the Princess in *Sweet Bird of Youth,* and Maggie in *Cat on a Hot Tin Roof* join her in using sexuality to generate and steer their wayward lives. Sex also steers the plays. The women's candor changes the weight of a scene and affects our sense of dramatic time: Languor alternates with breathlessness as the customary tempo of a Williams play.

That breathlessness, in particular, decisively changed theatrical form. "Horror of insincerity, horror of *not meaning,* overhangs these affairs like the cloud of cigarette smoke and the hectic chatter," wrote Williams about the

New York cocktail parties that both fascinated and disgusted him.[6] Yet he also could have been describing the atmosphere of his plays. His characters keep up the "hectic chatter" so that they can command attention, even if others are irritated. If they succeed, they have significance at least a tiny bit larger than what their self-pity and contempt has conferred upon them. For those afraid of not meaning, even notoriety or derisive laughter is better than invisibility.

So many of Williams's characters have a heliotrope temperament, drawn to the brightest eyes looking at them. They surrender themselves to the first person who lingers for a moment on their troubled faces, who pauses long enough to let them start a story. Because the one who surrenders in Williams's theater is usually a woman, and her listener a man, there's always an added level of danger to the exposure, a fear that too much might be relinquished, the possibility of more acute shame. When Williams lets his women loose, they burst out with a flood of huskily voiced needs, extravagantly described experiences, nosy questions, and fluttering self-deprecation, all with an explosive force that testifies to their long suppression. If the release is total, as it often is, their listeners' response invariably is startled bewilderment, a wondering silence that only spurs further exposure. This time, however, Williams's women reveal only inner emptiness, for everything has drained out in the first panic of confession. Spent, flayed characters lie about Williams's stage; few know how to let mystery protect them. "What can you do on this earth," says Carol Cutrere in *Orpheus Descending,* "but catch at whatever comes near you, with both your hands, until your fingers are broken?"[7]

Williams's chief contribution to twentieth-century drama looks unremarkable from our perspective: He wrote character-centered drama, a form we now take for granted. Beginning with *The Glass Menagerie,* Williams bucked convention and built up his plays around individuals, rather than trying, as so many other writers had long been doing, to fit his people into a plot. Even the greatest characters in theater history must be seen in the context of a story, a myth, a philosophical program. Williams stripped all that away to reveal the essence of his characters. He set aside "action" of the usual sort in favor of the internal catastrophes that sometimes can't be seen, can't be assigned to any clear source, or that follow small, seemingly inconsequential events. Electric encounters between men and women form the core of a Williams play, and the complications to these exchanges mark its progress. There are stories, surely, but they aren't as significant as the subtle modulations of temperament during conversations or awkward pauses, as what might happen after a missed rendezvous, or one that wasn't smoothly handled; a failure to recognize someone; inattentiveness during intimacy; a badly timed interruption; or being caught off guard, one's disguise for socializing not yet in place. "Time was," wrote the *New York Times* critic adversely of *Kingdom of Earth,* "when Tennessee Williams wrote plays, but nowadays he seems to prefer to write characters."[8] For Williams there could have been no higher praise; this was precisely his prime virtue.

The most memorable Williams characters stand out from their plays like lighthouses in stormy weather. No matter how ill arranged the rest of a play might be, they successfully direct attention to their own private, disaster-prone site, exacting sympathy even when other parts of Williams's art cannot. These characters are all wilfully ostentatious presences, casting their worlds into shadow. Williams called a late, failed play *Out Cry;* all his work could wear the same title. His characters call out for more room of their own, a release from claustrophobia. They want a place among the entertaining, clubby, satisfied group, but they always also doubt the possibility of ever belonging anywhere. Williams's people can't be other than they are, and that's what is so troubling. They are simply, inextricably, woefully *there,* resistant to analogy or a redeeming metaphor, surrounded by symbols but unfortunately not symbols themselves. They are all too human, with their dirty hair, halitosis, eccentricities, and all; their hiccuping laughs, leg braces, hothouse demeanors; their unsure senses of humor, just missing the mark; their lustiness always going awry. The sound of their pleas sets the pitch for others' speech. Likewise, the way they rush toward a visitor paces all movement, and the perimeter of their restless roaming defines the theatrical space. They all fear the possibility of being overwhelmed by their unruly feelings, and the panic that escalates as each play moves on shows how desperate are their struggles to master them.

These are qualities that Williams's central characters – all women – have in common. But in numerous other ways his characters diverge and resist classification. Williams's plays, for all their popularity, aren't really "universal," nor should they be. Of course, there are times when one's description of Blanche, say, could fit nicely on Lady, from *Orpheus Descending;* or when an aspect of Maggie seems part of *Orpheus*'s Carol Cutrere. Many of his characters betray something that all their spectators also endure, in greater or lesser degrees, and burrow their way out of conditions vaguely known to us. But the oddness of Williams's characters is really more compelling than their familiarity, and the traits that make them different from one another are usually more interesting than those they share. Those peculiar traits linger on in our minds long after our moment of identification has passed. If only they *could* be universal, maybe the pain of their idiosyncrasy would be mitigated, shared.

If Williams's women are ever going to fully escape the diagnosis that dismisses them as "neurotic," they deserve to be seen one at a time. It is necessary, I think, to begin speaking of individuals when discussing this virtuoso of the individual. Three of the most memorable women are worlds unto themselves; to understand them is to understand their plays.

AMANDA

It should go without saying that Amanda is the center of *The Glass Menagerie,* but sentimental productions often put Laura there, cued perhaps by the title or seduced by her vulnerability. Other, more literal-minded directors see Tom as the central figure, for the play is structured by his memory and saturated with his emotion, a version of Williams's own. For all her ostentatiousness, Amanda is easily shunted aside – perhaps because of our discomfort with her pathetic behavior or because we want Williams's play to be more bittersweet than it really is. When well performed, Amanda is a maverick, not the gauzy woman we have in mind from photographs of Laurette Taylor, who created the role. She doesn't let us pity her; and a good production of *The Glass Menagerie* doesn't leave us merely sorrowful. We should recoil from it a bit, just as we should always feel uncomfortable around Amanda.

Amanda is a mess of contradictions. One minute, she's shy and self-deprecating; the next, she's upset because no one paid attention to her latest bit of gossip. The actor shouldn't streamline her, as is possible, perhaps, with Laura – an altogether less fully imagined character. Amanda is too boisterous for any easy interpretation – by actor or spectator – and while she may pander shamelessly to her children and acquaintances, especially the Gentleman Caller, she never makes it easy for us to know her, much less feel superior to her.

Much is rotten at the heart of *The Glass Menagerie,* despite its reputation as a charming play. In fact, the "authorial voice" is unreliable. Tom sets the tone of rueful recollection, but what he remembers doesn't stay within seemly bounds. It's as though Amanda defies the way she is being imagined, always trying to bust out of Tom's memory and set things *her* way. She only ruins those things beyond repair – her problem all through life. She seems to know her own ineptitude, for she tries hard to distract from it, or prevent embarrassment with lots of talk about good intentions. She loathes vulgarity and works to maintain an air of propriety and delicacy even when the strain is most obvious.

Worse than vulgarity for Amanda is ordinariness – and so she pushes her children to be unusual, a cut above. She also twists herself to assume an unnatural elegance, always devising ways to elude predictability and mockery. She's not a cartoon – another frequent mistake seen in hastily conceived productions. She's vivid, certainly, but also subtly observed, presented from all angles, just this side of grotesque. One cannot describe Amanda without a stream of qualifications – and this seems to be her conscious strategy. She may be manipulative, but she's also vulnerable. She's anxious but also resolute. By such flip-flops, she succeeds in cheating those who mock her. She's more complicated a figure than can fit easily into their dismissive one-liners.

Amanda protects herself by being so mercurial; she knows a moving target can't be hit.

One remembers Amanda as always on her feet – a woman aflutter, cajoling her children or preparing for guests, scolding, dressing up or stripping down, gabbing on the phone. Her speed is surely an essential part of her character – her life is one long nervous run from humiliation – but Amanda is most compelling when she's least "theatrical," when she stops and pauses and lets herself step off to the side a bit, perhaps not noticed by everyone. It's then that we can hear what comes after the sweeping gesture, or see the expression that follows a loud declaration that nobody listened to.

Amanda is charming, in a bullish way, but when she drops the charm she tells us more. "I – *loved* your father," she says midway through the play, almost without warning.[9] The dash in the line is crucial. In that pause – perhaps it is even a gasp – you hear Amanda consider and reject the easier statement, something blithe and funny – and you also see her unable to come up with a proper alternative, a statement that would keep the conversation flowing. She and Tom started out talking about Laura, and then about Tom himself. Amanda now wants to discuss her missing husband, by way of urging Tom to change his ways, but all these subjects quickly fall away. She's left with no choice but to talk about herself – which is something, remarkably, Amanda rarely does. (She's often discussing her "glamorous" past, or her run-of-the-mill daily doings, but she never allows herself any moment of real self-assessment.) And so, with no options left, she can't help but speak the truth, plain as it is. Plainness won't do, though – so she artfully emphasizes the word "loved," and makes theater out of mere autobiography.

Without her sense of theater, Amanda couldn't bear the emptiness of her life. Williams compares the way Amanda sits on a fire escape to a Southern belle "settling into a swing on a Mississippi veranda." When Jim arrives, Amanda gets herself up in voile and silk, the dress she wore for *her* gentleman caller. By adding a bouquet of jonquils to her costume, Williams is cruel for the first time in his writing life. Those oversized, histrionic flowers make her a figure of fun – no longer just sad and trapped in illusions, but now garish too.

For all her talk, Amanda is most proficient at the instantly intelligible and often poignant gesture. She fully inhabits her body, whether sitting down or entering a room or, more commonly, making a face – letting her features sag in a look of calculated dismay or screwing them up to let someone know how hopeful she is, and how careful one must be not to disappoint her. She's not only a fiery intellect and imagination, as Tom is, nor just an acutely sensitive spirit, as is Laura. She's both those things, and a persuasive physical presence as well.

Her athleticism serves her well when it comes time to play the martyr or the mignon, two favorite roles. Appearance means a lot to Amanda, for she knows the schedule of ridicule: Once people have an opportunity to make fun of your looks, they'll go on to make rude assumptions about your intelligence and behavior and family and friends. Amanda nags Tom to fix his hair; worries over Laura's flat chest and won't let her think she's crippled. Amanda refuses to acknowledge any sort of debility. It's a quality worth praising her for: When you think of how often others must have made Laura feel worthless, Amanda's affected airiness must come as some kind of relief. But from another perspective, it's just another symptom of Amanda's refusal to accept the truth, and of the suffocating nature of her love.

Amanda fusses about her children so energetically that it's a shock when out of nowhere she stops short and says, "My devotion has made me a witch!"[10] She surprises us for many reasons. For one thing, it's a graceless admission, and Amanda is so fierce on the subject of grace that no matter how frequent are her lapses into vulgarity – and they *are* frequent – they always give pause. This is more than a lapse, however: It's a plunge, taken with full awareness of the desired effect. Many audiences will come away from Amanda calling her schizophrenic, but she is never out of control. Whether she's giddy or glum or racing between the two, she keeps one eye on the expressions of her children, gauging their reactions and figuring out what emotional state to hurl herself into next.

Amanda's statement can also make us rethink the way we have been evaluating her. Up to now, despite our sense of how calculating she is, we've thought she doesn't know the destructive consequences. Her self-condemnation suggests that she may be capable of change – something unthinkable for a woman so in love with nostalgia, so fixed on impossible, spun-silk futures for her children.

Amanda's understanding of truth is most fleeting with regard to sex. *The Glass Menagerie* has come to seem a remarkably sexless play over the years – a play about "feelings" more than urges. Indeed, there's little of the sexual candor that pervades all of Williams's later plays. But sex is a force in *Menagerie,* made important by the energy with which Amanada tries to deny its existence. "Instinct is something that people have got away from!" Amanda says approvingly. "It belongs to animals!"[11] But no matter how hard she tries to ignore instinct, Amanda always comes face to face with it – especially her own.

Her husband, an adulterer, has run away from home, this time for good. His picture, larger than life, sits on the mantle, a massive reminder of the power of flesh. Amanda's own behavior is at odds with the sermon she preaches: Her flirtiness, the sudden waves of girlishness, are far more convincing. She treats the Gentleman Caller as if he were calling on *her;* and, in a skillful production, her dealings with Tom should also have a faintly sensual undercurrent. Williams never again renders a mother as completely as he does here (few of his plays even have mothers in them). Only Mrs. Venable in *Suddenly Last Summer* comes close to matching the same uneasy blend of devotion and devouring. Amanda's children see this, and pass through the play in a state of constant embarrassment. They aren't just chagrined by their mother's theatricality; they also feel a deep, ineluctable shame at not being able to return her love. She makes them see their own hollowness.

Amanda doesn't know how to channel her considerable emotion or when to limit it. You sense that she is afraid to moderate her love, afraid that she'll wither up if she doesn't keep going at full throttle. If she weren't running after her son or his friends, she would find someone else to run after. What's important to Amanda is not the object of affection but how the experience of affection makes her feel. She constantly expects to be abandoned, so when she senses someone in her presence – whoever that may be (even a near-stranger on the phone) – she exudes a heartiness that comes more from relief than from real interest in the other person: relief that someone is simply there, and that she still can rise to the occasion.

Amanda is such an oversized character that she nearly banishes Laura from the play. Laura's shyness draws her to the shadows; Amanda's ego keeps her there. While Amanda says she wants a secure marriage for her daughter, she really loathes the thought of seeing Laura happier than she is; further, she wouldn't be able to stand the loneliness if Laura left home. In all situations, Amanda is practical at the same time that she is helplessly romantic. The two contrary forces vie with each other most strongly when it comes to envisioning the future. Laura may not be particularly glamorous company for Amanda, but at least she's someone who won't go unless pushed. So, for all her cajoling, Amanda never really forces change on Laura. In fact, Amanda makes a point of comforting Laura at the end of *The Glass Menagerie,* setting things aright again after Jim has revealed his engagement. It's the one place where Amanda drops her many roles and allows herself a moment of true feeling. After she wipes away Laura's tears, she glances briefly at the portrait of her absent husband. Tom, too, has now left. We can almost hear Amanda's sigh of thankfulness that her last possible companion won't be leaving just yet.

It never sounds completely convincing when commentators speak of how Williams's characters keep reaching out for connections with others; for just as desperately do they turn in on themselves, pull back from others, determined to possess themselves in case they can't have anyone else. Amanda at the end of *The Glass Menagerie* does exactly this. She's locked in for these final moments, suffering Laura's isolation with her; but that seems safer than trying to take up where she's not welcome. She suddenly seems to know just where she stands – on the edges of "acceptable" life and its conventional behavior, able to see its pleasures and privileges, and often eager to assume whatever disguise is necessary to enter it, but also deeply aware that she'll never be able to pull it off. Amanda has probably known this all along – only now she doesn't have to pretend that her life is any different. In this final scene, Amanda looks at herself and for the first time chooses not to flinch at what she sees.

BLANCHE

In many ways Blanche DuBois is a kindred spirit to Amanda Wingfield. Both are anxious about appearance and class – and so always look out of place wherever they are. Both suffer lasting humiliations from bad marriages. Both are emotionally unpredictable – flighty one minute, sulky the next. And for all their disgust at vulgarity, both are helpless to keep it at bay.

But Blanche is more volatile than Amanda. The difference is only partly due to Blanche's age. In fact, despite her relative youth, Blanche has a closer understanding of violence and real suffering, and so is less adept at presenting a show of charm. For all her theatricality, Blanche is not as artful an actress as Amanda. She is also too smart ever to believe in the parts she plays – the brittle, cool aristocrat; the sex kitten; the rebellious adolescent. But that doesn't mean she won't try to carry off the masquerade, and keep trying, for she knows that the effort alone can make her feel better. Blanche's common sense is considerable, a quality often missed by actors fascinated only by her neurasthenia. She isn't always clear about her ultimate objectives (as Amanda is), but she's more alert to subtleties of the moment; and when she does get something she wants, such as a suitor, she's wise enough to know that the satisfaction won't last.

A Streetcar Named Desire portrays only the final moments in the long history of Blanche's decline. Williams sets his best play in Blanche's last refuge and dramatizes her ultimate battle; her fate was settled before she arrived at the Kowalskis' home on the street called Elysian Fields. Much of *Streetcar* is taken up with Blanche's look back at a life of disappointed expectations and subsequent deceit – elaborate descriptions of the glamour of Belle Reve, the family estate, and the grief she felt as she watched her family die off and the estate slip out of her hands. The details of her story are questionable, but not its message of thoroughgoing loss. What matters is that Blanche *feels* pulled to shreds, even if her account of the causes isn't credible. Part of what makes Blanche remarkable, in fact, is that her dignity, or at least her stature, seems to grow as each lie she tells is more roughly exposed. Such endurance is the most incredible thing about her.

Most of the lies concern the life she led after Belle Reve: Instead of becoming a proper, prim schoolteacher, as she'd have her family believe, she wandered the lowlier parts of New Orleans, taking in men at a seedy hotel, seeking the affection she didn't find when she was married to Allan Grey, a homosexual who killed himself shortly after their marriage. She's now dog-eared and destitute but determined to behave as though nothing has changed.

By coming to Stella's home, she thinks she will be able to live more peacefully. Perhaps she hopes also to reinvent herself. Instead, she stumbles more often and finally falls.

Blanche is easily threatened at Stella's, but her fear doesn't make her pull back from life, as one might expect. Blanche is as resolute (even at times as vengeful) as she is hunted. She knows how to taunt and tease; she wounds as often as she is wounded. The way she dissects Stanley's personality in front of Stella, comparing him to a Neanderthal, shows that, for all her vaporousness, Blanche hasn't lost her presence of mind. Blanche isn't quite malicious, and she doesn't ever hate those around her; but everyone she encounters at Stella's seems to reproach her, usually unintentionally, and she lashes back to stop feeling the pain. People with money, or with stature of another kind – mothers, happily married wives, men in general – represent a condition of stability that Blanche has always longed for and that she once thought was assured her.

In traditional interpretations of *Streetcar,* it's Stanley who causes Blanche the most distress. After all, he is blustery, unkempt sensuality; he's from a class that Blanche fears; and he quickly sees through Blanche's disguise. But, the rape notwithstanding, Stanley's behavior doesn't rankle Blanche as much as Stella's: Her natural goodness might lead one to think that the sisters' bond is sturdy enough; but Stella represents an achieved sexuality. She has a rocky but nonetheless enduring marriage – and a pregnancy to prove it. Without intending to do so, Stella mocks Blanche's failure to be the woman she hoped to be. That's why Blanche tries to hurt Stella alone. The one person Blanche expects to be her ally abandons her. When the Kowalskis fight, and Stella leaves Stanley, Blanche does all she can to keep them apart, if only to have a companion in bereavement. Then she won't feel so freakish for being alone. The fact that Stella returns to Stanley hurts even more, for Stella does what Blanche has never been able to do: heal. Stella is capable of adapting to a host of new circumstances; she wouldn't have weathered the move from Belle Reve to Elysian Fields if she were not. Blanche, for all her protestations to the contrary and all her masquerades, is stuck. And so she has always been faced with the same afflictions, experiencing them over and over. Even though Blanche doesn't have to suffer Stella's sequence of abuse and recuperation, she does have to relive her own history and face the consequences anew in Stella's presence. She can't help but compare her sister's life to her own, and she winces at what she sees as her manifold inadequacies.

On her arrival at Elysian Fields, Blanche is close-coiled, wary, unable to believe she's finally reached a hospitable destination. It's a long time before the look of caution softens; only once or twice does it entirely leave her. Even at her most jubilant, she never relaxes entirely – for fear that her already weakened body will suffer total depletion. She downs several glasses of whiskey on first entering Stella's living room, but she doesn't drink to unwind. The liquor, she thinks, will make it easier to do the hard work necessary to hold herself together.

As *Streetcar* progresses, and Blanche settles into the Kowalski home, she begins to risk a little more. She deepens her intimacy with her sister. She learns to banter with Stanley's friends. One of them, Mitch, is easy to talk to, and she relaxes even more around him. Finally, she lets herself feel attracted to the primitive in Stanley. She can do so only because she has first learned the best way to combat the nagging feelings of vulnerability caused by his presence: She cultivates a parallel image of weakness, replacing real fear with managed, acted nervousness. If she can play this role successfully even for a moment, she won't have to experience actual pain.

Soon she has remembered all the other tricks of survival. She chooses not to see the world the way other characters do – that way, she can't be a victim of it. She creates for herself an entire alternative world, with different rooms, different light, her own kind of music, characters, manners, and rituals. It's a place where she can be charming, for she alone defines the meaning of charm. And if others enter her world and ridicule it, they are the ones who will feel foolish. For this time Blanche is the insider.

Like many of Williams's characters, Blanche is most adept at manipulating language. Words and phrases come in for swift renovation in her vernacular. When Stella refers to Stanley's friends as a "mixed lot," Blanche amends that to "heterogenous types." Her ancestors didn't just have sex with all takers; they perpetuated an "epic fornication." Blanche is drawn to lyricism partly because of what she's been witness to. Intimately familiar with death and decay, in all its unpoetic reality, she works hard now to bring some romanticism, some poetry back into her life. But poetry doesn't mean prettiness for Blanche. She doesn't want to gussy up the suffering, but instead to restore its true dimensions and feel through language its full horror.

A chance encounter with a newspaper boy midway through the play, just before she's due to meet Mitch for a date, gives her a chance to experiment with the potential of another kind of language. Luring the boy closer with rhapsodic descriptions of long rainy afternoons ("when an hour isn't just an hour – but a little piece of eternity dropped into your hands – and who knows what to do with it?"), she releases her sexuality into her language – a medium she can control, for she's too unsure, in this instance, of how to express her desire physically, and what the consequences might be.[12] (A few minutes earlier she had confessed to Stella, "Yes – I *want* Mitch . . . *very badly*!" – a sentence that tears through the velvet diction Blanche usually favors.)

Blanche assumes a prominent place in the long line of Williams's heroines who think that their sexuality is a curse and that they must always counter transgressions of the flesh. Blanche feels unfit, unworthy, dirty. Her emotional disarray comes from utter nausea at the sight of herself, of the mess she's made of a life designed in lily white. (Not for nothing is she named

Blanche; even her own name is mocking her now.) No matter what others say to her, no matter how steadfastly her sister assures her of her worth, or Mitch makes her see what's true and valued in her, Blanche seeks out the toxins, the blemishes; and if none are there, she inflicts damage on herself, for she believes she deserves it. She forces herself to do a brutal penance for the pain she has suffered. She knows she can never prettify herself, but she still hopes to discover some kind of purity, to perceive wholesomeness in someone else. She at least wants to know where goodness resides and how far away from it she is. Other Williams plays are more explicitly concerned with religion, but in Blanche, Williams finds his first and most probing seeker after grace.

Blanche is drawn to something she can barely express: It may be an image of an ideal self or of a more reliable companion, a more sensitive guardian. In all cases, hers is a voluptuous spirituality. In fact, "God" is too simple, and too authoritarian, an idea for the kind of sustenance she seeks. She is seduced outside of herself until the traps of her life are a distant memory, and she can understand what caused her ambitions for a satisfying life to fall to pieces. She *believes,* because not to believe is too frightening; to live her life without *something* overhead is too depressing. To have lost your god is worse than to believe in one that may not exist.

It's all too easy to ridicule Blanche for the flimsiness of her moral beliefs. "I have old-fashioned ideals," she says, and one immediately thinks of the hotel room in Laurel where she entertained man after man.[13] But such a dismissal misses the point. Blanche believes her ideals even if we don't. She knows how imperfectly she lives up to them, but that doesn't diminish their power as ideals, goals still to aspire to. They also stabilize her – all else in her life is transient, unreliable, easily corrupted and corrupting. An ideal remains pure forever – and as elusive as any other object of true faith. "Sometimes – there's God – so quickly!" she says, recounting the tragedy of her husband.[14] These visions of God are all she's looking for – the relief they bring is powerful enough to help her endure the multiple disappointments, the many times she doesn't see God but her own degradation, or the pitiful look of her supplication.

For all her self-involvement, Blanche moves beyond herself in these moments of waiting for God. And as she looks for some pattern in the series of destructions she has lived through, we see her vast reserves of pity and compassion, as though she feels herself to be representative of a whole race of troubled people, including Allan, Stella, poor Mitch, her family, and those she can only imagine. In fact, Blanche is theatrical only because she feels herself to be exemplary of a condition. She's that rare contradiction: an empathic, giving diva. (Not incidentally, her least admirable moments – when she's trying to keep Stanley and Stella apart, for instance – are her least histrionic.)

Blanche's belief in ideals doesn't mean she is ignorant of reality. Quite the opposite: No matter how enthralling her visions are at the lowest stations of her journey to Elysian Fields, she never closes her eyes to the threadbare curtains, the torn upholstery, the soiled sheets on the rented bed. Much confusion has come about because of the famous lines in *Streetcar:* "I don't want realism. I want magic! Yes, yes, magic! I try to give that to people. I misrepresent things to them. I don't tell the truth, I tell what *ought* to be truth. And if that is sinful, then let me be damned for it! *Don't turn the light on!*"[15] Audiences conditioned to see Blanche as unstable and emotionally reckless can miss the lucidity in this passage. She calls for magic from a position of complete awareness of reality and from disgust at the reductive, bloodless ways in which it has been understood and in which life has been lived. "She's mad," according to just about everyone in the play. "She's too fragile for this world," according to most of those who watch or read it. For Blanche, such madness is a form of self-protection, spiritual armor. Only by setting herself apart from the world and the way the world sees itself can she make her way through it. Madness could also be an exultant way of living – were people not so hemmed in by orthodox styles of behavior, a killing idea of "propriety." There's no doubt that, by the play's end, Blanche is destroyed. But hers is not simply a case of not fitting in. She knows what kind of life she is rejecting; she is just "passing through," she says as she's escorted out in a straitjacket. Perhaps her greatest moment of strength is this one, when she looks most weak. For it is here that she sizes up the world around her, relinquishes the fight to make it accommodate her, understands its limitations – and knows that its limitations are more ruinous than her own. By leaving this world, she declares that she's too big for it – and too proud and smart to ever cut herself down to its size.

"Blanche is me," Williams is reputed to have said. True or not, Williams shared his heroine's ambition to change the way we define reality. It shouldn't need restating at this late date that Williams was neither a realist, in the textbook sense, nor a pedantic naturalist. But the false impressions persist, domesticating Williams, sapping the allure from his work. Perhaps the usually misguided films of his plays have created the idea that he was more interested in outward verisimilitude than in emotional veracity. Williams was searching for a realism more real than what he saw on other stages, so he followed a policy of distortion, akin to expressionism but more substantive and subtle. Blanche's famous cry for magic was Williams's too, but unlike Blanche he didn't escape from people. He developed his theatrical magic to bring him closer to the hidden parts of minds and manners, families and those trapped in them – hoping to conjure up lives more vividly than orthodox realism ever could. His most memorable characters couldn't possibly behave themselves in order to fit into a "realistic" play. Williams wrote them in such a way that we feel we're seeing them up close – too close – and with the volume always up. They are instantly outré, and we're pulled deep into their lives. There's none of the polite distance between spectator and actor nor the chill of a clinical proceeding that characterizes most realism.

Many designers forget that Williams often asks for fragmentary scenery, sketchy rooms held together only by the efforts of inhabitants to feel comfortable in them. Wild, unmastered territory, urban or rural, is always just beyond the door, if there even *is* a door to offer protection. In *Streetcar,* the tuba-call of locomotives and the reproachful "Blue Piano" from down the alley regularly intrude, punctuating scenes or commenting on them. The blend of sounds and speech makes *Streetcar* more a collage than a narrative – representing known places, to be sure, but also suggesting some more profound configuration, a more ambiguous arrangement of experience. The world of *Streetcar* palpitates most severely toward the end when, in crucial stage directions often ignored, Williams asks for shadows to fill the walls and for broadchested echoes of everyone's speech to accompany Blanche's final submission. By now, spectators perceive the environment only through Blanche's eyes. She leaves a play she can't make sense of, can't even fully see, a room that refuses to correspond in even slight ways to her comforting memories of "home" – and presumably to *our* ideas of home as well.

In the years that followed *Streetcar,* Williams widened the gulf between our sentimental image of domestic life and its true image. He pushed his women toward even greater extremes of experience, starting from where Blanche left off. His next characters often suffer even harsher denunciation by those who uphold standard behavior. But the women also seem to know beforehand the price of their transgressions. It's as though they've witnessed what Blanche has gone through and are now able to pass by the obstacles she kept stubbornly running up against, hoping to make them budge. The heroines in these next plays know better than to even try. They understand their outsiderhood at the start, and each in her own way devises stunning reproaches to the world.

MAGGIE

No one is more stylish, or more savvy, in her defiance than Maggie the Cat. Her rage sustains her throughout *Cat on a Hot Tin Roof.* From the moment she enters, furious at the "no-neck monsters" for hitting her with a hot buttered biscuit, she keeps up an attitude of utter impatience, a deep disgust at the petty greed, social maneuvering, and small-mindedness that surround her. Maggie's anger doesn't come from her sense of superiority. Although she probably does feel more worthy than her husband's family, the well-to-do Pollitts, she also knows that such pride is unjustified: Having grown up in poverty, she has no standing. Maggie loathes this liability, so she bursts out in tirades against others to avoid attacking herself.

Her captive audience is her husband, Brick. Dependent on a crutch and everyone's ministrations after breaking his leg jumping hurdles on his high-school track, Brick is surly, silent company. He and Maggie have come to his parents' plantation, along with Brick's sister and her family, ostensibly to celebrate Big Daddy's birthday. In fact, they have gathered to preside over his death. Just before the play begins, the family learns that he has cancer, and the news sets in motion a mad scramble to soothe Big Mama's anxiety, to jockey for position in the inheritance, and to establish, at last, some truthful bonds between parent and child.

The difficulty of the latter task aggravates the tensions between husband and wife. Big Daddy wants his favorite son to provide him a grandchild, so that the line of succession will be assured. But Brick's marriage is frozen; he can't even speak to Maggie, much less sleep with her. Hatred, it seems, is all that keeps Brick from leaving Maggie – but it's shame that really holds them together. Maggie is the only one who knows Brick's youthful humiliation: His best friend in college, Skip, killed himself because he was homosexual. Brick feels implicated, with the nature of their friendship and his own sexuality called into question. His life with Maggie is a constant reminder of this experience; but Maggie also provides a place to hide, a place where he doesn't have to keep up a pleasant exterior. The pretense of his life, and also of their marriage, has already fallen away.

Maggie endures this state of affairs, but equanimity is beneath her. She fears reaching a point where she will calmly accept the status quo. That would mean she was fallow – as helpless as Brick, as close to death as Big Daddy. "I'm alive!" she hollers at one point, trying to beat back the conspiracy of neglect taking over the entire plantation.[16] She gets her nickname, the Cat, from her story of a cat trapped on a roof during a sizzling day. The tin heats up, but the cat doesn't jump. It scratches and claws and screams, but stays on. Maggie likes the example of fortitude. Later, she speaks of a scene that captivates her even more. She enjoys imagining that she is running with hunting dogs through cold wind, leaping over obstructions, pursuing feeble prey. For Maggie doesn't want merely to last out the family crisis. She wants to prevail, to come out ahead in the end. She wants to win.

Maggie is a political animal – and a clever one. She knows the ins and outs of the Pollitt family history better than those born into it and is able to distinguish between real status and mere inflated self-regard. She is also attuned to the ways in which the family members manipulate each other, and she can usually tell when they're concealing secrets. Maggie can move easily around the perimeter of whatever society she finds herself near, but for all her skill at analyzing personalities, she can never enter their circles. She lacks that attribute essential to any successful politician: magnetism. Certainly, she's a luminous, exciting figure for us in the audience. But she's easily overlooked by the other characters. In fact, they have turned their backs on her. Despite her theatricality, Maggie can never expect to be the center of attention.

Williams himself tries to defeat Maggie's need for the spotlight. In an important stage direction, he writes:

> The bird that I hope to catch in the net of this play is not the solution of one man's psychological problem. I'm trying to catch the true quality of experience in a group of people, that cloudy, flickering, evanescent – fiercely charged! – interplay of live human beings in the thundercloud of common crisis.[17]

Melodramatic language aside, this passage points to the remarkable tension between the playwright and the characters he has created. Williams is speaking here of Brick, trying to deflect attention away from the specifics of his sexual dilemma and onto the repercussions it causes in those around him. This is wise, for amateur psychologists in the audience are likely to forgo the play in favor of Brick's case study. The drama isn't with him. But it *is* with Maggie – and I think Williams has invented a character who defies his own intentions, much as Amanda defied Tom. For Maggie, the play is as claustrophic as the plantation. Maggie's vision of herself – as an interloper, a woman living on borrowed time, always in debt to others – determines everything she does. She is never unaware of her position, and she even seems to underscore it when others may have momentarily accepted her. She'll pick a fight with Mae or lampoon a Pollitt habit that only a newcomer would notice. Before long, she's drawn so much attention to her difference that she's not able to take part in the drama. She leaves one cold world for another – her own solitude.

When Maggie does try to break free of the family, she is rudely reminded that she never belonged in the first place. Blood determines rights in this world. Maggie only married into the family, so she is never far from the door. Maggie's understanding of this prejudice intensifies her yearning to have a child by Brick. As mother to a Pollitt, she would have a slightly more secure position. Maggie is the first of Williams's women who are caught between worlds: She is not yet a mother, like Amanda, so she doesn't have the power that comes with that responsibility. Neither is she a daughter – in the play's terrain, at least – so she lacks that easily accessible target for rebellion, a mother. Blanche may seem more alone than Maggie, but Blanche at least has the ability to affix herself to another person and stay there a while. Maggie can't even do that – she has no sister nor a likely suitor. If Brick even so much as notices her flirting with him, he's disgusted. Maggie always feels useless – never more so than when she's reminded that she's bound in a sexless marriage, and so is doomed to childlessness.

inders of the fleshly life are everywhere. In *Cat* Williams grows more ıble with sex and with the physical presence of his characters. The 't the corseted, invisible demon it is to Laura in *The Glass Menagerie.* s it always an agent of violence, as is Stanley's body. Nor, finally, is .. a freakish, subversive foreign object, as Blanche's body is to the men in *Streetcar.* In *Streetcar,* bodies are present only to emphasize points made dramaturgically – points about masculine power and eros, Blanche's emotional weakness, or, in the case of Stella's pregnancy, feminine virtue. In *Cat,* the physical life is presented more thoroughly. The first act has Maggie in a slip, Brick in pajamas. She's comfortable in such a state of undress; Brick is nervous. Both characters make us watch their bodies as attentively as we listen to their conversation. Brick is stolid, sheer mass, lumbering, sitting, making us aware of his size, letting us see the discomfort of being stuck in a leg-cast on a hot day in the South. Brick speaks little, but his body fascinates. He's an exotic creature arrested in midflight. Maggie, for her part, always touches herself, looks at her figure in the mirror ("Nothing's fallen," she says, admiring her breasts and hips); she fusses over her hair, lounges, twirls, and sashays. It's especially exhilarating when, midway through the act, Maggie powders her underarms: She even sweats!

The play's other bodies are just as prominent. Pollitt children are always underfoot, and their constant chatter and roughhousing noisily reproach Maggie for her abbreviated sexual life. Where are her own children to join the game? In addition, the Pollitt family is opulently proportioned. Flesh ripples out from bodices and T-shirts, strains against linen suits and silk, takes up a lot of space. It's not just the famous movie that suggests that, in any production of *Cat,* Maggie should be the smallest person in the cast. Her entire demeanor matches that of someone who literally has to fight for space.

Big Daddy's cancer draws particular attention to his body, since soon it will waste away. And his illness seems to have spread beyond his body and throughout his house, incapacitating every character, or simply throwing into painful relief those debilities that once went politely undiscussed. *Cat* is one of Williams's most sustained views of dying, a theme that would obsess him in all his subsequent plays. Williams doesn't make Big Daddy's condition the subject of the play – that would be to write just the sort of problem play he warns against in his note about Brick. Instead, he attempts a broader understanding of illness – which allows him to exercise his moral sensibility in addition to his usual theatrical flair. The most seductive Williams plays are the sickest – those, like *Orpheus Descending,* set in places beyond repair (what Williams calls "Dragon Country") or, like *Suddenly Last Summer,* in places so lush they seem poisonous. *Cat* has that decadent appearance, too – the plantation suggests its eventual collapse more than its wealth – but here Williams also has a surer idea of how such an environment affects its inhabitants.

Cancer isn't the only sickness in *Cat*. "Mendacity" is also endemic. The word is Brick's, and it refers not just to ordinary lying but to ingrained personal corruption. Characters so root themselves in an environment of distrust and dishonor that mendacity almost becomes an *ethic*. Seizing upon the idea, Big Daddy rails against the deception surrounding his illness (everyone has been telling him it's only an ulcer), his son's marriage, and the whole sordid family history.

In his bluff, snarling way, Big Daddy is trying to get at a problem that would affect many of Williams's dramatic families and societies. The way the family disguises its greed for Big Daddy's money as concern for his health mirrors a deeper willingness to see in another's vulnerability only an opportunity for gain. Likewise, Brick's refusal to own up to his complicated past is important only insofar as it points to a more troubling inability, shared by everyone in the family, to attend to the needs and pain being felt in the present. The lack of honesty suggests a wider failure of responsibility. The larger illnesses in *Cat* are blindness and paralysis – both of which set in when someone who is not "useful" calls for help.

Williams's critique of mendacity gives pause even to those of us who hope to interpret the play, and we should guard against loading too many meanings on the play's illnesses. Most viewers hasten to devise symbolic readings of Big Daddy's sickness, just as we are quick to speak of emotional debility when considering Brick's leg injury. Many of those readings are plausible, of course, and, after all, cancer is not the central subject. (To see *Cat* as a play about cancer or broken legs is as ridiculous as calling *Ghosts* a play about syphilis.) But illness in Williams isn't always a symbol of more abstruse problems. From Laura Wingfield on, Williams's characters ask only to be looked at for who they are, not what they represent. Searching for the deeper meaning of these conditions, we risk making the suffering less of a private matter – and so cheapen it even as we try to ennoble it. A character's pain may acquire stature in symbolic readings, but the character himself becomes irrelevant, overshadowed by politics or philosophy. One might just as well not even acknowledge the sufferer's presence, in the manner of the clumsiest sociologist. Williams protests the mendacity of those spectators who won't simply take aggrieved characters on their own terms – simply there, not referring to anything else. To view them otherwise, Williams suggests, is a subtle but real inhumanity.

A similar concern with inhumanity underlies Big Daddy's long exhortation to Brick. As Williams intimates, the dramatic tension in the scene should not come from our eagerness to learn whether or not Brick had an affair with his friend Skip. What matters more is whether or not *Brick* learns something. If he doesn't ackowledge his past – whatever its nature – he is not fully a son, a husband, a member of his world. He is not really present at all. Like Gertrude Stein, Williams was endlessly fascinated by sheer dramatic presence. Stein had a formal, mostly visual and spatial understanding of presence. Because Williams was a more psychologically oriented writer, presence for him also included the accretions of a character's long and varied history. All the traces of a life fully lived are visible in Williams's characters. In a way, Big Daddy is speaking with Williams's own voice – cajoling the rest of Brick's character onstage. Big Daddy reassures Brick that he won't be judged or interpreted out of all semblance of his real nature. Brick will simply be perceived; the family (and so the play) will make room for him. Brick will take his place fully assembled at last. What we see in Brick is a character resisting his dramatic life; the other inhabitants of the play try to compensate, try to find a way to give him back the dignity of presence.

Perhaps Williams's own experience of illness and despair makes him so protective about the dignity of his characters. For years he was beleaguered by everything from cataracts, at age 29, to heart trouble – and as he writes in his memoir, during one particularly bad period he lived and wrote with the certainty that he was about to die. During all this time, of course, his sexual identity was considered by the "establishment" to be another kind of sickness. The visions of defeat that surrounded him only affirmed his skepticism about the fortitude of one's body and soul. Two lovers died agonizing early deaths from cancer: Frank Merlo, his companion from 1947 to 1961, and, before him, Kip, his first love. In the background of these losses lay the other tragedy of Williams's life. His sister Rose, diagnosed with schizophrenia and then withering in an institution after a lobotomy, showed her brother how decay can slip into a life and flourish there. These circumstances surely affected Williams's conception of dramatic life, but even without them he probably would have settled into his long, unflinching contemplation of death. For he knew it was both another possible release from the anxieties of the spirit and the complement of sexuality – even its end, as it is so often in his plays.

The charnel house seems an unlikely site for sexual encounters, but for Williams it usually contains just the right amount of desperation and helplessness to cajole people into fleeting combinations. The grim familiarity with the body that such places require also makes any awkwardness swiftly dissipate. The couplings are fiercer, more impetuous, when suffering fills the background, as it does in *Orpheus Descending,* with Jabe dissolving in the murkiness upstairs, or in *Streetcar,* where the memory of the boy's suicide dogs Blanche, chasing her until she rushes toward Elysian Fields into the promise of another's life, and nearly ruins it too. The knowledge of Big Daddy's eventual demise makes Maggie's pursuit of Brick so rash and devious, as though his dying has set a deadline on her chances for fulfillment, or somehow made the eros of the encounter irresistible, so defiant would it be. Williams has often been criticized for the unconvincing alacrity with which his people achieve intimacy, but in such a context the speed seems sheer common sense.

Sex in Williams is never merely titillating, never without a deeper drive that goes beyond the physical. Norman Mailer once said that the thrill of watching Williams's plays in the fifties was that you could sense the homosexual subtext to all the erotic scenes.[18] But that seems beside the point. If there's any subtext to the sex scenes, it's a far less glamorous one: In all of these scenes, characters plead for acknowledgment from the person in front of them. Sex is simply the most direct, most forceful way to get that recognition. Maggie wants Brick to accept her presence in his life more than she wants any erotic frisson or even a baby. It's that simple – and that elusive. A sexual advance is yet another variation on Gertrude Stein's "listen to me" – here more openly anguished, more physically emphatic.

Given the ingeniousness with which Maggie tries to gain recognition, it's understandable that we remember her as ambitious and narcissistic. Understandable, but also unfortunate. True, she is thoroughly consumed with her own crises, but that self-interest is always at war with her innate curiosity and attraction to others. Maggie may talk a lot about survival and integrity and self-reliance, but she only feels able to know herself when she's involved in another's life. She needs to be needed, and is eager to throw aside her own anxieties and rush to the aid of others, if only given the chance. That chance is what she is so hungry for, not any sort of glory or adoration. Maggie is not suited to solitude; actors portraying her as proud and powerful miss her subtlety, overlook the woman who only wants to collapse in the presence of a trusted intimate, the woman who wishes she didn't have to be proud, hadn't had to learn self-reliance.

The clues to this tension can be found in Maggie's voice. Like many of Williams's women, Maggie loves the rush of speech, the thrill available only to those who know how to ride the waves of conversation. But Maggie has a harder time at it than Blanche or Amanda. Even when no one is listening, Amanda keeps talking happily, concerned only with her own amusement. Blanche may feel more wounded when her audience's attention wanders, but she is enough of a performer to move around until she finds someone who *will* listen. Maggie isn't as nimble as Blanche, nor as oblivious as Amanda. She is single-minded about her talk, and when she is crossed, we hear the frustration. She gasps for breath – when she suddenly becomes aware of Brick's inattentiveness, or when she can no longer fool herself that Mae cares what she says. Williams calls our attention to the "range and music" of her voice – a barometer of her mental state. At her most relaxed, she caresses Brick with her voice, purring "baby," toying with adjectives, drawing out the vowels of a word until she's luxuriating in sheer sound. When she's anxious, her speech becomes more athletic: She talks a blue streak, beating back her own demons and the possible threats of others with a gale of words.

Brick's silence only urges her on to greater revelations. When she's around him, she acts for two – speaking, then listening to what she's said, then talking back to herself – round and round.

Maggie talks herself dry in the opening scene of *Cat.* She is never again as voluble as she is here; and in only one other play, *Orpheus Descending,* does Williams display such a masterly feel for the spoken rhythms of desperation. Maggie is trapped in a cold world, and she warms herself with melodic speech. One utterance nudges her on to another. The few times she does sustain a monologue, she seems to get high. Yet even then, when she's trashing the no-neck monsters or talking about her early life of poverty, we can see how afraid she is to stop speaking and suffer the inevitable crash. The words almost don't matter in these scenes. (She rarely says anything profound.) Maggie's character comes through in the tone, the starts and stops. In *Cat,* speeches palpitate with more life than ever before in Williams's drama. "Y'know," Maggie says to Brick,

> Big Daddy, bless his ole sweet soul, he's the dearest ole thing in the world, but he does hunch over his food as if he preferred not to notice anything else. Well, Mae an' Gooper were side by side at the table, direckly across from Big Daddy, watchin' his face like hawks while they jawed an' jabbered about the cuteness an' brilliance of th' no-neck monsters! And the no-neck monsters were ranged around the table, some in high chairs and some on th' *Books of Knowledge,* all in fancy little paper caps in honor of Big Daddy's birthday, and all through dinner, well, I want you to know that Brother Man an' his partner never once, for one moment, stopped exchanging pokes an' pinches an' kicks an' signals! – Why, they were like a couple of cardsharps fleecing a sucker. – Even Big Mama, bless her ole sweet soul, she isn't the quickest an' brightest thing in the world, she finally noticed, at last, an' said to Gooper, "Gooper, what are you an' Mae makin' all these signs at each other about?" – I swear t'goodness, I nearly choked on my chicken![19]

Maggie does stop speaking eventually. After a fiery first act, in which she shares the stage only with Brick, Maggie recedes, and the play seems to close around the space she left vacant and move easily onward. Most of Act II is taken up with the long conference between Brick and Big Daddy. Maggie's presence in the act is minimal: She takes her cues from others. When she turns up in Act III, after a long absence, she has to fight for position with the entire family. The few times she speaks, she contents herself with one-liners, quick exclamations, small talk.

Maggie's diminished importance in the play may disappoint some readers and strike others as a flaw. But Williams seems conscious of the change. Only once or twice in his life did Williams show that he knew the value of underdramatization. By presenting Maggie as a forceful presence only at the start, Williams emphasizes her confinement to the margins of the family. He also makes sure that we'll always wonder what she's doing when she's offstage, and what she's thinking as she hangs back in the crowd, mute and watchful. He asks us to give shape to her silence, to devise a drama from it. We follow the gestural text of her performance as closely as we listen to what the other characters say around her. That silence is also something of a blessing for Maggie: She seems to nurse her wounds, to pull herself together and recharge as she lingers in the shadows; to assess her situation and make plans for her next move. Williams gives Maggie the asset of mystery – and she uses it.

The few times Maggie does speak in the second half of *Cat,* she disrupts the easy tempo of conversation. She doesn't get to set its pace, as she did in Act I, and she isn't able to catch onto it. Consequently, she speaks too loudly, or in a different rhythm, or at an inopportune moment – when it's not her turn. Conversation at the Pollitts is always a matter of compromises – for everyone would take the stage if offered it – and Maggie isn't one for compromise.

The most startling of Maggie's late exclamations is the announcement of her pregnancy. It's a lie, as it turns out. She merely wanted to make Big Daddy happy. She also wanted to regain mastery over the scene, now crowded with all the other characters. From the start of the play, when she was the victim of that projectile breadroll, Maggie has been at the mercy of others. It's perhaps sad, then, that she gains the most attention when she plays by the family's rules, chief among them a readiness to lie, "mendacity." Maggie sets herself up as a protector of truth – the natural role for the outsider. If only she can stick to the facts of her life as she knows them – can remember the poverty of her upbringing, the real story of Brick's past, the real dynamics of power in the family – then, she reasons, she'll survive. But ultimately, truth-telling gets her nowhere. Mendacity is the only way to prevail, and by lying about the pregnancy she *wills* it into reality.

Cat on a Hot Tin Roof is Williams's most cynical, pessimistic play, for Maggie clearly endures by adapting to a degenerate world. By throwing Brick's crutch out the window and locking the liquor cabinet, she finally makes herself needed. Endlessly resourceful, she makes Brick look to her for succor. Her own life broken, she promises to hand his back to him. The ending is one of Williams's most successful – and his most complicated. Maggie's words sound powerful and resolute. ("I'm stronger than you and I can love you more truly!") But her presence should be tentative. Her strength is self-constructed and is sustained only by sheer defiance. She has just recently emerged from the shadows of the play; she could easily slip back into them. Audiences used to Williams's graceful endings will have to adjust their expectations. Even the painful end of *Streetcar* feels like a conclusion: We know what fate awaits Blanche; we see the tentative repair begin between Stanley and Stella. Here, we teeter – for Maggie has uttered her last words a shade too urgently: "I *do* love you, Brick, I *do*!" What comes after Maggie holds out her hand to Brick? What will she say to Brick's mocking last line, "Wouldn't it be funny if that were true?" – a word-for-word echo of his father's derision of his own wife, heard an act earlier? (Maggie's words match those of Big Mama in that scene.)[20] The biggest explosion in *Cat* is yet to come. Maggie senses its approach, and as the play ends we watch her trying to prepare for the worst, trying to create an environment to cushion the blow. Fear should never leave her face, even as it twists itself into seductiveness. The tone might be tender, but Maggie's exhaustion causes her to panic – she'll be too vulnerable. Maggie can never let go, for no one but herself will care if she falls.

In a 1957 lecture on *Cat,* Arthur Miller faults Williams for not following through on the ambitions his play seems to contain. Miller finds in Brick's refusal to beget children a critique of Big Daddy's society and way of life: Brick declines to prolong a line of corruption he despises. Where the play founders – as it does, Miller says, in its ending – Williams has abdicated the so-called social responsibility of the playwright and has retreated into the world of small affairs and petty details. "If our stage does not come to pierce through effects to an evaluation of the world," Miller writes, "it will contract to a lesser psychiatry and an inexpert one. We shall be confined to writing an *Oedipus* without the pestilence, an Oedipus whose catastrophe is private and unrelated to the survival of his people."[21]

Miller is eloquent, powerful – and ultimately wrongheaded. For that private world is Williams's only true purview, the realm where his art is able to unfold most comfortably, where it seems most fully imagined and wide-reaching, and where he speaks most truthfully. At his best, Williams never generalizes about people. And while his plays are inseparable from what we have come to understand as Southern literature, he finds it almost impossible to imagine "societies." He knows they are too abstract to have dramatic life.

Williams's domestic, personal plays make us listen most attentively when the details are all in place. He has an uncanny sense of the small touch that can call up whole histories. Despite the extravagance in some of the settings and the angularity of their inhabitants, Williams in his best work never flattens people or portrays them only in broad strokes. He is sensitive about those aspects of appearance and accidents of behavior that ensure their uniqueness, prevent them from being just anonymous lost souls.

The ludicrous pink ribbons that festoon Miss Lucretia Collins's curls in *Portrait of a Madonna* and the kewpie dolls she cuts out of Campbell's soup ads express more about the sad delusions clouding the aging spinster than anything else said or done in the play. The desperation of Celeste in *The Mutilated* and Serafina in *The Rose Tattoo* comes through in similarly unobtrusive images. Celeste's hunger looks most pathetic when she pulls a garland of popcorn off a hotel Christmas tree and absently starts nibbling on it. And when Serafina succumbs to exhaustion after wrestling with her desire and sinks into a wicker chair, the way it lists to one side, precarious from losing a leg, gives just the right despondent humor to her awkwardness, her own snapped spirit.

The silly belch that Big Mama can't repress at the tensest moment in *Cat on a Hot Tin Roof* affects in the same way what would otherwise be an ordinary suspenseful scene. Her indiscretion ruptures the anxious calm before the revelation of Big Daddy's real, untreatable illness, and colors the whole affair with the sweet pathos of those more embarrassed than aggrieved by what they can't control. Big Mama's burp mocks the solemnity but, strangely, confirms the sadness. It twists the scene into something inappropriate, contradicts and subverts expectations, and so brings out the authentic suffering of the family.

With the patience to fashion such details, Williams could build a play around a single character and never risk reducing the scope of his art. But in many of his other plays, especially those from the sixties and seventies, Williams faltered. He jeopardized his art when he tried hardest to expand its form and reach after "big" ideas. With such ambition, he sacrificed his characters first: They ended up being little more than symbols or, at his lowest, mere decor. Williams made grandiose claims for the daring of those stylistic changes. *Camino Real,* produced in 1953, was "unlike anything seen on Broadway." *Two Character Play* (the 1967 version of 1971's *Out Cry*); *Small Craft Warnings* (1972); *Clothes for a Summer Hotel,* one of his last plays, completed in 1980 – all of these he deemed innovative departures, risky ventures into a kind of drama never tried before. The sense of exploration that he felt was surely genuine, but the plentiful infelicities in those plays make these chapters of Williams's career more warning than inspiration.

Camino Real is awash in sensuality, but the people are nowhere to be seen. The entire play is woven out of cobwebs. Characters from vastly separate contexts share the same space for a few fleeting moments and then disappear. Some of them are easily recognized (but never probed), like Don Quixote, Camille, Byron, and Charlus; others are archetypal, like the grim reapers in swallowtail coats, who wear their significance on their sleeves. The central character, Kilroy, comes closest to three-dimensionality, but he's more a gesture than a character – an exclamation point of a human being. Everything about the play remains incompletely defined, but the mystery dulls rather than enlivens the senses.

There is nothing wrong with drama that scoffs at traditional notions of character, of course. Some of the most exciting postwar work challenges psychological realism, as formal design grows as important as narrative, and actors make their presence felt with gesture and movement rather than just narrative transformation. But Williams wasn't temperamentally suited to such experiments, so he could never fully participate in them. He maintained his interest in emotional exposure, but he diminished the space for it in his plays, and so ruined his chances at excelling either in newfangled theater or old-fashioned drama. When he worked for formal clarity, the obviousness of his design ruined the truthfulness of the characters. In *Camino Real,* Williams was so caught up with misguided notions of epic theater that he didn't notice when the play fell into pedestrian intrigue and romance, played out by figures who have paled into ordinariness.

Summer and Smoke is held to such a naive opposition between Spirit and Body – Alma Winemiller longing for purity while battling her awakening lust for John Buchanan – that the play's considerable potential for poignancy is never realized. Later Williams works – like *Clothes for a Summer Hotel* and *Vieux Carré* – render the contrast between sex and death so starkly that the characters seem caught in nothing more mysterious than a diagram. His lovers make only a fatigued approach to each other, lacking any of the early conviction that succor may be found. Death happens just as effortlessly, almost like a tedious chore, or a garish, unseemly display, better not dwelled on for long. Williams's sense of craft dozed in these plays; he exerted just enough energy to take a shortcut, to cobble together notes for a play. The degree to which Williams abdicated responsibility is evident in this stage direction from *Clothes for a Summer Hotel:* "In this scene Zelda must somehow suggest the desperate longing of the 'insane' to communicate something of their private world. . . . The present words given her are tentative: they may or may not suffice in themselves: the presentation – performance – must."[22]

Williams would never escape his natural inclinations as an artist, no matter how hard he tried; he could never follow a fashion, no matter how attractive, as these failures make clear. If he had only had the courage to be left behind as the theater changed, had remembered that his style would follow inevitably from fulfilling his original commitment to render the dimensions of a beaten figure with the amplest sensuality. The Williams we see here approached his characters the way so many insensitive, hasty readers have: as a diagnostician, curious about them for only as long as it takes to classify their ailments. He lost sight of how complicated they are, how resistant to generalities. Caught up with the desire to be innovative, Williams neglected to find characters inside figures.

Only once or twice in his career did Williams devise a formal experiment that emphasized rather than obscured character, and so succeeded in beguiling his audience in a new way. *Suddenly Last Summer* (1958) is such a work, as is, on a smaller scale, *Talk to Me Like the Rain and Let Me Listen. . .* (1950). The design is simple (surely a key to its rightness) and flexible; in fact, in these plays Williams once again leaves himself open to charges of laziness, of not bothering to dramatize experience at all. For once, the lazy Williams is the knowing Williams, the generous artist able to let his creations speak for themselves.

Suddenly Last Summer is barely a play. There are characters and a setting, to be sure, and dialogue and suspense, as in most good realistic drama, but its central component is a long story, presented to us in undiluted form – as a tale that requires attentive listening, much like the long speeches that messengers deliver in Greek tragedy. Williams moves toward fiction in this play, but he arrives at a kind of theater containing dimensions of emotional, hypnotic power entirely new for him.

The tale concerns a promiscuous dilettante, Sebastian Venable, who tours glamorous capitals with his mother, a beautiful woman whom Sebastian uses to ensnare boys for his own delectation. When a stroke destroys his mother's looks, he enlists his cousin Catherine. On one tour to a poor waterfront village, he is pursued by starving children who tear him apart and devour his flesh.

The play would be nothing but a sensational anecdote, a kitschy curiosity, were it not for the manner in which the story is told and the setting Williams gives the speaker. Catherine is the messenger; her listeners include Sebastian's mother, who refuses to believe her golden boy could be capable of such "depravity" or could come to such a sickening end. Catherine has told her story before, many times; she tells it again in a last-ditch effort to convince Mrs. Venable of its truth, for Mrs. Venable has threatened to order a lobotomy for the girl, hoping to cut the craziness out of her and destroy the history. *Suddenly Last Summer* is a play about listening as well as telling – lives literally depend on these simplest of acts – and Williams does little to distract from the ritual. Indeed, Catherine's telling resembles incantation; she is possessed by sheer memory and by the desire to impart it. The seriousness with which the other characters listen to her serves as an example for us in the audience. We grow as entranced as everyone on stage.

The play's design proves so effective because Williams is thinking theatrically rather than theoretically. His formal conceit allows for a lively performance, whereas his other "experimental" plays look convincing only on paper – a series of dry oppositions, a set of gimmicks, abstractions barely given human shape. *Suddenly* begins and ends with human beings. It is impersonal (or lurid) only to those who think that the drama lies in Sebastian's experience, and so feel distanced from the real excitement. In fact, the play is

Catherine's, and more gripping than any event in Sebastian's last years is the phenomenon of her standing before us talking her way through the darkness of memory and coming out the other side.

The old saw about plays living more on the stage than on the page seems especially true when it comes to Williams. The very intensity of his characters' presence makes his theater occupy an ambivalent position between literature and performance. *Suddenly Last Summer* is a prime example of a work that, for all its literary competence, achieves its luster only in performance. With other plays, transition to the stage is even more essential. On paper, some of Williams's dialogue can sound forced, the tone ingratiating; characters appear either naive or sentimental, unable to secure our pledge of faith. There is not enough mediation to comfort those readers accustomed to the leisurely gait and more expansive scope of novels. But so much of what reads badly, mechanically, leaves the strongest impression on stage.

A crucial moment in *Orpheus Descending,* a play that can be chilling in performance, exemplifies this contradiction. Lady, a shopkeeper trapped in an unhappy marriage and about to lose herself to an attractive newcomer, accidentally encounters an old flame, David Cutrere; and in the few pages they share (he hasn't appeared before and won't be seen again), she hurtles headlong into recollections of their love affair and her unwanted pregnancy, later aborted. Without warning, she awkwardly cries "I hold hard feelings!" and then extracts from him the admission that his life, too, has been ruined.[23]

Everything happens too quickly in this scene, confessions and apologies don't feel justified, the ejaculations of love and anger read as though Williams didn't know where to put them or how to prepare for the entire encounter. But in the hands of skilled performers, willing to strip away the pretenses of orthodox acting, the very abruptness of the scene makes it affecting. Long preambles would only diminish the intensity of his characters' feelings, would suggest that they had the presence of mind to control themselves. People like Lady are at the mercy of their feelings, which here are carnal imperatives. In Lady's case, Williams writes the clumsiness into the text as a way of exposing on stage the reality of suffering – a reality that is never neat, never gracefully paced.

"All good art is an indiscretion," Williams once wrote, and as his characters unsoul themselves they help bring into view the artist himself.[24] After the disastrous opening of Williams's first play, *Battle of Angels,* his director advised him to stop wearing his heart on his sleeve, for "the daws will peck at it," and there will be nothing left to give. But Williams rejected such sensible advice and kept giving, forever indiscriminately, as though the mere act of revelation kept something alive in him. No matter how uneven, how unpredictable its quality, there is something inescapably impressive about the sheer volume of his writing: more than seventy plays in all; dozens of stories, poems, and essays; some screenplays, and a novel. In the memoirs, published in 1975, he keeps telling us that he's working on his "farewell" to the theater, *Out Cry,* his "last" play before he retires to Europe to raise goats and geese. (These forgotten animals seem just right for the Williams menagerie; he would never own sheep or swans.) Of course he wrote another, and another: some fourteen more before he died in 1983, accidentally choking on a nasal inhaler cap.

About a decade earlier, when he had finished a sorry play, *Small Craft Warnings,* he sent out importunate letters to friends and agents, saying how much he needed this play produced, pleading for the opportunity to unburden himself publicly once more. "I don't need more than the assurance that I am not prematurely counted out as an active playwright. Like swimming and love, it's all that keeps me going."[25] When *Small Craft Warnings* was foundering during its eventual Off-Broadway run, Williams himself stepped into the role of Doc to boost business: a gallant move, surely, a testimony to his commitment to his art, but also pathetic, one self-exposure too many. Couldn't he just stop? so many supporters must have thought. Didn't he realize he had done enough to be proud of? others (like Richard Gilman) would ask much later.[26] Didn't he know that by being so cavalier with his emotions and making such an abject display he was an easy target for ridicule? Didn't he understand that with every attempt to create he was really destroying more of himself?

Once again, he wouldn't listen, deaf when he wanted to be to the imprecations, more aware of his limits than others thought he was (as the *Memoirs* make clear), yet not seeing any reason to stop trying to push past them. That seriousness about his craft conferred upon him a dignity not even the most sensational portrait of him could damage – the alcohol-addled years in the sixties, the seedy hotel room, the drugs. (Williams's *Memoirs* is the only autobiography I know of with index entries for Seconal, Nembutal, Mellaril, and Doriden.) Even his bizarre death had a kind of disarming honesty about it, so like the fate of one of his defenseless characters. The stoned and stupid Williams may be one of the images that come to mind when we think of him, but thankfully it is not the most enduring. Rather, the person who wrote about how sure he was that succor would come if only he kept calling, kept communicating through art – that is the Williams who survives. His admission in his *Memoirs,* voiced more softly than his outrageous persona ordinarily allowed, that he still had no feeling of having arrived, no "sense of fulfillment as an artist" – and so had to keep working to achieve it – still lingers when his other declarations and stagey divulgences have floated away.

The memoir is bloated with that catty chat, its narrator playing the loudmouthed, rambunctious tattletale. The degree of sexual candor he had rescued for the theater had never been enough. Now years of suppressed discussion of "forbidden" loves and losses burst decorum; secrets flooded forth, unwanted by most. His heart was still on his sleeve; more daws kept coming. Williams himself, not the work he had made, became the curiosity. The unharnessed ramble of the book, so repetitious, so often shallow, reads like Williams's attempt to outpace the gossipmongers in pursuit. Did he think that if he only kept telling, telling all, no one could possibly hurt him? Did he think it best to make all the disarming confessions before others could make malicious accusations? Perhaps he hoped their wonder at his courage would replace derision or schadenfreude or prurient voyeurism.

Sex, he said, was never a private matter to him, but the writing was; and so the memoir would provide few insights into his craft. But frustrated readers used the sex talk to lead their way back into the writing. We started hearing knowing disquisitions from some critics on how all the women in his plays were stand-ins for the playwright himself, how every encounter was really a coded message about his own sexuality. True as some of these suppositions may have been, and despite confirmation, sometimes, from Williams himself, they miss the point. They also once again turn drama into case study, this time with Williams himself as patient.

Williams wrote about predicaments affecting every kind of exchange, regardless of the identity of the couplings, their real or presumed gender. So many readers thought otherwise that Williams finally had to state the obvious: "Homosexuality isn't the theme of my plays," he said to an interviewer in 1972. "They're about all human relationships. I've never faked it."[27] To fix his characters in a biographical equation is to make them too simple, to give them a clarity Williams knows they can never have. It is also, as I've said, to evade the reality of who they are and the disturbing experience of watching them play out their difficult lives.

"Make voyages, attempt them. . . ," says Byron in *Camino Real,* and Williams obediently did so, in art and life. But wasn't there always something in the work that cried out for stability at last? Characters who wanted nothing more than a sense of home, of having landed, exhausted by long vagrancy? Talking nervously so much of the time, Williams's characters really want nothing more than the chance *not* to speak. They are wise enough, though, schooled so rigorously in adversity, to be skeptical of any concept so flimsy as "happiness." That understanding gives them a different kind of pleasure: pride in their disillusionment – a delirious calm. This aspect of his art is perhaps the only thing Williams shared with the Chekhov he so loved and so misunderstood.

It seems we always live vicariously through Williams. Watching his work is chastening; his self-assessment implicitly asks us why we are not making our own. But we know we are too cowardly to match him. Williams keeps pulling himself into the unsparing light that bathes his stage so that we can sit contentedly in the dark. Our theater, now quick to pass by anything that isn't sensational, and impatient with characters who make only an oblique approach and mutter their stories haltingly – our theater has seldom known such generosity and such anguished benevolence.

3

SAM SHEPARD

SPEAKING TO AN INTERVIEWER some years ago, the English painter Francis Bacon described the perils of working with the obsessive rigor for which he was famous. He would often find himself trapped inside a canvas after long periods of frustrated work, not sure what lay before him, unable to mark his place in the painting and move forward. When this happened, he said, he would squeeze some paint into his hand, stand back, and hurl the glob at the canvas. More often than not, the random blotch opened up the finely designed, fastidiously executed surface, making it possible for him once again to "bring the figurative thing up onto the nervous system more violently and more poignantly" and to stress "the brutality of fact."[1]

Something in that impulsive gesture, dashing yet nearly destructive (what if the paint landed in a bad place?), corresponds to the theater of Sam Shepard. So many of his plays retain the restless energy that accompanied their creation, as though they were eager to elude the limits of their form. Shepard has often spoken of the fact that he feels confined by hoary ideas of craft – like Bacon, relying on them only for as long as it took to eradicate them – and so seeks out the right explosive agent with which to shatter theatrical surfaces. "The actor [is] trapped by the script," he has complained, and because of that the performance can never fully come alive and lift off.[2] But maybe it is possible to write one's way out of that jail, just as Bacon painted, or pitched, his way into another visual dimension.

The example of rock and roll is instructive – and humbling. Shepard has often wondered if any writer can match the liberating, raunchy irresistibility of the Rolling Stones or Bob Dylan or Jimi Hendrix. Part of rock's appeal is its immediacy – its passion makes itself felt all at once and lasts for just a few blinding minutes before being extinguished. Its emotions have to be brightly outlined, its ideas visceral, the performer's attitude unequivocal. Shepard learned to bring the same gimlet-eyed impatience to playwriting. In his early years he moved in and out of styles within a single play; he paced his action with abrupt shifts; his characters never let themselves become familiar – if they were predictable, they couldn't hold even Shepard's attention.

And when his early characters speak, their language is hot and nervous, even when the subject doesn't seem especially important. The words themselves might also be unremarkable, but the intensity with which they must be spoken creates their luster. A character's way of speaking – in language spasms or in the more sustained passages that Shepard calls verbal arias – has a way of making even the laziest atmosphere suddenly alarming. This kind of language, Shepard once said, has "the potential of making leaps into the unknown . . . it [can] explode from the tiniest impulse. . . . In these lightning-like eruptions, words are not thought, they're felt."[3]

His sensitivity to the instinctual life determined the way Shepard would go about putting together a play. "Ideas emerge from plays," he has written, "not the other way around."[4] He has said that he comes across a picture loitering in the margins of his consciousness – a picture of a character or a condition, a place or just a startling event that happened there – and from attentive contemplation of that picture finds himself led into an entire dramatic world. Throughout the writing, the euphoria of discovery never abates. The original image suggests another image. Then its shape requires a character who makes a certain action. The logic of that event leads inexorably to a broad new field of view. And so it goes until pictures, people, words, activities, and landscapes have been deftly strung together to suggest, however loosely, a theatrical event. In the earliest work it sometimes seems that Shepard has an entire cosmos at his feet: Characters move from the banks of a river in the nineteenth century to outer space without effort. They live dangerously but are never self-conscious about it. They are organically bizarre and shiftless, game for anything and full of good humor, just like the plays themselves. Shepard is cicerone to their journeys but also an eager spectator, as full of wonder as his audience, and as anxious to travel deeper, far from places he's already been.

That anything-goes technique generated an astounding number of plays in his early years and found its finest expression in a 1971 work (twenty plays after he started writing, in 1964) called *Cowboy Mouth.* It is Shepard's sweetest play and his simplest. Shepard, who wrote the play with Patti Smith (both also performed it), jettisoned fundamentals like plot and character and instead let his two figures, Slim and Cavale – essentially Shepard and Smith playing themselves – thrash through the space, a cramped rundown room. The play reads as though two people have nothing else to do for an hour but can't leave their apartment; so they set about trying to amuse themselves as best they can. Yet it's hardly a barren or dull play. Shepard may portray desultory lives and let events unfold casually, one thing leading to another, but the play quickly goes to extremes. It becomes a picture of pure delirium, impacted want – anger that only hastens to burn itself out. Slim rattles off a litany of ugly things at the start, letting the sheer momentum of speaking generate his images: "wolves, serpents, lizzards, gizzards, bad bladders, typhoons, tarantulas, whipsnakes, bad karma, Rio Bravo, Sister Morphine, go fuck yourself!"[5] Then he pounds on the drums, leaves them, goes to a mike and screams out a song, tires, goes to Cavale, curls up in her lap. When Cavale complains about an injured foot, Slim doesn't just offer solicitude. He licks her foot all over and then howls like a coyote. Shepard doesn't settle for half-measures, mere descriptions of states of feeling or notated actions; when Cavale says she wants to buy new shoes they do so, in a drama of their own making – pretending to walk up past Ridge Avenue and into the red-shoe section of the store, Slim shifting suddenly from companion to salesman. There's no particular reason for this digression – after all, the play is all digression. Slim and Cavale aren't confined by any external idea of what's "right" to do in a drama. Shepard doesn't appear to be following an intellectual idea while he writes; there's no trace of a plan or an outline. The structure is intuitive; the action looks improvised. The play exists in perpetual crisis. Shepard seems to answer each question as it comes up. It appears that the only rule in *Cowboy Mouth* is that the time should be used fully. There must be no dead air, even when Slim and Cavale have nothing to do. Slim may close himself off with his drum set, but Cavale won't sit idly by – she'll go through "a million changes," as Shepard notes in a stage direction. (Both characters love the catalogue form.) She "plays dead. Rebels. Puts on a bunch of feathers and shit to look alluring. Rebels. Motions like she's gonna bash the amps with a hammer. Hides in a corner. . . . grabs her .45."[6]

There's usually a special object of some kind sitting in the middle of Shepard's plays, and when his characters run out of steam or when Shepard himself finds that he's at the end of a detour, the object comes in handy as a new point of departure, suggesting fresh responses. In *Cowboy Mouth,* for instance, the prized object is a stuffed crow named Raymond that Cavale talks to and nurses when Slim isn't listening. In *4-H Club,* apples command most of John, Bob, and Joe's attention. In *Fourteen Hundred Thousand,* all of Donna and Tom's ill feeling goes into the piles of books they haul around. Kid's fate is triggered by hundreds of Ping-Pong balls in *The Unseen Hand.* In *Chicago,* the remarkable things are biscuits and fishing rods; in *Forensic & the Navigators,* Rice Krispies; in *Action,* another book; in *True West,* toasters. These catalysts have almost totemic status, or at least they contain so much ambiguous power that when a character uses them, or reacts to them, he is somehow expressing in the deepest way the essence of his condition. Despite their centrality in the plays, these objects aren't exactly symbolic – Shepard would never be so pretentious – but once we're brought up against the thingness of these things, neither are they quite familiar. Part of their unique theatricality comes from the combination of their everyday usefulness (and the associations that go along with that) and the preposterous new importance accorded them by the play. Their presence is deliberately inappropriate – that's what makes them so fascinating.

This is only one of the ways that Shepard exploits the theatricality of the inexplicable. How wrongheaded it sounded when the *New York Times* critic, Frank Rich, praised Shepard's memoir, *Motel Chronicles* (1982), for helping to "demystify the origins of Mr. Shepard's psychological obsessions and desolate frontier iconography" – as if such clinical clarity were desirable or possible.[7] "A character for me is a composite of different mysteries," Shepard has asserted.[8] For those of us who share Shepard's fascination with inscrutability and his understanding of its dramatic power, it is always disappointing when an overzealous critic translates Shepard's images into discursive "meanings" – denaturing the work by decoding it. *Icarus's Mother,* for instance, one of Shepard's most rankling works, is often subjected to this kind of treatment. The play ends with Frank's long monologue about an airplane falling into the sea (the one overt connection to the play's title). Something about that flyer going down, after dazzling the people on the ground by skywriting "E equals MC squared," sums up the crises affecting Shepard's characters. The catastrophe throws visible action into relief, conferring new meaning on it: the way the women chafed at the men's rule making; the longing of some characters to strike out on their own, and the need of others to keep the group together at all costs; Frank's delight at discovering a new beach, and Bill's dismissal of that delight with his hardbitten devotion to science – the viciousness beneath all of this petty banter surfaces when the action is set against the flyer's arrogant striving and subsequent disaster. Shepard charges his play with a simple juxtaposition, not with solemn, point-making scenes. The starkness of the juxtaposition is more disturbing than the violent content of the final monologue; mulling over the mystery of the juxtaposition is more compelling than labeling the play a parable about nuclear war, as many critics do. (That would be as simplistic as describing the profound yearning of the original Icarus as mere "ambition.") An apocalyptic interpretation is not wrong, but it domesticates the play, limiting its substance to the didactic and topical, so that its ending seems artificially conclusive. The characters themselves don't understand what has happened to them; the events terrify them because they are so resistant to interpretation. (Throughout his career, Shepard has heard critics complain that his plays don't end "correctly." Critics want to hear codas; Shepard gives them slams and crashes.)

This dissatisfaction with the familiar, this love of adventure – in narrative, characterization, and structure – and, even more, this buoyancy of improvised, homemade entertainment were pervasive when Shepard began writing plays. For the writers clustered in downtown New York City in the early sixties, theater making was a radical form of escape from regimentation of all sorts – not just from the mores of the mainstream but also from received ideas about proper theatrical subject matter (it must be tasteful), the party line on politics in drama (there shouldn't be any) and on structure (despite Stein and Williams, the cult of the well-made play persisted), even assumptions about length and breadth (two hours; big ideas). These theater renegades took refuge in the lofts, basements, church halls, and apartments that quickly became known, collectively, as Off-Off Broadway – its very name suggests remoteness, a place cut off from civilization, but also, in a reverse form of snobbery, what's "in," and a place where the fantastic might dwell.

La Mama Experimental Theater Club and Theater Genesis were the dual centers of Off-Off Broadway. They were also young Sam Shepard's two homes. Here a culture went about inventing itself, with few American models to guide it except the experience of the Beat poets of the fifties and the abstract painters of the forties. The scene was deliberately anarchic, welcoming artists pitched all along the spectrum of ability and sensibility, many of whom had little in common save their aversion to convention. Their activities obeyed no logic, served no grand plan for cultural renewal. Small, forgettable plays, no more than twenty minutes in length, shared seasons with epic spectacles; self-important efforts seemed, momentarily, to elbow aside other, quieter works whose landmark status would not be felt until a generation later. Whisked into this theatrical traffic, Shepard, a 19-year-old Californian, may have felt he had arrived "where it's at," but he would have been hard-pressed to say just where that was. He knew better than to try to find out, to fix something that changed so frequently. Instead, he worked to replicate this unpredictability, this spontaneous combustion, inside a drama counseled by instinct alone.

One of his earliest and most abiding dramatic choices might well have been shaped by what he learned in this environment. Shepard's first characters seem to take after this slowly gestating community of artists, always balanced precariously on the edge of oblivion. For those accustomed to robust, fully developed and documented characters, Shepard's theater will always frustrate. Most of his figures radiate powerfully, but few coalesce; their features remain malleable, their minds befogged. They are not anonymous, but neither are they readily recognizable. Identity is still negotiable.

Shepard's characters spend much of their time inventing themselves, however conditionally. The classic rebuke to a writer, that his works are "incomplete," becomes for Shepard a term of praise. Incompleteness means that characters may be busy with the act of creation itself, each character the artist of his own being. What Robert Hughes has written about the painter Frank Auerbach could easily apply to Shepard's work as well: "The key seemed to be wildness, so that the agenda . . . stayed open until the last moment of creation."[9]

Just when one of Shepard's characters seems finally rooted in one mode, he (or she) will assume a new posture, deploy an affectation, reveal a feature long concealed, change the pulse of his silence. Part of a character's long journey out of incoherence involves conscious experimentation with provisional selves. He will explore unlikely personalities, lingering in them just long enough to learn where the disguise begins. The correspondences between these impersonations and the actor's own craft are irresistible, and Shepard himself admits how fascinated his theater is with theater: He loves writing plays because only then can he "play" all the roles he wants to. But beyond these metatheatrical games, there is embedded in his plays a troubling understanding of identity. Troubling or liberating – it depends on one's perspective. Stu in *Chicago* often affects an old woman's voice and hunched sneer when he tells his stories. Chet and Stu in *Cowboys #2* pretend to be old men, then little boys, then cowboys attacked by Indians, until Stu is felled by an arrow. Characters make instant, agile transitions to new ideas of themselves, rather than gradually building themselves up. After a while, they cease to be characters at all: Each one is simply a collection of masks, or a force blowing through the play, a blurry gust of feeling. There are no centers to these Shepard figures; they are surfaces of the most beguiling sort, styles of energy that aren't easily harnessed, sites of crises that don't stop rippling.

Both Richard Gilman and Bonnie Marranca have suggested that Shepard's interest in transformation was sparked during his early involvement with the Open Theater, the collective organized by Joseph Chaikin that was most active in New York during the sixties. Shepard never had a central role in this theater, but he did participate in workshops and contribute dialogue to a few collaboratively conceived productions. (Some of his monologues for the actors survive and are collected in a volume called *Hawk Moon.*) During the months that Shepard frequented the Open Theater's rehearsals, he observed a style of acting that diverged radically from the conventions that most performers accept unquestioningly. The Method, which had been conceived by Lee Strasberg (adapting the lessons of Stanislavsky), was gospel among the actors who cut their teeth on Tennessee Williams and Arthur Miller. It demanded of the actor an arduously constructed sense of his role, one in which each action emerged out of a strictly logical, coherent understanding of motivation. The Open Theater dismissed much of that apparatus, declaring that it unnaturally encumbered the actor and sapped his spontaneity. Instead, the Open Theater proceeded from a fluid sense of identity, in which sudden change was the norm and a performer could mutate along a spectrum of temperament, bring many characters to life in a single piece, and remain always limber, limited only by his sense of possibility.

As profound as the Open Theater experience must have been for Shepard (and as lasting: he and Chaikin collaborated twenty years later on three performance texts), it wasn't the only influence on Shepard's art nor even the primary reason for his predilection for chameleon characters. The exigencies of his life in New York, where poverty was always close at hand, probably forced Shepard to learn adaptation and resourcefulness, always changing homes, jobs, circles of friends, schedules, and especially attitudes, just to survive. The drugs that helped him through those years, as he himself has suggested, also loosened his imagination, replacing an unforgiving world, stubbornly resistant to his attempts at living there, with a phantasmagoria. Music, too – Shepard's love – and movies, where he regularly sought refuge, demonstrated another kind of changeability: The careful progressions of jazz improvisation encouraged musicians to slip in and out of different tonal identities in a single jam; and the dizzying speed of cinema's montage allowed characters to be in one place and time for a few minutes and then, without warning, leap into another context, their age and appearance suddenly shifted.

The simplest explanation for the unpredictability of Shepard's art, however, is also the most likely. Like any good spectator, Shepard has a fierce aversion to boredom – or at least the pace of his plays suggests that he does – and so he has made a theater to surprise himself. Textbook ideas of consistency couldn't have sounded more staid to the neophyte writer, who cherished entertainment in the best sense of the word; even in his maturity he has demanded of his characters that they keep pace with his mercurial imagination. Some plays read as though Shepard led a character as far into a situation as he could go, found both himself and the character stuck, and so switched personalities and threw in a new context, like Bacon's blob of paint, as a means of escape. Fantasy has liberated his craftsmanship, ensuring that writing for him will never be a chore, but rather a constantly replenished amusement, always fresh.

His instincts, from an artist's point of view, are just common sense. Consistency, after all, is but one step away from stagnation. Any serious writer sees changeability not as mere perversion or recklessness but as essential to continued vitality. Since so many of Shepard's characters are artists themselves – some literally so, but all temperamentally – it's only to be expected that they should look after their own survival, shirking fixed personality as a way, ironically, of preserving their identity and integrity as creative individuals.

The Tooth of Crime (from 1972) is the most corrosive of Shepard's many plays about the creative crisis, since it demonstrates most explicitly the extremes to which an artist will go to keep his art alive. Hoss is a rock singer who enjoyed massive success until an upstart named Crow showed up on the scene with his own music, which has gradually been winning over many of Hoss's listeners. The rivals decide to meet and fight for the stardom each craves. Crow wins, and Hoss, broken more than merely defeated, kills himself. Surrounding this fairly schematic plot is a disturbing commentary on doubt and self-loathing, the often destructive uncertainty that accompanies so much creativity. Hoss complains that he's "stuck" in his image. He can no longer move through his art freely, nor can he manipulate the masks and manners once at his disposal to enchant his fans. He's trapped by the "code" – the rules of music making that now inhibit the very energies they meant to intensify. Hoss says to his friend Cheyenne:

> Can't you see what's happened to us. We ain't Markers no more. We ain't even Rockers. We're punk chumps cowering under the Keepers and the Refs and the critics and the public eye. We ain't free no more! Goddamnit! We ain't flyin' in the eye of contempt. We've become respectable and safe. Soft, mushy chewable ass lickers.[10]

Chewable. Hoss's determination to get some bite back in his act forces him to try to chew up and deny the person he's become. His confrontation with Crow doesn't merely pitch their musical talents against each other; it's a "style match," as Hoss calls it, and only the man who can deploy different personalities convincingly will prevail. Hoss plays a cowboy, a 1920s gangster, a blues singer, and a voodoo doctor in rapid succession, hoping to disarm Crow with the sparkle of his impersonations and to strike upon the character that suits him best. Crow chooses a subtler route: He plays Hoss, learning his walk, aping his way of carrying himself and speaking, "copping his patterns," as Hoss might say. This is a painful violation; Hoss finds himself unable to overcome the image of himself.

Seeing Crow as his mirror, Hoss learns how empty he really is. How durable can a self be if it's so easily appropriated? "IT AIN'T ME! IT AIN'T ME! IT AIN'T ME!!" Hoss cries, shortly before putting a gun in his mouth, fed up at last with all the imposture, refusing finally to let Crow "reprogram the tapes" of his spirit. But no alternative presents itself. "You'd be O.K.," he says to his companion, Becky, earlier in the play, "if you had a self. So would I. Something to fall back on in a moment of doubt or terror or even surprise."[11] Reaching for Dylan's grizzled charm, Jagger's greasy eros, or a vaguer romantic ideal of the Artist, Hoss has forsaken his originality – a prize he can only regain by destroying himself. Suicide is his truest gesture, anointing an identity inviolable for the first time.

Shepard is at his most protean in *The Tooth of Crime,* for the style wars are conducted with language, requiring him to move nimbly in and out of a range of tones and verbal rhythms. The play as a whole is volatile, impure, reluctant to settle. As if driven by caprice, Shepard melds together aspects of the crime novel, science fiction, sports, rock and roll, and the Western to create an argot that teases, suggesting one milieu for only a moment before alighting on another in the next clause, then lurching into a vocabulary impossible to place anywhere. "Got the molar chomps," says Crow, meeting Hoss for the first time. "Eyes stitched. You can vision what's sittin'. Very razor to cop z's sussin' me to be on the far end of the spectrum."[12] Language comes with its own attitude. Manipulated well, it can conceal as much identity as it reveals and can also throw a listener off balance, frustrating his attempt to understand, and thereby possibly to master, the speaker. Shepard's restlessly inventive exercise of language suggests that he, like his characters, fears being decoded, exposed too quickly, dismissed as a known quantity – for instance, as a writer whose language, exhausted, no longer glitters. The style of writing here is not subordinate to its content; style *is* content, the attitude that language projects its sole identity.

It has become fashionable lately to accuse Shepard of losing his ironic distance from the style wars he once chronicled so sharply. The acting career he began with such great success in 1982 now occupies most of his time; he's writing less (six years elapsed between his last two plays) and making more movies; he has become a heartthrob, trailing glossy magazines behind him. We could practically hear the groans of disappointment from long-time admirers when a coffee-table book of photographs appeared in 1990, featuring Shepard and his mate, Jessica Lange, looking rustic and sexy and clean for the camera of Bruce Weber, the photographer most associated with the vacuous glamour of fashion advertising. It was hard to believe that this was the same Shepard who once wrote of Hollywood: "People here / have become / the people / they're pretending to be."[13] Like Hoss and Crow, Shepard seemed in danger of disappearing inside his own aura, giving away what many had thought was his true identity – the writer forever a special taste, "our secret" – in exchange for superficial images of other people's making. "It ain't him, it ain't him, it ain't him!"

Such disappointment on the part of Shepard's faithful results, I think, from the mistaken reading of a moral message in his plays. Shepard has never pretended to more than a description of this image world. He unflinchingly has shown the lying and self-deception, the posing and posturing; but is always careful not to condemn. Far from it: The image world is the only world, as far as he can tell, and its traffic in disguise offers the sole possibility for unfettered self-expression in a society grown steadily more conformist.

There's a strange tranquillity to those Shepard characters who never settle into the "authenticity" of transparent, sincere selves. Hoss, after all, suffers for having a personality that Crow can copy too easily. Old-fashioned ideas about an inner self, the "real me" so sought after by actors and analysands alike, are, for Shepard, no more than red herrings – elaborate, seductive deceptions. "I'm looking forward to my life," says Jeep in *Action*. "I'm looking forward to uh – me. The way I picture me."[14] Here is the voice of someone delighted with the opportunity to create, not someone depressed by emptiness or satisfied with what he already knows about himself. "Just think of it!" says Kosmo in *The Mad Dog Blues,* surely Shepard's sunniest play. "We'll be able to go anywhere and do anything and be anyone we want to." "Who're you gonna be?" asks his sidekick, Waco. "I don't know. A different me."[15] Kosmo and another wanderlusty character, Yahoodi, hobnob with Jesse James, Marlene Dietrich, Mae West, and Captain Kidd, riding the infectious romp that Shepard arranges for them. They enjoy the freedom of their fantasy, trying out the new personalities each encounter suggests, following their impulses into the jungle, over the high seas, and onto deserted islands. There is little beneath the masks they assume except a forceful desire to acquire more varieties of being.

Niles, the musician whose absence lies at the center of *Suicide in B-flat,* learns this necessary talent too late; his fate, in fact, offers a useful lesson for readers intent on getting to the bottom of Shepard's fathomless characters. Niles has been losing his flair for jazz improvisation – his friends say he allowed himself to be co-opted by so-called healers, who promised him relief from the painful obsessiveness he always brought to composition – and for too long has been turning out predictable melodies, "pabulum," as another player calls it. A friend, Paullette, offers to purge Niles of his corrupting influences – all the borrowed forms and techniques clogging the flow of his originality. Under her guidance, he dons the chaps and hat of Pecos Bill, then the black tails of a big-band leader, and Paullette kills off each role. She doesn't plan to execute the "real" Niles, only the parasitic personas that have sapped his energy.

The procedure at first seems like a cure designed to restore the independence vital to a true artist, but before long it's apparent that "independence" remains elusive. "There's no guarantee I won't die along with him," Niles says, speaking of one role he's played. "I feel as though his skin is my skin."[16] His fears are justified: Niles's body is found with his face blown off, the "true" face his friends expected to find underneath the disguise. His identity *was* the identities he borrowed; in fact, he agreed to let Paullette eradicate the cowboy and the bandleader only so he could start the process over, compiling elements of other faces to construct a fresh self. He even worries that he'll find playing dead harder than "playing alive" – another acknowledgment that there's little spontaneity in any context, in any form of behavior, and that every action requires acting. The "natural" Niles never existed, nor could he, nor could anyone. Our identities can only be seen in the patterns of their permutations.

Shepard speaks of the necessity for a flexible identity in a wide-ranging interview from 1974. "You have this personality, and somehow feel locked into it, jailed by all of your cultural influences and your psychological ones from your family, and all that. And somehow I feel that that isn't the whole of it, you know, that there's another possibility."[17] The search for "another possibility" that fills his characters' lives isn't merely a picaresque adventure, conducted for the sake of the thrill it might give them, or the audience (although that is far from unimportant). Change is a way of life; it is the only way these characters can be sure they're living at all. The multiplicity of guises does not signify mental instability; rather, it indicates a commitment to experience as rich a history as they can find. In that same interview, Shepard says:

> You see somebody, and you have an impression of that person from seeing them – the way they talk and behave – but underneath many, many different personalities could be going on. . . . It's not as though you started out with a character who suddenly developed into another character – it's the same character, who's enlivened by animals, or demons, or whatever's inside of him.[18]

Given his understanding of character, Shepard's career as an actor should come as no surprise. He's escaping the strictures of one role and exchanging it for another. Those who chastise Shepard for becoming a movie star "when the theater needs him so badly" deny him the freedom he celebrates in his work.

Among Shepard's plays, *Angel City* is probably the most candid about the untethered life, its pleasures and dangers. In his Los Angeles, the animals and demons Shepard sees within all his characters have free rein – sometimes causing horrible disfigurement, sometimes liberating lively new styles of self-expression. In light of Shepard's subsequent Hollywood experience, it's tempting to see the play as an innoculation, as though Shepard were facing all the lures in advance and purging himself of toxins.

Wheeler is a studio executive looking for the right disaster movie to transfix (and make) millions. But as he tries to orchestrate entertainment and manipulate emotion he slowly rots away, exuding green slime. Meanwhile, the people he employs discover truer worlds of imagination. By Act II, Tympani, a drummer hired to hypnotize people with rhythm, has slipped into a role that brings more satisfaction: He pretends to be a swaggering short-order cook, monitoring imaginary burgers on his drums. Lanx, a director, puffs back and forth, lost in his vision of himself as a prizefighter. And Miss Scoons, a secretary, wears a nun's habit and scrubs the floor while singing in a lilting Irish accent. They're enacting their fantasies, but nothing in their behavior or the play as a whole suggests there's any "correct" identity to return to. Miss Scoons understands early in the play how genuine, yet how inscrutable, is each identity she and her colleagues project:

> I look at the screen and I am the screen. I'm not me. I don't know who I am. I look at the movie and I am the movie. I am the star. I am the star in the movie. For days I am the star and I'm not me. I'm me being the star. I look at my life when I come down. I look and I hate my life when I come down. I hate my life not being a movie. I hate my life not being a star. I hate being myself in my life which isn't a movie and never will be. I hate having to eat. . . . Having to live in this body which isn't a star's body and all the time knowing that stars exist. That there are people doing nothing all their life except being in movies. Doing nothing but swimming and drinking and laughing and being driven to places full of potential. People never having to feel hot pavement or having to look at weeds growing through cracks in the city. People never having to look the city square in the eyes. People living in dreams which are the same dreams I'm dreaming but never living.[19]

The joy of cinema, Scoons shows, inheres in its utter artifice. Her speech bursts the pretensions of those who insist that films (or plays, for that matter) must speak only "to our time," or portray familiar characters, in situations we recognize, with problems we know well from our own experience. Scoons longs to fly from her own experience, finding her way into unlikely versions of herself, impossible variations on the life she's supposed to live. The airbrushed image of the star may be "unbelievable" by puritan standards of verisimilitude, but Scoons knows how stifling verisimilitude can become.

The prominence that Shepard gives this yen for self-invention and the tirelessness with which he returns to it in play after play may account for the omnipresence of the term "American" in critics' assessments of his theater. Usually he's praised for "capturing our culture" or for being "uniquely American," but these encomiums are rarely followed by explanations of just what the critic means by "culture," or by "American." "America," it seems, is just as much of a cipher as "identity." Both are powerful ideas; characters and readers alike prize them despite their invisibility. We pursue a better knowledge of them and hope to locate their true nature, but we succeed only in discovering the limitations of our understanding.

The incompleteness of our definitions of the American idea is irritating, but it's also refreshing and inevitable, since a sense of possibility and the endless process of revision and addition remain hallmarks of the national culture. As Shepard's characters nervously scramble for open space, venting their chronic anxiety over what they're becoming, as they bulldoze inherited identities and set about building up new ones, they voice one unifying (and very American) idea: revolution. It's the central policy informing Shepard's ideas of dramatic structure – his sympathy with the revolutionary idea spurring him to write with that "open agenda." Dissatisfaction and idealism sweep up his characters and send them ricocheting through the theatrical fields he marks off for them. It's as though the cataclysmic energies that initially established American culture – severing it from its past and clearing space for its future – continue in the small insurrections set in Shepard's kitchens and living rooms, tacky motel rooms and vacant parking lots, or just in the buzzing imaginations of those stuck there.

Shepard lists "1968" as one of the inspirations for *Operation Sidewinder,* his play explicitly about revolution. It matches the tangle of warring initiatives and the jam of colliding crises of that year. Like *Tooth of Crime, Operation Sidewinder* is a stylistic hodgepodge, comprised of many disparate places and characters. Dizzy comedy adds levity to the conspiratorial air of an espionage thriller; blazing science fiction adds color and texture to mystical abstractions; rock music by the Holy Modal Rounders lifts political idealism out of arid rhetoric.

"Sidewinder" is the name of a computer (shaped like a massive snake) that has escaped from an Air Force installation. As the military sets out to recover Sidewinder, a group of black revolutionaries plans to steal it. Before either group succeeds, however, a tribe of Indians gets to the computer. With the additional aid of outer-space aliens, the Indians try to use Sidewinder to bring about their long-awaited salvation. Caught in the middle of this is a figure known only as Young Man. He embodies many of the desires consuming those who pursue Sidewinder, but also carries their hopes beyond that single object. He wants to "transcend barriers," as one of the Holy Modal Rounders' songs puts it – the limits set for him by other people's thought, systems of behavior, arrangements of society. "We can have paradise right now," runs another song, "Heaven is ours to make."[20]

The actual making of that available paradise proves more difficult than the songs suggest, however. The problem isn't one of ability: The Young Man has proved himself a forceful hero in the play's many skirmishes and shoot-outs. What's lacking, though, is a system of belief. He can't make a paradise unless he knows what it should look like. He easily rejects the sham ideas of American culture disseminated by the "establishment," and mourns a nation where the "soldiers are dying, the Blacks are dying, the children are dying." He lives in a place where the disempowered know only how to measure their loss, not how to remedy or even protest it, where "we become so depressed we don't fight anymore." But after naming what he's against, he can't say what he's for. "Oh please say something kind to us," he says whenever Hubert Humphrey comes on the TV, "something soft, something human, something different, something real, something – so we can believe again."[21] Whenever the Young Man's fellow revolutionaries do strike on something to support, the energy necessary to achieve their goals wanes from the same lack of conviction. A song from the Holy Modal Rounders later chastises them for just that: "Did you ever do whatever thing / it is you're for? / Or does an old idea like that have meaning / anymore?"[22]

What is to blame for this loss of faith? Throughout Shepard's theater, characters voice the same urgent need to feel sure about something, anything; to know the comfort that only comes when one is committed to an idea, a culture, another person, or just a manner of being, a way of presenting oneself. Cavale, in *Cowboy Mouth,* expresses their disappointment:

> We're earthy people, and the old saints just don't make it, and the old God is just too far away. He don't represent our pain no more. His words don't shake through us no more.[23]

Cavale puts all her hope on Slim – that is, on the person she hopes he'll become, a rock star to serve as her personal savior. When he fails, they both turn to the Lobster Man, a delivery boy who promises more than just seafood.

Like the Young Man in *Operation Sidewinder,* Cavale and Slim look outside themselves for salvation. So many Shepard plays, in fact, send characters on the road in search of some vague promised land or at least the education that the long ramble confers. But rarely is life elsewhere after all, and in fact travel threatens to destroy whatever paltry sense of self and history the traveler began with. The Young Man in *Operation Sidewinder* seems to sense this danger when, in a climactic moment at the end of his speech about belief, he blurts out: "I am! I am! I am! I am! I am! I am! I am! I am! I am! I am! I am! Tonight. In this desert. In this space. I am."[24] He understands who he is by marking where he is. He may not know what he believes, but he can ground himself and escape suspension, letting the simple language of "I am" separate him from others, and establish his dimensions and dominion, a sense of mastery.

The arrival has been a long time coming. In the Young Man's desultory existence (not much different in nature from Shepard's own), he has been like the nomad in the Holy Modal Rounders' "Alien Song":

> This is the place I was born, bred and raised
> And it doesn't seem like I was ever here
> . . . Now I can see my whole body
> Stranded way down by the creek
> It looks so alone while it looks for its home
> And it doesn't hear me while I shriek.[25]

Nation has ceased to mean anything to the Young Man. He's able to list the clichés of America ("lace doilies and apple pie") and its standard scandals ("incest and graft") but finds none of them particularly compelling. He wants to place himself anew, escaping those old settings whose claim on him is now merely a formality. He's interested not only in where he is, but also in where he belongs. Stuck between home and the world, he doesn't know where he's meant to live anymore, but neither has he learned how to address the beckoning wilderness.

If there is one quality of Shepard's vision that has seeped into general consciousness, it's this ongoing perplexed interrogation of the land, the Great Outdoors. "What's the most frightening thing in the whole world?" asks Rabbit in *Angel City*. "A space." Shepard's own early life was one of perpetual travel. He was an Army brat, living on many different bases around the world; in later years he remained restless, moving to London for three years in the seventies, going on the road with Bob Dylan in 1975. (The *Rolling Thunder Logbook* records that adventure: As usual, every trip becomes a narrative.) These days, he shuttles between coasts of the United States. (Despite all his travel, he's famous for not wanting to fly. Perhaps trains allow for greater connection to the landscape and force a closer awareness of the span and significance of the journey.) Almost every Shepard play contains characters celebrating the rambling life, wishing to escape – Jeep in *Action,* Henry Hackamore in *Seduced,* Emma in *Curse of the Starving Class,* and dozens more. In *La Turista,* Kent ends the play by swinging on a rope through the back wall, leaving a hole shaped like his body. (Formally, the play itself breaks free, too: Its second half bears only superficial resemblance to its first. Although the characters are the same, and their conditions related, the feeling and tone have shifted radically, as though the work and its writer were bent on escaping from expectations established at the start.)

Shepard doesn't celebrate freedom the way a homely patriot might, in a dreamy daze. Escape appeals to him in a deep, natural way, but he also asks critically what happens to a sense of fellowship if everyone is always striking out for the open road. "What's a community?" asks Jeep in *Action*. He has lost that knowledge (if he ever had it) by concentrating too much on expressing his individuality. He doesn't know himself in relation to a society, a home, or a family, so he's filled only with a passionate longing for wholeness. Many of Shepard's characters eventually retreat from expansive outdoor spaces into safer places, where claustrophobia seems a small price to pay for security, the comfort of feeling (however mistakenly) that your body and especially your mind are in some sense inviolable.

Stu, in *Chicago,* won't leave his bathtub; Shooter, in *Action,* huddles under a big overstuffed chair, declaring that he's never coming out. Dodge rarely leaves the moth-eaten sofa in *Buried Child;* and Jake vows never to emerge from his womblike childhood bedroom in *A Lie of the Mind*. Perhaps most knowingly, Cody defends his psychic territory in *Geography of a Horse*

Dreamer: Only in his mind is he truly at home; only there can he find the right weather for his special creativity.

Other characters restrict themselves to verbal travel, chronicling even the most insignificant action with such ardor that a whole world of experience opens up. Sensual and imaginative landscapes replace geographical ones; the frontier of the narrative beckons more forcefully than anything on a map. Shepard's plays honor articulate fancy. "I've had a vision!" Kosmo exults at the start of *The Mad Dog Blues.* "Sing it," urges Yahoodi. Characters mark off protective forums for themselves – in *Red Cross,* for instance, Jim and The Maid use beds as their stages; in *Angel City,* the space inside a big picture frame and a magic circle that Rabbit makes are privileged territories – in which they can let their imaginations loose.

The self-ordained naïf of Off-Off Broadway, who once proudly said he rarely reads or attends plays, Shepard ignores that hard and fast "rule" of playwriting: Show, don't tell. Shepard doesn't merely insert long stories in the midst of plays; he makes telling the salient activity. His plays aren't narratives so much as plays about narrating. The process of description becomes athletic, propulsive, rather than merely expository, something to get over with quickly before moving on. Shepard's plays *don't* move on after the narrative ends. The stories only lead to more stories; the tellers get swept up by the telling, and transported out of the very forum they mean to address.

Stu, in *Chicago,* is one such airborne reporter. Wallowing in his bathtub for the entire play, he nonetheless ventures into disparate arenas of experience simply by describing them – lushly, in the language available to his imagination. Often the least promising topic snares his enthusiasm and launches him into narrative orbit. Speaking about a train ride, Stu says:

> They have one whole car where you eat. And another car just for drinking. The tables are nailed to the floor so they don't jiggle. You can buy a whole dinner for about five bucks. They even give you a full pitcher of ice water. They just leave it on the table so you don't have to keep asking for water. And a silver cup full of toothpicks. You sit there and pick your teeth and look out the window. Then you have to leave. They force you to leave because there's a whole line of people waiting to eat. They're all hungry. . . .[26]

And so it goes, for several more minutes. While Joy prepares for a real trip, piling dozens of suitcases onto a trolley, Stu makes more elaborate journeys, unencumbered. The Chicago of the title is never explained, nor need it be. This play resides only in cities of the mind. Soon Stu is on the edge of an island fantasy all his own, where he wanders into a densely detailed region and records the tides, the comings and goings of the boats, the liaisons of sailors and young virgins, and the eventual decline of their lives. The story continues inexorably until Stu has surrounded the others with his self-made verbal territory: His friends pretend to go fishing in an ocean teeming with his words; then, in unison, they breathe in the air his telling exhales.

In other plays the narrative urge, though less mannered, is no less pleasurable. If a story is well told, it can be lived, and the experience will shape a new aspect of identity. The events in the story will become lasting memories, changing the person who guards them. In *Icarus's Mother,* Pat makes a trip to the park in language alone, imagining, then telling of, a Fourth of July fireworks display. When characters in other of Shepard's plays describe actual experiences, recalling them for their own benefit or to astound disbelieving listeners, they speak with zeal, carefully going over every cranny, lavishing attention on minor facts, often repeating themselves. (In *Cowboys #2,* Chet doesn't just ask for some milk with his breakfast; he describes "a tall glass of milk with water on the outside of the glass.")[27] Events in Shepard's world don't fully exist until they're discussed. Reality is always provisional until an impromptu historian records it. Shepard's characters grab at and anxiously grapple with the phenomena before them, worried always about the inadequacy of the intellect and the senses to seize upon them. As often as language takes off in exhilarating bursts of energy in Shepard's plays, it also quietly fixes experience in place, to shore up a pleasing thing or charmed place and prevent it from crumbling away.

Language also helps characters attest to the reality of their own bodies. *The Rock Garden,* the earliest of Shepard's plays that survives, begins with a boy sitting in his underwear, listening to his mother tell him how much he looks like his father. After she mentions a feature or limb where the resemblance is most striking, he leaves and returns with a piece of clothing covering that part up. Finally, he gets a chance to tell the history of his body himself. He explains what his orgasms are like, what sexual positions he prefers, what he feels like when he's inside a lover. Each admission brings more of him into focus. At last, he really possesses himself, really inhabits his flesh. He speaks himself into presence.

Shepard has said that *The Rock Garden* is about leaving his own parents. The process of taking that distance would continue in the next forty plays he would write, through *A Lie of the Mind.* His surrogates often return to examine their origins, the strange combination of forces that made them, and then to assert differences. These characters need to know who they are *not* before they can say who they *are;* and they have to look first at the ground beneath their feet before they're able to see, and recognize, the body standing upon it.

"I feel there are territories within us that are totally unknown," Shepard said in an interview:

> Huge, mysterious, and dangerous territories. We think we know ourselves, when we really know only this little bitty part. We have this social person that we present to each other. We have all these galaxies inside of us. And if we don't enter those in art of one kind or another, whether it's playwriting, or painting, or music, or whatever, then I don't understand the point of doing anything. It's the reason I write. I try to go into parts of myself that are unknown.[28]

The journeys that Shepard's characters make have much in common with his own artistic adventures. And the attendant fear leads the artist back indoors just as quickly as it does his creative progeny. He may want to reach another dimension of being, like the Young Man in *Operation Sidewinder;* but "as soon as that world opens up," Shepard admits, "I tend to run the other way. It's scary because I can't answer to it from what I know."[29] Maybe that terror explains why Shepard advises new writers to start with the body, using it as the first source of images and impulses, of questions that the writing will address, just as he did in *The Rock Garden.* "The more you penetrate into the smallest thing, the more it sends off sparks to the biggest."[30] By making the body the object of close inspection, Shepard suggests, the drama will maintain the sensuality essential to its artistic life. And the writer, like the characters about whom Shepard has written, will for once feel placed, related to palpable history and culture, instead of spinning blindly toward abstract "ideas" or "meanings."

In *The Tooth of Crime,* Hoss rattles off some of his models in an inspired burst of rage – James Dean, Duane Allman, and, most unexpectedly, Jackson Pollock. What they have in common is a bewitching self-destructiveness, a knack for "breaking it open," for "pulling the trigger," as Hoss puts it, a conviction that only when they have pitched themselves toward the extreme of ecstatic suffering, of painful bliss, can they create. They are making art with their lives, not only with their minds. The entire body – especially in Pollock's case – risks annihilation so that a song or a painting can emerge. The work of art is the engraved trace of a carnal event.

Shepard is not as self-destructive as these artists, but much of his work reveals a similar search for the perfect gesture. In a 1971 program note, Shepard wrote: "I like to yodel and dance and fuck a lot. Writing is neat because you do it on a very physical level."[31] Despite his deliberate impudence and the apparent simplemindedness of his assertion, Shepard here provides a key to the peculiar power of his writing. And, perhaps unwittingly, he exposes the central deficiency of the theater surrounding him. It shouldn't sound so radical when someone suggests that theater making is a physical act. Isn't that what distinguishes the form – its kinetic force, its temporality, its three-dimensional life, vivid and moving before us? But the degree to which theater had ossified by the sixties wasn't really apparent until Shepard shook and rattled and careered around the stage. He restored the theatricality to the drama; the body to the costume; the tremulous or booming voice to the dialogue; the wind to the way an actor crossed the room.

Actually, the life in Shepard's writing owes a lot to Tennessee Williams. At first glance, the elder writer seems an unlikely kindred spirit: Williams looks too soft to be the father of an artist who is all electric guitar and leather, swagger and spitfire. But both writers have conceived characters bent on chronicling their physical lives and, further, on articulating with their bodies what language can't express. As in Williams, Shepard's characters speak obsessively about bodily forms and functions, charting their corporeal terrain, as if they must assure themselves of its presence before they can engage with another person, or travel to bigger places. Jim in *Red Cross,* for instance, goes into great detail about his crab infestation; Henry, in *Seduced,* maniacally takes inventory of the contents of his body, monitoring the flow of fluids, supervising the minute changes in pallor and weight. Like Howard Hughes, whom he clearly resembles, Henry is crazily afraid of disease, constantly purifying the places he occupies, draping himself with Kleenex. Henry hopes for total control; like other self-conscious Shepard characters, he suffers from an unslakable need to be certain that the body he occupies is actually his.

The flesh demands attention with greater ferocity in later Shepard plays. Kent reaches a kind of catharsis in *La Turista* by surviving a brutal illness. The family members in *Curse of the Starving Class* just about buckle under to hunger until they too achieve a strange peace. Each mindlessly checks the refrigerator over and over; when there's nothing to eat, they attend to the body's demands in other ways. Emma bemoans her period; Wesley pisses on the floor, and later strips off his clothes and walks naked outdoors in the cold, testing what his flesh is capable of, what it can survive.

Fourteen Hundred Thousand begins placidly enough: Tom and Donna paint a new bookcase for the fourteen hundred thousand books Donna owns. Suddenly, Tom swings a soaking brush at her, and a paint fight ensues. The outburst is shocking, for it erupts without warning or apparent motivation, but it's just business-as-usual to these characters, who accept the violence easily into their lives. No one registers surprise in the aptly titled *Action,* either, when Jeep lifts up a chair and smashes it on the ground for no visible reason. His companions calmly replace it, and he repeats the tantrum. In *4-H Club,* rage is simply the most direct and unfussy way for John, Bob, and Joe to communicate with each other. Ordinary conversation doesn't express quite so much as the gusto with which they smash plates, kick around the trash, wrestle, pretend to shoot guns, stomp their feet, yell, swing a broom against the door, bang a coffeepot on a hot plate, and noisily crunch away at an endless supply of apples.

Pervasive as this violence is, it's rarely out of control. Even in *4-H Club,* or in *True West,* where Austin smashes toasters and Lee pounds a typewriter with a golf club, the rage has an agenda to be satisfied. It is not quite intellectual, but it is focused, purposeful. Violence is never less than violation.

The violence in Shepard's plays is part of an extreme approach to characterization. Rather than the give and take of ordinary dialogue, the pedestrian tempo of entrances and exits, battle is the favored mode of exchange for his characters. They collide verbally, their speech more assault than address, in a dramatic arena where entrances are always invasions of some sort and exits are frenzied wall scalings.

This ever-present tension suggests that Shepard lives with an excruciating frustration while writing his characters, that he's perpetually dissatisfied because he can't get near them, or inside them, in the way he wants. Shepard seems always to be trying to close in on his figures, to reduce the distance between himself and his surrogates, to get *at* his characters in ways other writers never even try. For Shepard, characters exist to be sparred with, to be backed into corners and exposed. Some of his violent characters are more interested in testing their strength than in hurting anyone; and alongside them Shepard is also taking stock, measuring just how far his imagination can take him.

The objects of such abuse aren't always women – *Suicide in B-flat, The Tooth of Crime,* and *True West* are only a few examples of plays in which men are the primary victims – but the particular pain the female characters seem to suffer, and the greater candor they have about their fears, is telling. Shepard doesn't give his stage over to blatant brutality, but even his men's small gestures, contained in quiet moments, can trigger wracking crises in his women. The severest violations are always muted. When Eddie, the cowboy manqué in *Fool for Love,* starts lassooing the bedposts, we see his longing to rope and hog-tie May, along with the pain of not being able to approach her directly. Less obliquely, Bradley colonizes Shelly's body in *Buried Child.* The middle brother in a burned-out family, Bradley is a terrifying presence – big, gruff, and lumbering; missing a leg. But nothing in his appearance causes as much fear as when he asks Shelly, his nephew's girlfriend, to open her mouth, and then with utter control and calm, inserts three of his fingers inside.

Such scenes of violence have contributed to a prevalent belief that, in Shepard's world, women are more often acted upon than active, with men assigned the central place and function. Bonnie Marranca writes that in Shepard's plays "women are the background . . . always treated as subservient to men, their potential for growth and change restricted." According to Marranca, Shepard is unable, or reluctant, "to create female characters whose imaginative range matches that of males."[32] Joyce Aaron, an actress who performed in many early Shepard plays, ends her own assessment of his work by exclaiming, "I wish he'd write a play for women!"[33] There *is* an essential masculinity to Shepard's dramatic world – as might be expected from an artist so skilled at projecting the crises of his own artistic, sexual, and psychic life on stage – and the emotional center of the plays usually does rest within his male characters, especially the ravaged ones, overwhelmed by the confusion around them. But in many plays the women are more autonomous, wiser, and more self-reliant than many observers give them credit for. The world may be masculine, but it's the women who are able to see what that world lacks, to understand its inadequacy and poverty, to expose its soullessness and predict its inevitable demise.

Shepard's women adapt to hostile, unforgiving climates more readily than his men. Shelly in *Buried Child* takes refuge in tasks (she says she shucks corn "to survive"), then eases into a commanding role in the household, eventually commandeering the absent mother's bedroom. The mother, meanwhile, forsakes a rotten household. So does Ella, the mother in *Curse of the Starving Class*. Ella's daughter Emma follows suit, riding out to the horizon on a horse and leaving her father and brother behind to patch together some kind of existence inside the shell of what was once a family. The women in these late plays escape the past and the confining present – something the men dearly want to do but rarely can. Lorraine, in *A Lie of the Mind,* burns away all the remnants of her former life, eradicating the memory of her late husband and eagerly planning a future; her son remains trapped with the false icons and romantic memories of past glory. Lorraine endures – just as May withstands Eddie's torture in *Fool for Love,* refusing to pin her hopes on some change of heart Eddie might have, readying herself to leave the instant she knows he won't return to her. Even the subservience that Marranca detects can be interpreted, alternatively, as self-sufficiency. In *Action,* while Scooter cowers under a chair or Jeep paces the room like a helpless animal, the women (Lupe and Liza) find equilibrium in household chores – doing the laundry, cooking, restoring whatever Jeep wrecks. Likewise, in *Buried Child,* Dodge lies prone on his couch waiting for Shelly to bring him soup; and Baylor, in *A Lie of the Mind,* can't get his boots off, and his frostbitten fingers ache, until Meg helps him into his slippers and rubs balm on his skin. Women master the space in *A Lie of the Mind,* and in *Action* and in *Buried Child.* Men are victims of it, forever uncomfortable.

That dependence rankles: It draws attention to the larger ruin of their entire lives. It's out of this awareness of failure, never soothed, that Shepard's men resort to violence so regularly. Their outbursts do not announce strength, but rather, as Shepard notes, express only how weakened they've become, the degree of their psychic damage.

> In full force [violence] is very ugly, but there's also something very moving about it, because it has to do with humiliation. There's some

> hidden, very deeply rooted thing in the Anglo male American that has to do with inferiority, that has to do with not being a man, and always, continually, having to act out some idea of manhood that invariably is violent.[34]

Once again, Shepard's characters succumb to role-playing, not able to know themselves apart from the disguises they've inherited.

It would be a mistake, then, to assume that Shepard endorses the violence he so graphically shows. In fact, he's critical not only of the abuse but also the entire ethos of masculinity that sanctions it. As he said in a recent interview:

> Machismo may be an evil force, but what in fact is it? I know what this thing is about because I was a victim of it, it was part of my life, my old man tried to force on me a notion of what it was to be a "man." And it destroyed my dad. But you can't avoid facing it.[35]

Shepard's work certainly testifies to his deep fascination with the masculine mystique – the farmers and cowboys, the rock stars and space heroes. But alongside the fantasy runs a strong current of skepticism. Shepard is attracted to and repulsed by the same images, and as a way of understanding this contradiction he writes his way toward its source: "my old man." If he can finally know his father, Shepard may finally know what to do with his legacy, the lessons in behavior.

Motel Chronicles, the closest thing we'll probably ever get to a memoir, suggests one reason why Shepard's characters are determined to return to their origins. The book, a collection of verbal snapshots written on the road while Shepard was acting in his first film, has at its center a series of encounters with his father, who lives alone in the New Mexico desert. Shepard finds him in order to assess the significance of their connection, to reaffirm it in some way – but also to acknowledge finally the distance between them. One photograph from the memoir, of the two Shepards looking at each other, captures their estrangement: Shepard warmly regards a man he barely knows; the father, in a cowboy hat, stares, uncomprehending, in the direction of his son's throat, not meeting his gaze. Showing off the pinups on his wall and his collection of cigarette butts in a Yuban coffee can, the elder Shepard says that he doesn't "fit with people" – not even, it seems, with the child he left behind.[36] In the plays that Shepard wrote just before and after these visits, he tried to figure out why that had to be so. What are the consequences of losing a father? How can a son who still wants that relationship feel bound to an absence? Because these questions can never be answered adequately, and because the father always eludes his son's reach, these plays show Shepard at his saddest, most resigned.

For perhaps the same reasons, he has also grown more accessible. The newer, family plays, from *Curse of the Starving Class* in 1978 to *A Lie of the Mind* in 1985, earned Shepard popular acclaim, but also caused, among his admirers from the sixties, some quiet disappointment. *Buried Child* may have won a Pulitzer prize, *A Lie of the Mind* a New York Drama Critics Circle award; but it seemed that Shepard was paying for such honors by giving up his artistic delinquency. There is less anarchy and purely theatrical imagery in these later plays; the gestures are more controlled, the structure more formal; a narrative is sustained. These plays are also more generous to the reader and spectator. For the first time, Shepard includes characters who are outsiders to his dramatic world. The Mom in *True West,* the lawyer, Taylor, in *Curse of the Starving Class,* and most articulate, Shelly, who can't reconcile the people in *Buried Child* with her expectations of a Norman Rockwell family: They are *our* surrogates; they express all our confusion and wonder.

Surely the later plays stand apart, but they signify less a break with Shepard's past than an extension, a focusing of his interests, examining the same issues of identity, role-playing, and placement in the smaller arena of the family. Unfortunately, family drama has acquired a bad name after decades of banal naturalism. But it's precisely because the family is such an overworked theme that Shepard's response to it is so impressive. He plays off our familiarity, subverts our expectations, and exposes the underside of images we've grown accustomed to – so that his family dramas exhibit much the same strangeness as an early play such as *Icarus's Mother* does. His theater now also has a genuine emotional center, which grounds the imagery and adds weight to the mystery. (The emotion in the early plays is often all on one level – usually up high – or all Shepard's, ecstatic with creativity.)

In *Buried Child,* Vince describes how the known became unknown for him during his second ride home:

> I could see myself in the windshield. My face. My eyes. I studied my face. Studied everything about it. As though I was looking at another man. As though I could see his whole race behind him. . . . And then his face changed. His face became his father's face. Same bones. Same eyes. Same nose. Same breath. And his father's face changed to his Grandfather's face. And it went on like that. . . . I followed my family clear into Iowa. Every last one. Straight into the Corn Belt and further. Straight back as far as they'd take me. Then it all dissolved. Everything dissolved.[37]

The dissolution continues at the house. *Buried Child* is a dusky play, gray save for the brilliant orange carrots and yellow corn that Tilden improbably harvests from the backyard. The play's interior is deliberately hollow; characters circle a void left by the play's two fathers: Vince's father, Tilden, and his grandfather, Dodge. The men are present only as stunned, gutted bodies; their bewilderment has taken the place of paternal attachment. Tilden has returned home because he had nowhere else to go; but he remains hunted by the recollections of a vague crisis he just fled. Dodge, even more empty, despite the ferocity of his claims that "this is me! the whole shootin' match!," is a strawman whom the other characters torture and humiliate. Bradley, the more visibly mutilated son, shaves his father's head until the scalp bleeds; Tilden covers Dodge's sleeping body with corn husks at the end of Act I; an act later, Bradley covers Dodge's head with a fur coat.

Dodge's two burials nicely match the child's internment: The corpse lies under the corn crops, its birth and death remaining mysteries throughout the play. Who are its parents? Was it murdered? By whom? The answers are not as significant as the way the family refuses to address the same questions, refuses even to acknowledge the corpse's presence. That neglect is only one of many severed connections in the household: The dead child offers a silent reproach for all the ruined responsibilities. Dodge won't accept that Tilden now lives with him; Tilden can't recognize Vince as his son; Halie exaggerates the memory of Ansel, another dead child, hailing him (falsely) as a war hero and basketball pro.

Faced with so much willful, blinkered isolation, Vince declares, "I've gotta carry on the line," trying to reestablish ties and claim his inheritance. He does so violently – the only way to force anything through the entropy around him. Drunk, he crashes about the porch, toppling furniture, smashing bottles, then cuts through the screen into the living room, destroying the house as a way of asserting his ownership. Finally spent, he lies down on the couch, replicating his grandfather's position. He achieves kinship with his family – but at what cost? For what purpose? Vince only learns a different loneliness, a variation on the feelings of deprivation he lived with before rediscovering his father. Tilden shows solicitude only for the corpse of the hidden child, which he disinters at the end and returns to Halie's room. Vince becomes the invalid father to a family that he never knew.

The sons in *Curse of the Starving Class, Fool for Love, True West,* and *A Lie of the Mind* settle accounts with their fathers in different ways, but all share Vince's fever, as well as his fear that nothing will change, that they will feel just as barren after facing their fathers. That worry, in fact, makes the sons' searches all-consuming, an ultimate test of endurance and resourcefulness, more than merely a domestic problem. Their journeys, in this regard, are allegories – drawing together many of the concerns in other Shepard plays to subsume them in this highly private experience. And the encounters between father and son – or between the son and his memory of a father he cannot retrieve – become final reckoning places, opportunities for Shepard to sum up and evaluate everything he had been trying to achieve as a playwright.

The desire of Shepard's characters to find that one remarkable gesture has never been as acute as that held by a son anxious to win his father's attention, or else banish his ghost for good; to demand his interest, his shock, or just to force him to witness a son's anger. The ardor with which Shepard tries to penetrate his characters is mirrored most vividly in these men as they run themselves up against granite figures, refusing to quit until they at least know the degree of their fathers' resistance. That devotion to lost causes helps explain Shepard's abiding interest in the mutability of character and structure: For while these late plays may *look* more stable than the early work, it is only because the sons are so obsessed with reaching their fathers that no action seems improbable. A son will go through an entire catalogue of behavior until he strikes the one approach that might carry him right to the deep center of his family. He even impersonates his missing father, as though to conjure him up in absentia, and then to feel a replica of the relief in finding him.

Shepard's interest in the body also acquires a new dimension when seen in light of the drama between father and son. Eddie and May in *Fool for Love* share the same father (a wanderer who watches from the margins). Their romance is a way to reach *him* more than each other. In *Curse of the Starving Class,* Shepard's exploded version of the save-the-farm play, Wesley finally knows his father, Weston, only after putting on Weston's clothes, settling himself into that discarded shell, since no other connection is possible now that his father has left home. "Everytime I put one thing on, it seemed like a part of him was growing on me," he says. "I could feel him taking over me."[38] Abstractions like affection or pride or concern – all the clichés of parenting – don't have the same reliable fleshiness as the sweat and dirt in Weston's clothes that Wesley mingles with his own, or the poison Weston refers to as his link to his own father: "I saw myself infected with it. I saw me carrying it around. His poison in my body."[39] In Shepard's world, blood and bone determine who is bound to whom, and who is excluded; the family is an "animal thing," Weston insists, not just "a social thing."

A Lie of the Mind, Shepard's longest work, is a compendium of all the family plays. Here there are two absent fathers – Jake's, long dead, run over by a truck; and Beth's, alive but emotionally detached, given to vanishing in the woods for long periods of hunting or hiding in a hut, more comfortable with slain animals than with his relentlessly living family. Jake and Beth, married but driven apart by Jake's abuse, loiter around the voids where their fathers should be, and only discover their own vacancy. Beth's emptiness is most severe: She has suffered brain damage from Jake's beatings and actually cannot recall exactly how she fits into her family.

Like Shepard's other sons, Jake wants both to retrieve and to bury his father. His sister says he sought out their estranged father only to see him die, but when Jake returns home he dons the medal-laden army jacket his father wore. It's a stifled sort of tribute. He clutches the box that contains his father's ashes, but when no one is looking he opens it and blows some dust away. The contradictory responses should be familiar to students of Shepard, as should the violence, which here returns (albeit more viciously than in his earlier plays) in a network of ruinous attachments. Jake batters Beth; Mike, Beth's brother, hunts down and beats Jake; Baylor, Beth's father, accidentally shoots Jake's brother, Frankie; and on and on through the many smaller skirmishes, emotional and physical.

Some of Shepard's favorite public icons, such as the American flag, also appear (as garb), enlarging the strife from the domestic to a broader cultural arena. Alas, the imagery alone can't do it: By now, after other Shepard plays have winnowed the sham from the genuine ideas of Americanness, such pictures look glib, facile, unable even to communicate their own emptiness.

Despite these refrains, *A Lie of the Mind* is a searching work: It manages to push into a new corner of Shepard's world. He seems to be running through his obsessions in search of a deeper level of thought, a new stage of artistic maturity. Shepard goes beyond merely exposing the anguish of his families; he explicitly offers reasons for it (only rarely *too* explicitly) and, most astonishing, even proposes a way to begin repairing the injuries. *Lie* is also an unusually moving play – in a hushed, unobtrusive way, leaving us wondering how Shepard manages to find a place for unadorned affect in a landscape of such hardness. Despite the sovereign detachment and independence from ordinary ethics that this, as all plays, must claim, *A Lie of the Mind* is also curiously "responsible."

One hint of Shepard's change is the setting. Claustrophobic spaces enclosed many of his earlier plays, but never so functionally, nor so self-consciously. The need for security, or its opposite, the nervous longing for escape, seemed vivid enough in the earlier plays without further comment. They summed up well a troubled existence or a battered mind and heart; and once Shepard had those pictures in place, he ended the play. In *Lie,* Beth and Frankie, Baylor, Meg, and Mike are trapped at home by a blizzard; while far away, Lorraine and Sally have walled themselves up in Jake's old room. But this time Shepard's characters capitalize on the confinement, using it for self-examination, and for a series of family negotiations. Some characters in *Lie* do try to flee engagement of any sort – as did the hermits and vagabonds in early Shepard plays. The difference here is that they are stopped. Someone like Beth will hold them back and cajole them into conversation; someone like Sally will ask, "what are we supposed to be hiding from?"

The families in *Lie* retreat from places that don't make any sense, milieus less hospitable than hoped, a culture that they don't recognize. Beth is the most stranded – but she doesn't reiterate the despair of other Shepard characters. "This is where I need to be," she says, using her rootlessness to prod herself toward attachments, making of the hostile home a place to work her way into. Rather than mourning the lost ideal of a family, something that no longer corresponds to reality, she refashions what she's given, builds a new shelter up again around her.

At every juncture the play offers opportunities for emotional reform and testifies to Shepard's renewed spirit. It's fair to say that the outlook is rosier in *Lie* than in his other plays, and even that the optimism is not yet persuasive, given the ruin that surrounds it. But *Lie* must be seen as a tentative start on a new project for Shepard – not, as its size and setting led so many to believe, the culminating work of Shepard's family cycle. *Lie* has less in common with *Buried Child* and *Curse* than one might think. The endings of those plays show families torn asunder, scattered, or else holed up in catatonia. The characters have become ciphers – stripped of encumbering identities, and naked beneath the essential falseness of their lives. *Lie*'s characters reach that blankness, gaze into the void of their lives, but then pull back and turn around. In a fragile but real way, they survive.

> BETH: (*Very simple to Frankie*) This – this is my father. He's given up love. Love is dead for him. My mother is dead for him. Things live for him to be killed. Only death counts for him. Nothing else. This – This – (*She moves slowly toward Frankie*) This is me. This is me now. The way I am. Now. This. All. Different. I – I live inside this. Remember. Remembering. You. You – were one. I know you. I know – love. I know what love is. I can never forget. That. Never. (*Lights fade.*)[40]

Lie closes with a silent picture of Baylor and Meg folding the flag peacefully, and Frankie and Beth piecing together a relationship, gently embracing, after Jake relinquishes his claim. The tableau would be sentimental, as would Beth's speech, were the characters not so uncertain about their actions and emotions. It is a "happy ending," at least in the context of Shepard's other work, but it comes out of such suffering and is so tentative (as though the characters themselves didn't quite believe they were doing these things) that it's not really pat – and far from enduring. *Lie* ends with an image of healing, not of health: only the beginning of a long recovery.

"I know what love is." Beth's assertion, simple and beautiful, contains no self-satisfaction or evangelical ardor. She sets herself against the acceptance of emptiness in Shepard's theater. With a manner that is persuasive by being so humble, she declares that ideas mean something after all; that bonds among people endure; that an overused, abused concept like "love" is still viable, along with "family" and even "America." (Her force of belief recalls Chekhov's Sonya.) Perhaps most startling, she shows that there is such a thing as identity: The face that she wears is real. The debris of her life lies around a core of undamaged feeling – something so ineffable and radiant that it shames all those Shepard characters who had faith only in masks.

In *Lie* Shepard resembles Francis Bacon again, but for a different reason: Bacon had always shied away from abstraction, preferring to work a plodding path through figurative painting. For him, abstraction could not reach the grimy realities he was drawn to; there was more mystery in flesh than in a dance of brushstrokes; a rendered face, for him, plumbed deeper spiritual depths than a screen of paint ever could. There's also a genuine sense of commitment in figurative painting that appealed to Bacon – not in terms of politics, but as a belief that the world deserves to be engaged, and that a painter can meet people and things head on and still maintain his freedom.

A Lie of the Mind reaffirms Shepard's own faith in realism. The play is full of answers to the Young Man's plea, fifteen years earlier in *Operation Sidewinder,* that someone "say something human, something real – so we can believe again." How unseemly to want such certainty, such meaning, or at least the possibility of them, in a culture so entranced by simulated experiences, celluloid paradises, glossy personalites – all the coy duplicities bundled into what's come to be known as postmodernism. There's a fed-up, plain-speaking tone to *A Lie of the Mind,* as though Shepard were irritated by the evasions of his own past work and wanted finally to settle himself into some kind of artistic home, or at least burn away the reminders of who he has been, as Lorraine does, and start a new history. The rough-and-tumble early years – when his plays never stopped shaking and, as Michael Smith put it, his sense of structure was "hunchy" – were heady enough while they lasted. But now, some thirty plays later, Shepard asks for nothing so much as a real destination for that energy. This play tries to answer a question Shepard refused to utter in the early work: What does it all add up to? Where are his characters going after they flee entrapment and greet danger? Questions like these are too weighty to be worked through in one play, and *Lie* is most significant for the plays it prepares Shepard for, the suggestions in it of things that won't fully coalesce until future days of writing. For all its apparent conclusiveness, *Lie* is really as open a play as some of his first efforts.

Shepard once wondered aloud if he had written himself out; if, after all those plays, there simply was no more he wanted to say. The six years of relative silence after *A Lie of the Mind* appeared in 1985, years in which he devoted himself mostly to film activity, led many winking observers to agree. There was often a scolding tone to these appraisals of Shepard – as though there were something inherently wrong with being depleted, as though artistic lives don't have their own cycles apart from biological ones, and so can't be forcibly resuscitated.

In fact, recent years have proved that reports of Shepard's playwriting demise have been premature. In 1991, he presented a short play, *States of Shock,* in response to the Gulf War. He completed a longer work, *Simpatico,* in 1993, and has begun collaborating again with Joseph Chaikin. It is too early to assess the significance of these latest plays, but with their arrival it *is* possible to rethink assumptions about Shepard's hiatus from playwriting. A silence that had looked like writer's block or imaginative sterility, or merely Shepard's enchantment with the distractions of celebrity, now also seems to have been a necesssary pause for self-questioning.

The wary pace at which Shepard is returning to the theater may be an inevitable consequence of *A Lie of the Mind* itself. That play teaches patience; its characters insist on responsibility for behavior and speech; its aching tone asks for careful listening and considered reflection. From this perspective, Shepard's long silence after 1985 appears part of the very substance of *A Lie of the Mind* – its contrapuntal response. In order to honor his characters' demand for sincerity, Shepard begins with himself – welcoming a period of lingering, of looking closely and slowly at his surroundings, of waiting to speak until his ideas and images are weighted adequately, and until writing feels necessary. Perhaps it is no longer possible for Shepard to write with his early hurtling, heedless ardor: He has learned the lesson of *Lie* too well. Usually hidden from view now, Shepard seems to insist that his new work earn its presence – and, as each play emerges from an inscrutable, expressive stillness, that it also retain the ample space in which to be fully perceived.

4

MARIA IRENE FORNES

THE PLAYS OF MARIA IRENE FORNES insist that small things matter. She is not a miniaturist – at least not in the condescending sense that often accompanies the term – so much as a writer for whom the imperative to draw out the nuances of experience is particularly pressing. Fornes's plays are easily overlooked, or looked through, by readers in search of more ostentatiously declarative art. We can often find ourselves just to the side of her work, even after the most sensitive of readings, unable ever to feel that we have really been inside the play, or even held onto it for more than a moment before it floated away. Was that all there was? Was it even there at all?

Reading Fornes slowly, however, or with the kind of languor that sharpens the senses, we are gradually initiated into her way of seeing. A long stay with Fornes's drama makes us alert and newly articulate – and also more comfortable with silence, able to pause and consider what formerly we tried to unwrap or, maybe, wrap up. Her approach to observation is so rigorous that even her most lighthearted plays have a deep seriousness, as though the writer's very life depended on the accuracy and the economy with which she sets down the phenomena before her. Some of her characters, it will be seen, do in fact live under this pressure: They record their lives to defend themselves against those who cannot see their worth, articulating the present and the past as a way of securing a possible future. Fornes's anxiety is every writer's helplessness in the face of so much life to respond to – but, like her characters, she never seems to panic: Her plays have a disarming gentleness even when they're set in an atmosphere of brutality and indifference. Fornes doesn't know how to be indifferent. Her drama everywhere attests to the responsibility with which she takes care of the people and events spawned by her imagination.

That constant receptiveness to detail, not automatic in the ways of false hospitality, gives her work its considerable clarity. Her theater is deceptive: It looks more spare than it really is. She builds many of her plays with short, self-contained scenes, some without any dialogue at all, others with just a word or two, or with an abrupt declaration and stunned response. Those sentences are just as unembroidered: Their syntax is elementary, the words are well polished from frequent use, their tone unfussy. Since 1968 Fornes has been directing her own work, and so these scenes now look as clean as they sound: She eschews clutter; the actors are given ample space between each other; their gestures are sharp and strong, without being flamboyant or gratuitous. Fornes's scenes breathe easily. They're full of light and freshness; they're bracing, compelling as more labored events could never be.

Because Fornes strips away excess and aerates her scenes, the subtle aspects of a character's personality and the minute gradations of behavior stand out clearly. An action that would be inconsequential in a more ornate play has the power to startle when there's little else to look at. A thing or a person can simply be present, regarded, without having to take its functional place in a complicated plot. Single occurrences become more significant than the narrative, and more complicated. A figure demands to be seen in all her complexity when she stands alone in a big white space. Meanwhile, despite its apparent starkness, Fornes's theater is profoundly sensual, aesthetically concerned. She is passionate about surfaces and worried about shapeliness. Her theater is the gift of someone who regularly lets herself be astonished.

"I write these messages that come," Fornes once said when asked to explain her process.[1] The sentence is characteristic Fornes – downplayed, obvious perhaps, yet truly explosive. Fornes discards the seductive image of the writer as a forger of resounding truths; she doesn't see herself rigging up an ideology, much less a theology, the way so many proselytizing writers do. She is always the spectator, especially when inventing the most fanciful worlds. Instead of starting a play with an idea, she'll retrieve a phrase, remember an arrangement of people, or just look more closely at the memory of, say, the angles formed by a man in a chair, and then allow the associations to course by. The ease that so many Fornes plays have, their self-possession, stems in large part from this confidence that a well-formed picture or a nicely turned sentence is its own justification; that one good utterance will simply demand the right words to follow; a beautiful gesture will elicit the next one automatically, and Fornes won't have to force her play to unfold.

Fornes's plays take time – she makes time her own, resets the clock to accommodate her habit of lingering around the things she loves. She encourages us to relax along with her: It's impossible to predict where a Fornes play will go, so spectators are better off contemplating the images as they come, resisting the urge to hitch them to the engine of a plot, disregarding the itinerary in favor of the attractions it holds. She has said that she abhors deliberateness in writing, any passage that exudes a fretfulness about conveying its substance or importance. To stave off her own temptation to elicit meaning artificially, she throws her plays open to seemingly accidental events, the moments that sober writers would call extraneous. There's a scene in *Fefu and Her Friends,* Fornes's 1977 masterpiece, that shows this openheartedness particularly well. Just before a character named Cecilia is about to deliver a speech, another woman starts playfully humming the Simon and Garfunkel song "Cecilia," and before long the other women have joined in, singing it through to the end. Then the scene proper – the business at hand, as it were – resumes, untroubled. Fornes is a patient enough writer to allow for such interruptions: She knows they won't derail her play. If anything, they give her theater its particular honesty and its tenderness.

Maria Irene Fornes was born in Havana, Cuba, in 1930. When she was 15, she emigrated to New York with her mother, just three months before the end of World War II. She enrolled in high school, but dropped out a month later, and went to work in a succession of factories and offices, until, at age 19, she realized that she wanted to be a painter. Night-school art classes encouraged her to seek out Hans Hofmann, and soon she was studying with him in Provincetown. That experience, in turn, prompted her move to Paris, where she enjoyed three years of bohemian living before returning to New York in 1957 and going into business as a textile designer.

Three years later she understood she never would be the visual artist that the perfectionist in her demanded. She had done little writing up till then – just some translations of letters written by a cousin to her great-grandfather, which taken together conjured up for her a fascinating lost world – and read nothing in dramatic literature except *Hedda Gabler.* She had been living with Susan Sontag, then an unknown lecturer at Columbia, and while presiding over the beginnings of Sontag's career as a writer, Fornes suddenly hit upon the idea for her first play. Nineteen days later she had finished *Tango Palace.* She was 30 years old.

It's hard to comprehend the velocity of her creativity, for Fornes was writing in English, her second language. Fornes has said that she never writes her plays in Spanish, that the rigors of working in a second language keep her honest: They enforce the discipline any writer hopes to practice. Fornes won't force a drama to occur if one doesn't suggest itself naturally, but once images and dialogue do surface, she is fastidious about them. She worries over each word longer than she might if English were a language she took for granted. The fine curves to her sentences are the products of intense pruning and paring ("Words that are useless, like 'actually.' I take those little words out," she has said): There's little possibility, after all, of getting wordy when one's vocabulary is still incomplete. The struggle pays off: Her paragraphs have poise.

Fornes has often spoken about how words can only *evoke* experience, never capture it, much less re-create it. "Words change the nature of things," she writes in her play *Dr. Kheal.* "A thing not named and the same thing named are two different things."[2] Such awareness accounts for the extraordinary humility of her plays, and also their enduring freshness: One feels that the play is still evolving; the language is still stretching itself toward the things it's meant to encircle. Fornes's plays have an unsatisfied air to them: When characters speak, one almost sees them compromise, accepting, for now, the imperfections in what they are able to say, but determined to be more eloquent next time. Every sentence in Fornes bears the traces of all the other possible sentences rejected or postponed.

Five lines from a recent play, *Mud,* seem to have this kind of history:

MAE: (*She kisses him again*) . . . I want you here.

HENRY: Here?

MAE: I want you here.

HENRY: To live here?

MAE: If you will.[3]

Mae's restraint speaks volumes: She sticks to her carefully fashioned sentence – "I want you here" – when she could easily let loose with supplication or earnest declaration. Fornes could also have given her a less controlled last line – something casual, like "Yes" or "Please," or something passionate – but instead chose "if you will" – a phrase so awkward, so retiring, that it suggests what Mae can't have, as much as it suggests what she wants.

Fornes is such a generous writer that it seems odd that her first play is such a harsh examination of manipulation. To hear Fornes set *Tango Palace* apart from the rest of her work, and express her skepticism about its vitality, would lead one to believe, falsely, that the play is something of an anomaly, a failed start. In fact, it's one of Fornes's surest efforts, and a central work of the American theater of the sixties: an amazing first play. Thirty years later Fornes still hasn't abandoned the subjects she explored in *Tango Palace.* She may have altered her approach, and shifted her perspective, but recent works like *The Conduct of Life* owe their forcefulness to the early fascination with the mechanics of attachment and the terrifying ease with which people abuse one another. In *Tango Palace,* Fornes may have purged herself of the manipulative tendencies she feared in herself (never again, she said, would she work so programmatically, fitting a play to a predetermined conception), but she wouldn't be able to leave behind the play's substance or find satisfying answers to her troubled inquisition of the condition she portrays: Why does this have to be so? Why must people do such things to each other?

The Tango Palace itself is a cavelike room where Isidore, pudgy and soft, his face painted to give him the rotten prettiness of a crushed rose, keeps Leopold prisoner. Isidore wears high heels and a blouse, and he pouts a lot, but little else about him is delicate. He whips Leopold and smacks him when he talks back, punctuating the violence with mottoes like "All is fair in love and war" and underscoring the obvious – "that is pain," Isidore says after seeing Leopold nurse his wounds – making the humiliation sting even more.

Isidore's sadism is more insidious when it's psychological. He not only tells Leopold what to do and where to go, but also thinks for Leopold and controls his every response. Whenever Isidore says something particularly epigrammatic, he flings a card to the floor, as though the gesture ensures that the statement will be indisputable. Isidore's smugness doesn't stop Leopold: He routinely challenges Isidore's pronouncements – feistily, until he picks up some cards and finds out that his *own* statements are printed on them. When he tries to escape, Isidore knows exactly what Leopold is thinking, and announces his movements just before they occur – denying Leopold even the pride of making an independent protest. "I am the only voice," Isidore declares.[4]

A few years before writing *Tango Palace,* when she was living in Paris, Fornes had her first significant theater experience: She saw the world premiere of *Waiting for Godot,* Roger Blin's now-famous production. The experience has stayed with her to this day, she says, but nowhere is its influence so profound as in *Tango Palace.* The world in Fornes's play is gaudier, more vibrant and campy than Beckett's ever would be, but the older writer's example taught Fornes that madcap vaudeville could share space with emotional truthfulness and not jar it; that little was needed materially to express whole washes of experience; and that a writer's compassion for his characters displays itself naturally when the play is simply conceived and sharply focused. *Tango Palace* opens with Leopold writhing in a sack and Isidore calmly watching – the same kind of pathetic behavior Beckett's characters know so well. Pozzo's torture of Lucky recalls some of Isidore's tricks, just as Estragon's sufferings match Leopold's own: *Godot* must surely have shown Fornes how dependency can alternately sustain and debase those too vulnerable to exist alone.

Tango Palace gains in significance when considered as the first stage of Fornes's long, ongoing sifting of the dirt of human exchange. The dirt is real: Toward the end of *Tango Palace* Leopold rhapsodizes about his bowels, Isidore's smell, dust and sweat. He says he wants to "live with that loathsome mess near me, not to flush it away . . . [to] let the dirt rot inside." Leopold embraces the pollution surrounding him, but his spirit struggles to remain immaculate. He says to Isidore, "I will not become rotten for you," and rejoices when Isidore acknowledges the difference between right and wrong – at least Isidore is open to reform; he concedes the reality of goodness despite being unable, yet, to uphold it.[5]

All of Fornes's subsequent work reiterates this longing for a moral life, a whole, healthy one, as her characters devise ingenious new ways to beat back the physical and spiritual filth encroaching upon them. The typical Fornes character is a beguiling mix of sobriety and romanticism; delicacy and a winning resilience; fluent charm and a temper that bristles efficiently and unforgettably. All these qualities serve the cause of survival: Fornes's characters are master strategists, agile adapters, canny about the possibilities before them, but unwilling to compromise about their determination to endure with their dignity intact. *Tango Palace* is so claustrophobic that it shows off this range of behavior particularly well. Backed into a corner, Leopold tries anything to keep Isidore at bay; by turns he's petulant and winsome. He lashes out at Isidore, then whimpers "Tell me that you love me." Leopold has been laid siege to; Isidore hunts him down; so Leopold keeps his character in flux, trying to elude Isidore by remaining unknown, fluttering about the cave like a canary minutes away from suffocation. Isidore, for his part, shuttles along the spectrum every sadist knows – smug about his power, telling Leopold that "you are just what I want you to be," until the brutality starts coming too easily to him. Then he abuses himself, giving Leopold a sword and saying "gore me," so that he can feel the perverse thrill of first suffering, then rising up from the ground and lording over Leopold once more, empowered by the aphrodisiac of humiliation.

Tango Palace is certainly grotesque, and handled by a director sensitive to the modalities of fear and pain, it can be deeply upsetting. But it is also strangely enjoyable: It's fun to watch Isidore literally make a spectacle of himself – posing in his shrine, for instance, or hamming up the martinet turns. And Leopold's predicament is only partly horrifying: He's also ridiculous – almost a burlesque of real suffering. For all its claustrophobia, *Tango Palace* is remarkably lighthearted: Fornes gives it a buoyant atmosphere, where everyone is effortlessly ingenious. No single abuse of Isidore's lasts long; no cry by Leopold is so piercing that we stop our ears. *Tango Palace* isn't a dark night of the soul, where the characters' faces are always ashen and their voices broken. Leopold and Isidore are full of color and spirited good humor. And that's what makes Fornes's vision of hell so bewitching: The despair is delirious.

Fornes returned to this mix in most of her plays from the sixties: Her characters' whimsy was their way of masking psychic sickness. (Only later, in the late seventies, did she choose to expose the pain fully and describe the damage done.) In the early work, the brio that Fornes brought to the theater was enabling her to examine desperate conditions without producing static, heavy drama. The upbeat tempo made her engagement of her characters' troubled lives especially intense; she could cover whole stretches of their experience without getting bogged down in any particular increment of pain (the "mud," as a later play would call it). Not incidentally, the airy persona also won Fornes her widest audience – and established her as one of the most exciting writers to emerge from Off-Off Broadway.

Promenade, in 1965, made the biggest "splash" – the adman's word is particularly appropriate, for *Promenade* was a full-blown hit, drawing audiences from far beyond the usual cozy confines of downtown New York. And it was a musical, the first of what would be Fornes's many experiments with the form. *Promenade* proved that musical comedy doesn't have to be vapid or merely spectacular. With extraordinarily modest means, Fornes rescued the musical for more considered purposes. Together with her composer, Al Carmines, she set about to find an American equivalent for a kind of song already well known in European and Latin American theater: charming and wistful on the surface, anxious underneath. "Sometimes it hurts more than others," sings one woman, "Sometimes it hurts less. / Sometimes it's just the same. / Sometimes it's really just the same."[6] Fornes's lyrics helped ensure that her theater would never become orthodox psychological realism, the self-indulgent variety, where all the contradictions of behavior – like those between euphoria and depression, the perfect state for song – are smoothed over. Because Fornes used the musical form to take distance from the characters, she was able to render their emotional turmoil more accurately.

Fornes has said that she started writing *Promenade* by first listing eight different places on one set of index cards, and eight different kinds of characters on another set, and then pairing them up at random. The first two cards she picked were "Aristocrats" and "Prison," and so *Promenade* began with Convicts 105 and 106 digging their way out of jail and hastening to a black-tie party at which they felt they surely belonged. Fornes quickly abandoned the mix-and-match process after *Promenade* got going in her imagination, but the manner of one ready for surprise infused the entire action.

Convicts 105 and 106 sweep through high society (where all the men have names of consonants – Mr. R, Mr. S, etc. – and all the women vowels), the political machine, the military, and the urban poor. They don't stay with anyone for long, for a jailer is fast on their heels, but they often find themselves crossing paths with a philosophical mother in search of her lost children. The encounter teaches all three an important lesson.

"When pain bites you don't look away. You pull it toward you," the Mother advises, quoting a story about a fisherman who finds wisdom. "And when it's right on top of you, and it starts flapping, and almost knocking you down, that's when you have it conquered, because it's out of the water."[7] Convicts 105 and 106 have a different strategy: They choose a self-protective giddiness:

When I was born I opened my eyes
And when I looked around I closed them;
And when I saw how people get kicked in the head,
And kicked in the belly, and kicked in the groin,
I closed them.
My eyes are closed but I'm carefree.
Ho ho ho, ho ho ho, I'm carefree.[8]

The two approaches to pain shouldn't reconcile; one should prevail. But Fornes is such an accommodating writer that she doesn't make the choice for us. We do the thinking, educating ourselves as we go along about the contradictory urges that characterize the typical experience of hardship. In the end, both the Mother's courage and the convicts' obliviousness seem appropriate, even shrewd. For Fornes, there is no party line, no such thing as "correct" behavior. One way of thinking doesn't cancel out another. She's attuned to the way circumstance affects choice: One may need to affect ignorance in one kind of dilemma; in another, defiance may prove more comfortable. The important thing is the freedom to think for oneself – to think at all in such a condition of privation. Despite the difference in their responses, the Mother and the convicts share a belief in the right of a human being to design his or her life independently, free of dogma and able to resist the seductions of acquiesence. And they join in awe of the power that comes to those who exercise that right. The convicts may close their eyes, but at least they elect to do so on their own.

Toward the end of *Promenade* the Mother articulates this idea plainly: "I have to live with my own truth."[9] There's nothing particularly ostentatious about her assertion – it's not accompanied by any chest pounding or fist raising. Fornes isn't that kind of political writer. Even the syntax conveys a strict humility – a simple announcement, spoken with the quiet strength of one for whom the idea has long been gestating. It only now comes to speech, and when it does the belief is so solidly grounded that no embellishment is needed: It is simply a fact, a fait accompli. Later in the same song, the Mother says she wants "to go where a human being / Is not a strange thing." Taken together, her two declarations make a compelling ethic. The Mother speaks for all those Fornes characters who can't fit comfortably into other people's systems – be they on the right or left, "with us" or "against us." Fornes is acutely sensitive to the differences among people: Her characters are never voice boxes for ideology, nor are they "types" – indistinguishable from every other spirited fighter. The nature of the awful condition may be familiar – depressingly the same from play to play – but the way those circumstances affect her characters always varies. Her women (for they usually are women) make themselves unique, independent, in the way they search for a way out, hunting for that place the Mother imagines in which individuality won't leave them open to assault.

Fornes takes such care making sure that each of her characters has a life all her own that her plays become virtuoso displays of a writer's compassion. "Madness is lack of compassion," Convict 106 sings. Fornes keeps sane simply by letting her characters tell her what to do. The idea sounds silly – Fornes probably knows readers will be skeptical when she explains it to them – but it does approximate the way Fornes elicits genuine *identity* from the collections of words and gestures that make up all characters. She's so good at it that critics often find themselves writing about her characters as though they were real people.

Fornes is a remarkably hospitable writer: She gives her characters space and sets them moving through it. "Being there" becomes a radical act in her theater. In a valuable essay establishing a critical vocabulary for Fornes, Bonnie Marranca suggests something similar when she writes of the "loveliness of presence" in Fornes's theater.[10] But "loveliness" may connote too much relaxation. Fornes's characters have often had to fight for their place on stage; they usually can claim for themselves only a tiny square of light, the corner of a room, and must guard it jealously. Presence can never be taken for granted; the loveliness is but the welcome dividend.

It is Fornes's awareness of the difficulty of simply being present that makes the theater a perfect form for her imagination. Theater encourages in spectators an awareness of place more forcibly than fiction or poetry: Characters aren't bustling about in one's mind or easily leaping from one context to the next. In a play, characters are inarguably *there,* rooted, expectant. Being so exposed and so observed, trapped by the stage and the light that fills it, they are instantly poignant. It took a writer as subtle as Fornes to see the theatrical value (and emotional power) of such a simple truth – forgotten in all the years since Gertrude Stein wrote a play telling us just where one of her four saints, Therese, stood and how she felt there.

Stein could easily have been the one also to give Fornes her love for the way people mingle with one another. *Promenade* is delightful partly for the skill with which Fornes directs its traffic: Like the thirties film comedies that inspired it, *Promenade* is all bustling crowds and fleeing felons; the moonstruck colliding with the woebegone; and witty repartee keeping pace, crackling by. Fornes seems to take great delight in bringing together characters from disparate worlds and watching the fireworks of their encounter. What better forum than a theater space? Only in performance is the craziness of the cohabitation among the plutocracy, the convicts, and the sad mother so evident – closed in on a (most likely) tiny stage, they can't help bumping into one another. Each one forces the others to notice him – literally to feel his impact.

The collisions are more than physical. Just as important to Fornes as the way groups form and scatter are the minute exchanges among individuals. All of her work scrutinizes the transmission of experience: Characters find listeners and pass on their stories. Usually, those stories are autobiographical, but the important aspect of the conversation isn't so much the personal history per se as the way that telling the story affects the speaker and listener. The crucial moment in any Fornes scene is often what comes after the long speech – the way a speaker may suddenly look astonished at her admissions or changed by having made them, or how a listener might avert his eyes or change the subject or suddenly blurt out his own startling confession. Fornes looks to see how relationships are made between her characters; then she isolates the moment of contact and exposes its strengths or vulnerabilities. In a recent talk, Fornes underscored this process at work in a passage from *Abingdon Square*, a 1987 play, in which a girl named Marion passionately declares her love for Frank, a man she sees when her husband isn't looking:

> MARION: How I wish I could spend my days with you and not have to lie. (*There is a pause*) Frank, wouldn't you like it if we spent all our time together, day and night? If we traveled together? If we walked on the street together, holding hands? If we spent the evening together sleeping in each other's arms? How would you like that? (*There is a silence*) Frank . . .
>
> FRANK: We have to be careful.[11]

Frank's hesitation marks the beginning of the end to their liaison.

Fornes is so beguiled with the way people work their way into each other's lives that she often includes scenes where that process is explicit – meetings, as in *Fefu;* a staged diary, as in *Evelyn Brown;* a marriage ceremony, in *A Vietnamese Wedding;* and meals, in many of her plays. *The Danube* is filled with all the small rituals that accompany getting to know one another – telling about one's family, origins, likes and dislikes. And *Dr. Kheal* is set in a classroom. It is in this last play, from 1968, that Fornes initiated her look into another perennial, inexhaustible theme: education, the by-product of all the conversations in her theater.

Dr. Kheal is a feverish, absent-minded, mercurial teacher – and the only character in the play, which makes sense, for he seems scarcely interested in engaging his students: Indoctrination is more his style. In the course of his brief lecture (the play is only seven pages long), he is often aggressively inane – "Balance can save your life . . . . Balance is keeping my pants up, my groin in place" – and always self-important: "I am the master . . . . How could my answer be wrong?" But buried in all the cant is a simple faith in logic and the rightness of his intellectual quest. He ends the play by saying "man is the rational animal," and while his bluster may ruin his credibility, you still can't quite dismiss the conclusion.

Kheal is a smart teacher because he understands the limits of the intellect. The realization doesn't mean he lets himself rest in the pursuit of knowledge. Rather, he teaches himself how to be a more delicate thinker – gingerly assessing the objects of inquiry, careful not to tear them apart with his penetrating mind. Dr. Kheal admonishes his students not to define Truth too narrowly: "The moment you name it, it is gone . . . . Surround it, and you'll have it. Never touch it. It will vanish." Likewise with beauty and love: Dr. Kheal says he doesn't know how to talk about them.[12] Fornes's teacher is not one for easy answers; he pursues a real knowledge, which must include an awareness of what's unknowable. That's the only kind of education Fornes hopes her characters come away with: an understanding that they'll never fully leave helplessness behind.

As though she herself felt the need for a fresh education, Fornes tried out a new vocation shortly after *Dr. Kheal.* With fellow-playwright Julie Bovasso, she founded the New York Theatre Strategy in 1971 as a cooperative run by and for new playwrights. The work proved so time consuming – Fornes was the theater's chief administrator as well as muse – that she did little playwriting until 1977. She had perhaps been ready for a hiatus: A revival of *Promenade* in 1969 was a dizzying event, with uptown producers and designers transforming the original into a much bigger affair. Fornes had only just recovered from her other mainstream endeavor, *The Office,* a play that Jerome Robbins directed on Broadway for a small number of preview performances in 1966 before the producers closed it down. Never again would Fornes venture into the commercial theater.

When she did find time to write, Fornes presented her work at her own theater. It was there that Fornes began subtly to expand her vision of what plays could be. Fornes's retreat from the mainstream has meant that even now, seven Obie awards later and after inclusion in the American Academy of Arts and Letters, she is generally ignored by most critics and audiences. But the coterie that follows her work knows that she is as important as Tennessee Williams, Sam Shepard, and David Mamet have been in expanding our idea of realism – taking it further and further away from its nineteenth-century origins, its staid, often laughably fastidious temperament.

A hard-to-shake fallacy about Fornes's evolution as a writer makes it difficult to relate her early plays to her late ones. Many critics term her work from the sixties "absurd," more romp than rumination. The recent work, beginning with the stunning achievement of *Fefu and Her Friends,* is described as more realistic, contemplative, or, most patronizingly, "mature." Surely there are distinct differences, and in some plays Fornes's tone has indeed mellowed into a minor key more suited to the longer look at anguish. But all of Fornes's works are of a piece, issuing from a whole imagination. They are the offerings of someone who keeps trying out fresh ways to summon onstage the elusive states of experience – those easy to name but hard to show, like real glee or rankling unhappiness, tenderness that isn't maudlin, anger that hasn't yet turned explosive. There's no lack of moral discourse in *Promenade* or *Tango Palace,* just as *Fefu* and *Sarita,* a musical from 1984, possess their share of loopiness. Often the plays that deserve to be seen alongside one another come from distant places in her career: *Tango Palace* has much in common with *The Conduct of Life,* an acclaimed 1985 work (both take on sadism); *Lovers and Keepers,* her 1986 musical celebration of coupling, echoes the tone of *Promenade;* 1983's *Mud* pairs nicely with an early play, *The Successful Life of 3,* from 1965 (Ross Wetzsteon, one of the first critics determined to see Fornes whole, calls them mirror images of each other); *The Danube,* from 1982, develops themes first raised in *Dr. Kheal* (they share a fascination with language and learning). No writer who as recently as 1986 wrote a play in which the main characters are potatoes (*Drowning*) can be said to have fully relinquished her love of the non sequitur.

It would be sadly ironic to split up Fornes into little parcels of identity, only tangentially related, for she often writes about characters who long to be integrated. It's their feeling of inner fragmentation that makes them want to educate themselves. These characters from the seventies and eighties are all those unseen students in Dr. Kheal's classroom. They seemed to have learned his lesson well: They don't so much want to acquire facts and figures (although those are welcome) as to learn how to think. Once they have mastered the skill of reflection they can relate the bundle of experiences and memories and sensations to one another, detect the pattern of their lives, make distinctions, analyze the choices before them. They won't just absorb life; they'll shape it – and so shape themselves.

"I prefer to have my actors reflect than emote," Fornes once said.[13] Her theater is an overwhelming emotional experience, but its depth of feeling comes from those moments when characters finally arrive at a long-awaited realization. There's a swell of understanding that's both exhilarating and heartbreaking. Yet Fornes is careful not to let thoughts ossify into theses: The act of reflecting is continually renewed. Fornes's writing, despite what Susan Sontag rightly calls its "elaborate sympathy with the labor of thought," is not a theater of ideas. It's more dynamic, nothing is yet certain or conclusive; characters make propositions, or consider those of others; they don't demonstrate them the way more programmatic art does. "It is the characters themselves who appear to be thinking," as Marranca puts it in her own discussion of Fornes's reflective theater, "not the author having thought."[14] This approach makes for devastating theater, precisely because the characters are so calm, so methodical. Chekhov wrote of how whole lives can fall apart during something as placid as the evening meal: People are drinking their wine and dully cutting their meat, but they crumble inside. It's not surprising, then, given her own feeling for the indirect, that Fornes adapted and staged *Uncle Vanya* in 1987. Both writers know how barely visible are the truly momentous passions.

The spectacle of a character sunk in thought isn't usually as doleful for Fornes as it often is for Chekhov. She finds those periods of reflection uncommonly joyous and always beautiful. There is little actually to see, but much to feel, as a woman (again, the one favored for thinking, and often the one deprived the chance) surveys all that she's been through, sifts the places seen and people met, and tentatively proposes to herself the next thing she'll do. Little else in the way of action is necessary: Fornes writes the scenes other artists pass over or forget – those places in a play others would call dead, empty or, most wrongheadedly, static. The crytallization of sensation into thought, and thought into speech, are shattering events in a Fornes play.

Such a description of what, for other writers, are merely the givens of drama – listening and speaking – may sound extravagant. But the experience of Fornes's characters merits the emphasis: Many of them live in strictly curtailed worlds, unable to venture freely, bound to housework or stifling marriages, cut off by poverty from the culture of inquiry they dream of joining. So when they do find a quiet minute for meditation, there's a huge feeling of elation. And when they're able to give a name to those thoughts that arise, they enjoy an even greater rush: The act of speaking is precious for these characters in a way it is for all accustomed to the oppresion of silencing parents, spouses, employers – or just the reproachful inner voice of one's own personality. Fornes's theater is mostly talk, though not of the bubbly, effortless sort one associates with writers like Bernard Shaw. For her, talk is careful, always mindful of and showing the struggle that preceded it, a hard-won reward for those not used to speech. This quality makes the conversations in her plays vibrate even when the subjects under discussion aren't particularly exciting: With every utterance, one senses that an entire character is being born, and a world of perception is coming into view. Fornes describes it thus:

> The action of the words coming out or forming in the brain is a delicate one. It is as if words are dampness in a porous substance – a dampness which becomes liquid and condenses. As if there is a condensation that is really the forming of words.[15]

Fornes shows how much work that process takes in *Fefu and Her Friends*. The seeds of all her later work can be found in this beautiful play, alive as it is with the thrill of discovery – as the playwright finds other cadences in her distinctive voice – and also the most dense of her plays, big and ambitious in a way Fornes hasn't been before or since, yet ever lucid.

Fefu brings together eight women, many of whom are old friends, for one afternoon in 1935. They have come to Fefu's house to organize a meeting of their educational society, rehearsing speeches and assigning responsibilities for the evening. That project helps focus another kind of education – *Fefu* shows women learning simply to be together and speak freely and directly to one another – no easy task, according to Fefu:

> I still like men better than women. – I envy them. I like being like a man. Thinking like a man. Feeling like a man. – They are well together. Women are not . . . . Look at them. They are checking the new grass mower . . . Out in the fresh air and sun, while we sit here in the dark . . . Men have natural strength. Women have to find their strength, and when they do find it, it comes forth with bitterness and it's erratic . . . Women are restless with each other. They are like live wires . . . either chattering to keep themselves from making contact, or else, if they don't chatter, they avert their eyes . . . like Orpheus . . . as if a god once said "and if they shall recognize each other, the world will be blown apart." They are always eager for the men to arrive. When they do, they can put themselves at rest, tranquilized and in a mild stupor.[16]

Fornes draws attention to the importance of clearing space for that interaction in her customary no-nonsense way: She arranges her stage so that, in the second of the play's three acts, the audience will move from place to place in the auditorium, observing four scenes in four different sites. Emma, the budding actress among them, and Fefu will play croquet on the "lawn." Cindy and Christina will read in the study. In the bedroom, Julia will describe with nightmarish clarity the accident that has left her wheelchair bound. And Paula, Sue, and Cecilia will commandeer the kitchen, there to run down their various romantic misadventures as they refill the icetrays and sip soup. The women are not just sharing stories; they're also making each room their own, designating it as the appropriate setting for their revelations. Fornes senses how even the most trivial comment demands the right environment: "It's a kitchen joke," Paula says when her jest falls flat on the retelling in the living room.

Only when the space is really theirs, Fornes suggests, can the women talk easily to one another. Some critics have suggested that the dialogue in *Fefu* is distinctly "female," by which they mean, in part, nonlinear and "organic." Fornes disavows most gender politics as it applies to her work, and won't let herself be called a feminist ("If I were limited to writing plays to make points about women, I would feel that I was working under some sort of tyranny of the well-meaning," she once wrote), but she does acknowledge the significance of putting women, and women's speech, at the center of her theater.[17] One would be hard pressed to say just what *Fefu* is "about," for Fornes seems to let her characters talk about whatever is at hand, serious or ostensibly trivial. "Who's ready for lunch?" asks Fefu at one point, and there follows a fugue of responses – "I am," "I'd rather wait," "I'll have coffee" – which somehow leads to another snatch of small talk about clothes.[18] Readers who speed past these passages looking for the core, or the plot, of the play will be disappointed. For it's just in these seemingly trivial exchanges that one can best see how the women have chosen to present themselves and the nature of their feelings for one another – who's comfortable and who's not, who's tuned in and who's distracted, who's using the small talk to couch larger issues and who couldn't care less. The rhythm of the dialogue and the music that the women's voices make are often more significant than its substance: Just the fact that they are able easily to talk back and forth says something about how much they have learned about being together. The horseplay that periodically breaks out is significant for the same reasons. Someone starts a water fight in Act III, and in a matter of minutes it has taken over the whole play – Fornes *lets* it take over the play, establishing physical connections to match the emotional and intellectual ones.

The fight also allows the women to make fools of themselves, without the fear of reprisals or mockery. *Fefu* doesn't just give its women characters space to speak calmly and listen sympathetically; it also allows for outrageousness. "I'm strange, Christina," Fefu says,

> But I am fortunate in that I don't mind being strange. It's hard on others, sometimes. But not that hard. Is it, Cindy? Those who love me love me precisely because I am the way I am.[19]

Fefu's friends never stop loving her, but they also constantly fear for her and are frightened by her. In the privacy of the study Christina tells Cindy that Fefu's way of thinking and behaving "endangers" less "adventurous" people like herself. Does the adventurer have "less regard or respect for things as they are?" Christina wonders. Fefu probably wouldn't think so, for all her energy is directed to exposing life as it is, in all its beauty and ugliness. At the start of Fornes's play, Fefu announces how excited she gets from feeling revulsion. Revolting things are for her "to grapple with" – ignored at one's peril. "That which is . . . underneath is slimy and filled with fungus and crawling with worms. It's another life parallel to the one we manifest . . . . If you don't recognize it . . . (*whispering*) it eats you."[20]

As one might expect, bodily realities are the most vivid, and also the most frequently disregarded or distorted. "Each person I see in the street," Emma says, "I keep thinking of their genitals; what they look like, what position they're in. I think it's odd that everyone has them . . . . [But] people act as if they don't have genitals."[21] The body is outrageous simply by virtue of its existence: It shouldn't be seen, runs the conventional wisdom; it's a necessary evil, and only the perverse draw attention to what is evil. The flesh must be disguised and disinfected, if possible rendered invisible, in accordance with aesthetics. It takes Fefu's affection for a diseased cat, mentioned late in the play, or, more forcefully, Julia's unwavering gaze at those physical facts that "shouldn't" be seen, to demolish such sham ideas of decorum.

Julia's long speech in the second act is the emotional center of *Fefu,* if it is even possible to determine a core of a deliberately multifocused play. Fornes calls for her to be "still and luminous" – and the message she delivers to the empty room is just as quietly compelling. She insists, as Fefu might, or Emma, that "the stinking parts of the body are the important ones: the genitals, the anus, the mouth, the armpit." A woman's "entrails," Julia laments, will always rankle those under the sway of orthodox ideas of gracefulness: "Isadora Duncan had entrails. That's why she should not have danced," Julia says, mimicking the logic of such thinkers. "But she danced and for this reason became crazy. She wasn't crazy."[22]

Julia seems to be paralyzed but, as we learn later, doctors never found any real damage done by the hunter's bullet that accidentally hit her. Her peculiar debility teaches its own lesson about the body: It can't be separated from the spirit and, in fact, acquiesces to the mind's demands. Fornes isn't enclosing in *Fefu* a vague, feel-good tract about organic living or homeopathic biology; she's far too specific a writer for that. But she does see clearly the way her characters split themselves apart, trying to keep what they feel separate from what they think. Julia makes the simple point that women's sexuality is not just physical (as it is, she says, for so many men), but also profoundly spiritual. Yet most of her fellow women, she seems to suggest, don't acknowledge the link, so they continually feel themselves lost in places their bodies have taken them, or unsure how to compose themselves in the places where their minds must take the lead. Faced with these warring impulses, they can't feel whole – or even really present.

The woman in *Fefu and Her Friends* who is most in danger is Fefu herself. It's surprising to hear a character mention Fefu's unhappiness or to see even the flashing glimpses of that pain, for Fefu seems sunny, possessed by unassailable good humor. What could Julia mean, one wonders, when she asks her imagined interrogator, "why do you have to kill Fefu, for she's only a joker?" and then warns Fefu that "they want your light." Fefu's cheeriness, it seems, is subversive, and so such bad behavior will leave her always vulnerable. The playfulness of *Fefu and Her Friends,* orchestrated in large part by Fefu herself, disrupts theatrical decorum, but it also exposes just how shattered many of the women's lives are and how anxious they are about repairing them.

Fefu's life is one busy search for the right mix of thoughtfulness and euphoria – too much of either would tear her apart. Fefu can be manic – shooting blanks at Phillip (her husband, who's perpetually outdoors); playing croquet; zooming through the room carrying pitchers and glasses, a lunch tray, coffee all around. But she can also stop short, and arrest us with a sudden acknowledgment of what she's running from. "I am in constant pain . . . . It is as if normally there is a lubricant . . . not in the body . . . a spiritual lubricant . . . and without it, life is a nightmare, and everything is distorted."[23]

Except for Julia, the women in *Fefu* come upon their pain unexpectedly, as though they have been trying to crowd it out of their lives with constant activity and much company, but find they can no longer keep up the dodge. In the midst of friendly preparations for coffee, Paula suddenly confronts Cecilia with the fallout of their recently ended affair; and, a little later, Fefu blurts out how much she needs Phillip. Throughout the play, the women unobtrusively acknowledge just how severely they depend on each other as confidantes, guardians, friends of uncommon watchfulness and understanding. These moments aren't climaxes to scenes nor the center of them: The "serious" exchanges have to fight for attention just as earnestly as the frothy ones. In *Fefu*, scenes of joyousness and those of deliberation comment on each other; the former keep the latter from getting too pious.

The exclamations in the middle of scenes are also moments where characters break free of prescribed modes of behavior and thought: They speak out when they "should" keep the patter of conversation flowing effortlessly. These models are just as much self-imposed as inherited. The meeting itself is a form that begins to feel stifling as the day wears on. When one woman breaks away from the responsible talk (organizing schedules, making agendas) or even when she pulls out of the "irresponsible" small talk and forces the others to listen to more momentous admissions, Fornes shows just how complicated is the process of achieving identity and "taking stage." Not only do the women have to distance themselves from society's definitions of propriety and bad behavior – the definitions that term Isadora Duncan crazy or a woman who simply speaks at all as impudent. They also have to find an identity separate from the standards of propriety their fellow women want to enforce: Those who resist desultory, pleasant conversation display a different kind of courage and discover patterns of thought all their own. (This is another way in which Fornes takes distance from feminism: She has said the movement suggests too much homogeneity for her taste, policies of behavior that threaten to obscure individuality.)

Fornes has a faceted way of seeing the world, and after a while her spectators learn to share it. Because the second part of *Fefu and Her Friends* is composed of four sites, there are four different styles of perception. The sequence in which you see the action depends on what quarter of the audience you are in. There is no "right" way to see the scenes; their order in print is no more than a compromise with the limited possibilities of texts. Meaning is in flux during performance, always asking to be assembled. Some spectators come to Julia's chilling speech after Fefu's admission of her own barrenness, and so might make conclusions about the characters' resilience that wouldn't occur to those whose passage between the two scenes is reversed, or those for whom the sequence is interrupted by two other scenes. Yet those other spectators will, perhaps, hear Fefu's words after first absorbing Christina's warning about Fefu's dangerous liveliness and will thus bring a more critical sensibility to Fefu's scene.

Because the variations are numerous, the field of interpretation is expansive and thrilling: The spectators become active participants, not just recipients for a playwright's bromides. Fornes doesn't have to work out strict causality, or submit to corseting ideas of "motivation." If she did, she might find herself writing the kind of thesis play she despises. In Fornes's theater of thinking, the spectators also must work to break out of old patterns of behavior – intellectual patterns, to be sure, but also physical ones, for they are on their feet in Act II, walking from scene to scene.

Each scene is but a glimpse of a relationship, an illuminated aspect of a life, and so suggests a larger, denser world. "I don't like scenes to build up or peter out," Fornes has said.[24] The scenes she chooses to show us always point to what can't be dramatized, and so always lead us to wonder about what's missing. Each scene leads the play in a different direction or suggests how various are the routes it could take. After a while we learn to focus our minds on only the events before us. What do the arrangements of people and intensities of expression in each discrete scene have to tell us? We learn to register these detached moments without an expectation that the ending will reveal a recognizable pattern. With a few exceptions, most of Fornes's plays are thoroughly democratic systems: Each scene carries its own weight. They accrue, and by the end our perception of things has changed, but it's impossible to say just where the change occurred, what scene was the hinge.

The action in *Fefu* spreads out before us rather than hurries along in a straight line. Her plays aren't easily charted; they are never the sum of their parts. The characters themselves work their way step by step through their lives, always asking questions about them, guessing at their layout. Moments of dramatic life remain distinct, even as they proliferate, and each contributes essentially to the play's emotional persuasiveness.

Fornes's graceful evolution into a writer of great poignancy didn't happen without trepidation. The mix of the serious and the trivial in *Fefu* shows how cautious she was, as though she were not yet ready to relinquish the jaunty spirit of *Promenade*. She once spoke of how worried she had been that her work was getting sentimental. It wasn't until she showed a friend a manuscript and heard the appreciation that she understood the significance of the unfamiliar creative drive overtaking her: "Why should anyone be embarrassed about exposing their feelings?" she asked herself.[25] She didn't so much change her style or redirect her attention to more "profound" matters as simply see more of the characters already before her. She made herself look at them longer and from all sides. *Fefu,* she once remarked, was the first play in which she created last names for her characters.

The delight in style – often and unapologetically for style's sake – that characterized Fornes's early work still served her well when it came to writing *Fefu*. She says she started each day of work on the play by first going through a file of notes about her own moments of unhappiness and disappointment – her folder of "sufferings," she called it. This would put her in the right pensive mood to conjure the anguish of her invented selves. But she also knew that unalloyed suffering on stage wouldn't do – it had to be given form – and so she would also spend those hours of preparation listening over and over to a favorite record by the Cuban singer Olga Guillot. The songs touched many of the same subjects she had written about in her folder, but they also possessed a hard-won clarity and sober elegance. The music taught Fornes how lyricism can discipline emotion, keep it from being sloppy or self-indulgent, while also intensifying its effect on audiences. Beauty is not a dirty word for Fornes; it never signifies superficiality. Quite the opposite: "To respond to the beauty that's around you," Fornes has said, "there's no deception in that."[26] In fact, her quick responsiveness to what's sensuous about a character or a condition keeps even her most searing work from being didactic.

Almost all the plays that followed Fornes's return to writing in 1977 contain moments where characters come to a new awareness of their language. But none is as detailed about the journey as *The Danube,* from 1982, the next major Fornes play after *Fefu*. For the reader who comes to it directly after *Fefu,* it's as though Fornes has contracted her imaginative scope and intensified the light on a small, essential fragment of the panoramic experience seen in the earlier work. As befits the scientific tone and atmosphere of *The Danube,* she breaks down a community into atoms.

Fornes says she got the idea for the play while out walking one day in New York City. She came across a thrift shop, and in one of the record bins found an old set of Hungarian–English language lessons. She bought it, and listening to the records later felt an overwhelming awe of the fragility of this lost age and sadness at the thought that her own world could disappear as easily. *The Danube,* set in Budapest just before the Second World War, was the result of her anxieties, and the forum in which to face them.

In *The Danube* Fornes replicates the form of those vintage language lessons. Her diction, customarily uncluttered, here approaches the pristine. In most scenes, Fornes employs only the most elementary sentences; characters declare themselves baldly; there is little in the way of nuance or ambiguity to their exchanges. And yet no scene is without grace. Speaking their platitudes about the weather, the city, or their families, Fornes's characters seem also to apologize for the clumsiness of their speech. They sound hapless, but determined to preserve their dignity with the scant verbal means available to them.

The linguistic austerity of *The Danube* actually gives the play its nervous, passionate energy. The dialogue inches along, building itself up gradually, as if the characters held in them so much feeling striving for expression that they could explode at any moment. That proximity to danger is real, for *The Danube* contains, inside the pretty simplicity of its language tapes, an awful vision of the end of the world.

There is little plot in *The Danube*. It starts in a café in 1938, where Paul, a young American, meets Eve, a Hungarian, and her father, Mr. Sandor. Paul and Eve quickly fall in love and marry; but shortly after their wedding Paul becomes ill, fainting, suffering convulsions. He blames Eve for "polluting" him, and plans to leave her. By now she, too, is ill, as is everyone else in the play. Their bodies are covered in spots. Their clothes are layered with soot and their speech is garbled; they wear goggles as the unnamed disaster nears. The play doesn't end so much as stop in its tracks: Just as Paul and Eve decide to leave Budapest together, *The Danube* is arrested by a sharp blinding burst of light.

Most critics interpret *The Danube* as a play about nuclear war, although the bomb is never actually mentioned. Whatever the origin of the characters' sickness or the meaning of the final blast of light, its effect is certain: The cataclysm shatters the delicate balance among the characters, tearing asunder freshly made attachments, scattering the pieces everywhere. Fornes shows how vulnerable those connections are at the very start. With the formal inventiveness that by now one has come to expect from Fornes, she integrates the language-lesson tapes into the performance, so that many exchanges are interrupted by the dull, relentlessly pleasant voices of a couple demonstrating, first in English, then in Hungarian, the way one establishes contact.

"Good afternoon, Mr. Sandor," Paul says at the start, but not until the same sentence has been heard in both languages on tape. "Here comes the waiter," he says in a later scene, just as patiently – his words a translation of a translation. The convention becomes chilling in a love scene between Paul and Eve: "Marry me, sweet Eve . . ." "Oh, Paul, you love me. You do." There's no spontaneity to these scenes – worry over precision replaces passion. And yet, in the very worry and care, we can read more genuine engagement than there might be were the declarations of love to come blithely. Paul and Eve demonstrate their love, work it through, rather than plunge into it impetuously. They have to take time, waiting for the tape to run before answering each other, and so enjoy moments of contemplation, gain space to evaluate what they've heard and consider what they'll say next. They are given time to attend to the details of love. (It's possible, also, to see these scenes as Fornes's exploration of techniques that Gertrude Stein introduced in plays such as *They Must. Be Married. To Their Wife.*, where the punctuation – the full stops that enforce breaths in the middle of sentences – made one more acutely aware of how the couples actually fit themselves together.)

Fornes's characters bring so much thoughtfulness to every one of their sentences that even at their most candid they are never unseemly. Eve flatly says, "You will be happy since I love you so," and, remarkably, her frankness sounds normal, unforced. Fornes knows the strategic value of tactlessness. When her characters speak out simply, they are at the same time expressing how few alternatives are left to them: Eloquence, of the elaborate sort, isn't accessible, not in their condition, where just the time to talk at all is precious. Their statements accompany a latent text that tells of how dangerously close they have come to being rendered silent by their experience, of how long and hard they have thought of what they need to say, and of how much they want you to listen attentively.

The Danube is the first of a strong series of Fornes plays from the eighties – work in which she seems to hit her stride, to explore most fully the ramifications of her vision of the world. *Mud* (1983), *The Conduct of Life* (1985), and the most disarming in the series, *Abingdon Square* (1988), are harsher than any other Fornes plays. "I'm a Romantic," Fornes breezily announced in one interview. But, she said a year later in another talk, "I don't romanticize pain."[27] Neither does she lecture about it, although she surely is a teacher.

"You have to know how to enter another's life." Marion's admonishing words to her stepson Michael, who catches her writing in her diary and asks prying questions, don't only articulate the challenges facing the characters in *Abingdon Square*. They also sum up the ethic of respectfulness that informs all of Fornes's theater: Her scenes present us with examples of discretion. But in these recent plays it becomes harder for her characters to respect boundaries or to have faith in the discretion of others.

The pressure to be civilized grows intense; and the possibility of finding the right, comfortable way of being with others has only looked so remote in Fornes's work once before, in *Tango Palace*. There seems to be a code for social interaction which all but Fornes's central characters are privy to; only those lost women have to renegotiate their lives every day. Over and over in these plays you hear the women lament their incompleteness: Sarita, in the 1984 musical bearing her name, calls herself a savage; in *Mud,* the profoundly intelligent Mae wants only to free herself of the humiliating association with her half-wit husband, Lloyd; Nena, the 12-year-old girl in *The Conduct of Life,* is the victim of Orlando's abuse, raped repeatedly and kept in a dark cellar, but still she refuses to vent her own aggression, vowing to live in dignity: "If someone should treat me unkindly," Nena says near the play's end, "I should not blind myself with rage, but I should see them and receive them, since maybe they are in worse pain than me."[28] If we place her at the center of *The Conduct of Life,* instead of Orlando, the play's title sounds proud, no longer a resigned admission of incurable corruption.

Mud and *The Conduct of Life* are plays in which Fornes also most fully explores questions of evil. Evil has concerned Fornes in earlier work, but she never had this explicitly exposed and named it (*Tango Palace* notwithstanding). Here her morality is toughening, her ethics coalescing. The women in earlier plays came to recognize the possibilities in their minds and bodies; now they discover their souls.

On the surface, Mae in *Mud* is another of Fornes's perpetually dissatisfied students. Like her fellow students in earlier plays, she isn't content with mere information; she wants the tools of analysis as well. She also wants to learn something unteachable, something the women who preceded her never even found time to yearn for: a sense of decency. When a friend, Henry, offers to educate her, she doesn't just see it as a way to break free of Lloyd and acquire her own presence of mind. She sees him as offering an entire alternative world – one where she isn't besieged by base instincts, where knowledge serves action, where she doesn't live like a dog (what she calls herself when she's with Lloyd), where values and standards exist and have meaning, and ideas of spirituality aren't just empty chatter. Only there can she talk about her "soul" and not be laughed at by someone more fascinated by her shape.

On the one hand, such a desire is simply put: "I'm going to look for a better place to be," she says matter-of-factly to Lloyd when things look desperate.[29] And yet, because such a search involves more than one's body, satisfaction is always elusive. In the end, she's more capable than even the man who educated her (Henry has a stroke halfway through the play), but Lloyd and Henry both refuse to grant her her wish for freedom. Lloyd shoots her, and as she dies she speaks in language as transparent as Fornes at her best, but somehow more disturbing:

> Like the starfish, I live in the dark and my eyes see only a faint light. It is faint and yet it consumes me. I long for it. I thirst for it. I would die for it. Lloyd, I am dying.[30]

The passage is subtly composed: As in the rest of the play, in which she fends off her tumescent husband's advances in order to complete her self-education, Mae remains entranced by spiritual goals in these lines, refusing to acknowledge the body's demands until she says her very last word – "dying." (The vision of death in the penultimate sentence is held at bay by the conditional tense.) Until her final breath, Mae always finds time for a liberating metaphor.

The darkness and light that Mae speaks of are also the hallmarks of Fornes's structure in this play. Fornes's love of the short, self-contained scene here has added thematic value. For in this highly spirit-minded work, these tiny scenes function like epiphanies or stations of the cross – Mae's agonizing Passion. The scenes are like gasps, moments when light falls suddenly and without warning on the waiting penitent, illuminating her distress for a moment before being snuffed out. Characters freeze at the ends of scenes; the lights go down; then, after a moment, the actors move to set up the next scene.

As with *The Danube,* the steps of a character's descent are painstakingly worked out – modulated finely so that nothing is left unexamined or misunderstood. But in *Mud*, what happens in the darkness, unstaged and unspoken, is just as important as what's seen and acted out. Since Mae longs to escape a muddy world, we can only look in the interstices, the gloom surrounding the bright room, for places where she unfolds her consciousness and works toward decisions about her future. Those dark blank spaces are crucial, never empty. They are pauses filled with the momentous preparation for revelation. Fornes's technique here is like what Joseph Conrad wrote about *Heart of Darkness:* "The meaning of the episode was not inside like a kernel, but outside, enveloping the tale which brought it out only as a glow brings out a haze, in the likeness of one of these misty halos that sometimes are made visible by the spectral illumination of moonshine."

Abingdon Square doesn't have any of the physical brutality that makes *Mud* and especially *The Conduct of Life* disturbing; the tone is muted and the characters are privileged: Fornes sets the play in the perfumed townhouses of turn-of-the-century Greenwich Village. But Marion deserves to be considered alongside Mae and Nena, Sarita and Evelyn Brown, even Rachel, the ebullient adventurer in *A Visit.* She may be the most articulate of them, but she's no less overwhelmed by the combined pressure of society's expectations and her own demands for a fulfilling life. At 15 she married Juster, a man thirty-five years her senior. Fornes chronicles the next nine years of her life, dramatizing only those moments where she winces in her position as wife and leans almost imperceptibly toward an alternative she can't even name; and those other times when she lacerates herself for her insufficiencies and sees with sudden clarity the necessity of her fate.

"Fate" might seem too lofty a term in the world of Fornes's other plays, where her women's suffering is all too secular, its origins all too clear – Lloyd and Henry's indifference in *Mud,* or the wracking self-doubt that makes Orlando ferocious in *The Conduct of Life*. But the crisis in *Abingdon Square* is harder to isolate. Marion, its heroine, is overtaken from all sides, and no single explanation for her anguish seems adequate. Marion herself yearns to understand what is happening to her, but ordinary methods of inquiry aren't working. "Fate" does seem responsible, and to counter it, or at least face it, she prays.

In one particularly arresting scene, Marion has hidden in the attic, her arms stretched out, standing on her toes, her forehead perspiring as she recites cantos from Dante's *Purgatorio*. Then she collapses. Marion strives for a vision, and for light, abnegating herself in order to change. Her life consists of numerous forms of penance: One of the more absorbing is writing letters over and over again to her dead mother. After writing one, she'll memorize it, and collapse again. She gets up feeling stronger in spirit, at least, if not in body.

"I have a bad destiny," she realizes in one scene, and if she can't change it, she wants at least to be so nimble that it will never take her by surprise. Even though the soul presumably matters to her more than the body, she lets herself start having an affair, and eventually leaves her marriage. Everything she does betrays her frustration with what she calls her "vagueness": "I feel I have no character," she says. If she acts with vividness and confidence, regardless of the outcome, she will at least have substance.

In much of Fornes's work, the women are deliberately reckless, while the men are fretful about maintaining order. Marion and Juster are no exceptions. Marion may long to be civilized, but she knows better than to think Juster's pedantry is any example for her. Marion may want to devise her own form of morality, but she avoids ideas of "moral balance." That's one of Juster's specialties: He's proud of his perfect digestion, his clockwork schedule, his socks that fit him so well and have never known a hole. There's a wildness to *Abingdon Square* easily missed in the charm of its old-world setting. Fornes's genius here is in showing that having "morality" doesn't necessarily mean that one acts consistently or even rationally. Her characters question the very definition of rationality in order to reach more accommodating moralities. And so one's quest for spiritual replenishment can't possibly be a quiet, delicate process, conducted by candlelight. It's hearty, dangerous, full of risks that test one's mettle. Only then, Fornes suggests, will rebirth feel genuine and lasting.

And yet, if Fornes had left *Abingdon Square* at this – with Marion struggling to break free and partly succeeding – the play would not be as distinctive as it is. Fornes also shows how the fear of loneliness can affect one's behavior as decisively as can one's yen for independence. Toward the end of *Abingdon Square*, Juster has a stroke, but the event brings no release for Marion. Her last line is "he mustn't die!" Fornes declines to resolve this moment of crisis – she holds the scene aloft, as she did more theatrically in *The Danube* – ending the play with the dramatic equivalent of an ellipsis. It's part of Fornes's characteristic honesty, which unfailingly tells her just where to end a play, that she leaves this one so open. Anything more than that would turn it into a sentimental fantasy – or, worse, a how-to manual: How to get out of a repressive marriage, and so on. In this and other Fornes works, an ending can easily be seen as an upsetting beginning. In Marion's last line there's a disturbing question – not whether or not real freedom is possible, but whether the solitude it requires can be endured.

"What is it that makes someone a link between you and your own life?" a character named Pea asks in *Drowning* (1986), a short, nearly forgotten play that Fornes adapted from Chekhov's story. Fornes tries to find an answer to this question in every one of her plays. If Pea's behavior is any clue, one can gain an awareness of one's own life, and its significance, by simply perceiving another person fully, as if for the first time.

> She is a mystery to me. I look at her as one looks at an animal, loving those eyes, the look in them, the breath as it goes into her shirt, her lips as they close and then part, her mind, the way her body moves. I love her. She is close to my heart the way only an animal can be. And as unfathomable. Looking into her eyes is so quiet – like sleep, like a bed. And she, she is wild like a tiger. She smells like a lion, and she claws like a lion, and yet, in her eyes, she is quiet like a fish.[31]

The eloquence of this description doesn't restore to Pea the woman he misses, nor does it make the memory of her any less baffling. But by speaking about her so well he knows that the beauty he saw was real. That's no small accomplishment for characters constantly beset by uncertainty. All that Fornes's characters can really do is describe their feelings of awe and frustration in the face of inchoate experiences. But this they do with such passion that they reach some tentative kind of mastery: Characters are careful to note specifics, how what confuses them is different from everything else; what the exact dimensions of the conundrum are. Fornes's characters never throw up their hands and let the mystery envelop them.

The smallest human unit is two people, not one, Brecht reminds us, and Fornes's theater shows why: Only in the abrasions against another can a person find out who he is, what he looks like, and what he feels. Fornes herself says she can write only for the theater, because she cannot work in isolation: She needs the pleasurable interference of her actors and designers – and, presumably, her spectators.

The idea of one's life as a brave new world, undiscovered territory until one finds the right guide – this sentiment lies behind all those scenes where Fornes stages the gestures of wonder. And it's also heartbreaking. Pea's words have the numbness of one who has known the pleasures of that companionship but doesn't count on finding it again. It's not so much to relieve loneliness or escape their demons that Fornes's characters keep trying to perfect their sociability. Those had been some of the motivations in Tennessee Williams. Fornes's characters want to be with others because then they can see things differently, and any change in perception is a pleasure: It expands one's sense of possibility.

Many of Fornes's characters spend their entire plays searching for the right combination of people, the right human landscape and emotional weather, in which best to receive the multiple sensations of the world. The act of looking is often shocking and explosive in Fornes; and, since the characters' field of view is usually curtailed by other people, it demands rare courage really to look at one's surroundings. Fornes's characters are forever looking over their shoulders or past the heads of those in front of them, stealing furtive glances at what they're not meant to see, too much the aesthetes to let anything beautiful, or compellingly ugly, pass unnoticed. Once they succeed in seeing what they want, they are transformed – enriched by things seen. And so, in some real sense, the simple act of looking is redemptive.

Fornes once tried to describe how thrilling such looking can be and how the thrill, in large part, comes as much from the company of another watchful person as from the thing perceived:

> We were in a bar, we were drinking beer, and I said, "Have you ever been with a person when just being with them makes you see everything in a different light. A glass of beer has an amber, a yellow that you've never seen before and seems to shine in a manner that is – " and she said, "Yes!", and I said, "That is romantic! That is romance!" and she said, "Well, in that case . . . ." I said, "It *is* more beautiful. It isn't that you want it to be more beautiful or that you are lying to yourself. It *is*."[32]

Such words capture the special joy of being with Maria Irene Fornes and her work. She is the theater's sweetest alchemist, intimately familiar with the mud of our world, but also promenading in the direction of the stars, beckoning us toward things she wishes we would look up and see.

5

ADRIENNE KENNEDY

THE STAGE IS VAST and filled with shadows. Windows at the top of the set's soaring wall let in the dull light of street lamps; snow falls steadily in a darkness that suggests an immense outdoors. Those who enter the stage look lost, unwelcome, still cold long after they have arrived. Only the middle-aged woman sitting in the center of the room seems to have settled, made a place for herself in the forbidding murk. Suzanne Alexander, the central character of Adrienne Kennedy's *The Ohio State Murders,* gathers around her what little light there is. She has burrowed behind the books of this university library, trying to turn the shelves into barricades against an unspoken threat from outdoors. Suzanne treats her space on the stage as though it could serve as a nest, a hiding place. As we watch her, the smothering darkness becomes a cushioning chiaroscuro, and an overwhelming space gradually becomes small – inhabited.

Suzanne's tentative efforts to be at ease, stymied at frequent intervals, are the most highly charged actions in *The Ohio State Murders,* deliberately made more vivid than the "dramatic" events suggested by the play's title. The shift in emphasis – away from external circumstances, onto a character's private, difficult maneuverings toward domesticity – is typical of what gives the theater of Adrienne Kennedy its particular febrile energy. The characters in many of her plays have the pantherlike watchfulness of prisoners pacing around cells; when they come to a standstill, they acquire a weightier weight, a clarity consisting of sharply defined lines, newly audible tones of their speech and even of their breathing, a brightness that is the product of their long negotiation with the space around them.

In all her plays, Kennedy takes great care in negotiating the relationship between characters and their environments – so much care, in fact, that one often remembers her plays best by the rooms they inhabit: the classroom in *A Lesson in Dead Language,* the sick bay in *A Movie Star Has to Star in Black and White,* Sarah's bedroom in *Funnyhouse of a Negro,* the Tower of London in *The Owl Answers.* (It is possible, also, to think about the plays by the colors in those rooms: the browns of the rats in *A Rat's Mass* and the owls spoken of in *The Owl Answers,* the black-and-white of the old movies flickering through Clara's memory in *Movie Star.* Kennedy's palette always consists of faded colors, shades of gray, evocative sepias.) Her theater is obsessed with rooms, with the capacity of rooms to solidify characters and establish their places in life – or else, in many instances, to suffocate them and cut them off irretrievably from life. "After years of searching . . . for their environment," Kennedy writes in her autobiography, *People Who Led to My Plays,* "my characters live in powerful, influential rooms, almost to the exclusion of the outside world."[1]

For Kennedy herself, the rooms in which she has lived and worked, been forced to flee or sought refuge in, retain a strange radiance in her memory. In the preface to her first collection of plays, she writes fondly of "the shuttered guest house surrounded by gardens of sweet smelling frangipani shrubs" where she wrote *Funnyhouse.* And there's "our wonderful brand new apartment in New York in the Park West Village for *A Rat's Mass* and the enchanting Primrose Hill in London for *Sun* (sitting in the dining room overlooking Chalcot Crescent)."[2] These are memories so evidently treasured, it is as if the rooms themselves, in the shine of their floors, the caprice of their fixtures, the way the windows refract light, and the scents in the air, created the plays as much as she did – or that only the rooms possess the secret of the plays' meanings.

The plush, almost erotic mysteries of rooms and houses have been well described by Gaston Bachelard, and the philosopher's *Poetics of Space* could be read as a compendium of Kennedy's preoccupations and a guide into her plays.[3] The interiority of Kennedy's theater seems to confirm Bachelard's insistence that writers "know the house" before attempting to "know the universe" – for, as he writes, the house is our "first cosmos," and without attending to the effects on us of its architecture, all our speculations about the outside world of experience and ideas will be mere abstractions, lacking any origin.

Yet Bachelard offers more to Kennedy's readers than mere writing lessons. He also directs us to see how rooms are linked to memories – and, by implication, how Kennedy's theater of rooms consists of memory plays and dream plays. Most of Kennedy's writing begins with her own recollections, often kept explicit in the plays that result. "Autobiographical work is the only thing that interests me," she has said. Each play is an "outlet" for "questions stemming from childhood."[4] Her characters, in turn, spend most of their time also remembering, turning over and over the troubling, unknowable events of their pasts. The process of remembering eventually becomes so all-consuming that it seems hallucinatory. Memories of the past can't be separated from hallucinations about the present, nor from dreams of the future. The setting – a house or room or bed or desk – becomes a stabilizing force, keeping these various visions contained and accessible. Bachelard envisions the house as a site for the "integration" of "the thoughts, memories, and dreams" of the individuals housed there, and, considering each room a "psychological diagram," calls for a "psychology of the house."

Memories, Bachelard understands, have their strongest life when attached to places, or the things and sensations associated with those places. The Proustian echoes are deliberate. A recollection of breeze passing through a bedroom, for instance, may call up a particular bygone sexual anxiety. The image of a drawer opened with its usual difficulty may spark understanding of some aspect of family strife. The memory of kitschy wallpaper may sum up more directly than could a protracted case study the stifling isolation that a child once felt. Rooms contain what Bachelard calls "compressed time" ("that is what space is for"); they are, in fact, the only memento of time, offering the only way fully to reenter the past. "Memories of the outside world will never have the same tonality of those of the home," Bachelard writes. "For a knowledge of our intimacy, localization in the spaces of intimacy is more urgent than determination of dates."[5]

The notion of "tonality" is especially important. *The Poetics of Space* reminds us that memories are phenomena with shapes, textures, and temperatures. For a theater artist, beholden to the visible and the aural, they could hardly be otherwise. By creating in one's theater a space that is emotional as much as merely scenic – personal, not merely for show – perhaps the writer's more elusive memories will emerge into three dimensions. Memories are also physical. Bachelard celebrates the "passionate liaison of our bodies, which do not forget, with an unforgettable house" – and Kennedy demonstrates this truth through characters who remember with sensual as much as meditative force, and whose every thought returns them to past moments of bodily trauma or, more rarely, bodily exaltation. They scrutinize their bodies and the places their bodies have lain for the keys to self-knowledge that their minds and spirits have lost.

Rooms often retain their power in our imaginations because they call up the all-too-rare experience of safety: the remembered comforts of a nursery, say, or the one-room apartment that is one's sole familiar haven in a confusing city. Bachelard extends these associations to matters of the imagination. Rooms protect the imagination as it conducts its nervous explorations, and "allow the dreamer to dream in peace." They enable us to "concentrate" ourselves, to coalesce into an identity made up of a completed past and a carefully monitored present. We can mold our thoughts to the shape of a particular room, or tether ourselves to it as we venture imaginatively further afield. In such a safe zone, the writer finally can discover a sense of self. Kennedy returns us to this knowledge by always presenting characters whose fate is bound up inextricably with that of their places, yet she qualifies Bachelard's view of a room's inherent safety. Her rooms can also threaten and bewilder. Characters can long to feel at home but never succeed, or work hopelessly to escape inhospitable sites. Whatever its nature, each location in Kennedy's theater is as much an active character as the people caught there.

Kennedy writes of the chambered emotions, the impulses and preoccupations that are most difficult to explain adequately in public language. She finds in her characters the face one sees only when gazing a long time into a mirror – long enough for the face to change shape, to seem alien. She gives her characters the deportment one only experiences in private. The stillnesses between movements run longer. Sometimes the limbs move more slowly, without the forced grace they often must acquire in the presence of others. At other times, bodies allow themselves eruptions that would also have been stifled in public. The air around the body seems to change, no longer an invisible element taken for granted, but now a strange force to be pushed through, wedged against, stirred up – one of the few things left to feel in Kennedy's cloistered world, and so felt intensely. (This tension between control and chaos has led Elinor Fuchs to compare Kennedy's work to Maeterlinck's tragedies of daily life, and Gerald Freedman and Gaby Rodgers, Kennedy's frequent directors, to link her with Robert Wilson.)[6]

Kennedy's rooms give her the occasion to define a fresh theatrical image of intimacy – a rare thing on stage, where usually it is confused with mere sexiness or the predictable motions of confession. Intimacy, for Kennedy, is never so self-indulgent. There is nothing misty or sweet; her characters don't let down their guard with the swift ease one sees in conventionally intimate situations. Boundaries between people dissolve roughly in Kennedy's theater, as they often do between her people and places, yet this sensation of blurring is rarely pleasurable. Characters experience vertigo more often than ecstasy, claustrophobia more often than coziness. Kennedy envisions intimacy as an anxious state, its violence barely concealed beneath her plays' placid surfaces. Some characters, despite their physical proximity, seem to move further away from real engagement with one another as more is exposed, protecting themselves with diffidence. Other characters move so emotionally close that they can no longer see clearly, and no longer distinguish present occurrences from their visions of past and future ordeals. The resulting panic only intensifies the pain of not having any space on stage to call one's own. Kennedy's intimacy is something to be suffered, not luxuriated in; its characteristic rhythms are hesitant, stumbling, thick; never lissome, never soft.

The clarity with which Kennedy dramatizes the dusky, painful moments of experience, and her fascination with sequestered lives, has unfortunately made it easy for audiences and readers to pass over her work. It is too bleak or esoteric, one hears, too marginal or peculiar. Kennedy's work is rarely produced today, and over the past decade she has had to withstand as well the wounding neglect of most serious critics. Kennedy insists she doesn't really like the theater anyway, that she would have preferred to have been a short-story writer, "sitting alone in my room, writing out stories and sending them to my publishers" – someone like Edith Wharton or Gwendolyn Brooks, she says – "then I wouldn't have to be with all those people in the rehearsal hall."[7] Her comments aren't without self-irony. When asked why she stays with the theater, Kennedy jokes that anonymity would be worse. But even as she speaks warmly of her life whenever asked and brings into print volumes of her autobiography – *People Who Led to My Plays* in 1987; "A Theatre Journal" (part of *Deadly Triplets*) in 1990 – she makes clear how deeply she feels the importance of privacy, the restorative capacities of seclusion; and how vigilant she is about the ways her identity is shaped by the people she meets and the places she lives in.

There's nothing odd about a fine writer like Kennedy missing out on the popular success and lucrative rewards that come to more commercial writers. Kennedy should always be grouped with Maria Irene Fornes, Sam Shepard, and all those other writers whose idiosyncratic sensibilities seem to ban them from many regional theaters and Broadway. But what doesn't make sense is Kennedy's exclusion from even the alternative ranks. She is missing from David Savran's *In Their Own Words,* his valuable collection of interviews with contemporary writers, and missing, too, from *The Oxford Companion to American Theatre,* a book aspiring to be a standard reference work in its field. Errol Hill left her out of the otherwise useful *Theatre of Black Americans,* and few of the many recent anthologies of black drama find room even for one of her shorter plays. Judging from these books alone, and the many theaters that never consider her when it's time to plan seasons (in New York she hasn't premiered a play, apart from academic commissions, since 1976), one could easily conclude that Kennedy had fallen right out of our theater's history.

What accounts for the neglect? Surely it has something to do with her distrust of linearity, her way of fragmenting experience and emotion. The way the elements of her plays hold together isn't always evident to her readers. Also, the mix of surreal imagery with passages of corrosive naturalness must trouble those guardians of consistency lurking in her audience, wondering just what "ism" she fits into. But more troubling to the theater community is Kennedy's intensity. Her works are short and clenched tight – sharp flarings of anxiety, smothered only with difficulty. As such, they're easily undervalued by those whose idea of drama is the leisurely, lumbering three-act play, seducing us for a while, then ushering us politely out. Kennedy's work doesn't beckon us in; nor, once we *are* in, does she make it easy for us to leave without persistent questions about what we have seen.

Kennedy is a difficult playwright, but not in a way that leaves readers wishing they knew more about history or literature, or for that matter about her private life. Hers are not erudite, reference-thick plays. In fact, they are remarkably uncluttered, which is precisely why they are so taxing. One prefers to read them in small doses – a single ten-page play is enough for a sitting. In performance, they are equally difficult to absorb, but not, for all that, unabsorbing. When sensitively produced, with a minimum of theatrical apparatus to distract from the characters' inner ordeals, her plays can be exhausting, testing one's attention span in an hour to the same degree an opera four times its length might.

There are deeper reasons for Kennedy's frequent inaccessibility. She seems to know that a too-candid presentation of her characters and their concerns would likely destroy their very substance. Like a veil worn by the easily abashed, the mystery surrounding the characters protects as much as it obscures. It enables them to come forward the short distance they do. Moreover, the interruptions to their speech and the abbreviated quality of their gestures provide important clues about their lives. Such irregularities may be symptoms of the devouring persistence of a character's conscience, for instance, or another's incurable inability to adapt to the dominant tempo of everyday life. To explicate such behavior, to clean it up with one's interpretations, is to suggest that the "real" characters lie beneath their difficult presentation. Nothing could be more misleading. What Kennedy shows about her characters is all there is; *how* she shows them mirrors how her characters see themselves, and how they are seen by others.

Finally, Kennedy's inscrutability forces readers and viewers back upon themselves. This exercise is one of the main pleasures of work so resistant to our attempts to enter it. Finding no easy access to the plays, or, rather, never feeling that we can reach their center, we are left to meditate more closely than we might otherwise on what little we *can* see. We also have time to speculate on possible correspondences between these images and the scattered images from our own lives. Kennedy obstructs ordinary acts of interpretation, but she does open up avenues of self-reflection usually closed to audiences busy traveling through someone else's story. Bachelard's comments on difficulty are to the point:

> The real houses of memory . . . do not readily lend themselves to description. To describe them would be like showing them to visitors. We can perhaps tell everything about the present, but about the past! . . . All we communicate to others is an *orientation* towards what is secret without ever being able to tell the secret objectively. What is secret never has total objectivity . . . . What would be the use, for instance, in giving the plan of the room that was really *my* room, in describing the little room at the *end* of the garret, in saying that from the

> window, across the indentations of the roofs, one could see the hill. I alone, in my memories of another century, can open the deep cupboard that still retains for me alone that unique odor, the odor of raisins drying on a wicker tray. The odor of raisins! It is an odor that is beyond description, one that it takes a lot of imagination to smell. But I've already said too much. If I said more, the reader, back in his own room, would not open that unique wardrobe, with its unique smell . . . . We have to induce in the reader a state of suspended reading. For it is not until his eyes have left the page that recollections of my room can become a threshold of oneirism for him.[8]

Set against Bachelard's complex imagery of interiority, how inadequate it sounds when critics blithely describe Kennedy's theater as "dark." The term does suggest how the plays are touched with anguish, filled with images of violence or physical suffering – looking inward to private landscapes, not out into a world others might easily recognize. But as one moves further into the plays, the darkness doesn't lift, the way out is obscured, the situations don't clarify. They do grow more familiar; some landmarks and characters coalesce, but at the same time the imaginative jungle becomes denser. Her plays don't follow a forward trajectory, nor even a circular pattern. They move back into themselves, regressing to the forgotten, abandoned regions of Kennedy's consciousness. Perhaps this technique helps explain why she has written so many plays on ostensibly the same subject (and why so many share the same tones and temperaments). One play brings her down to a point in her psyche from which she can't find an exit, so she writes another to help her look for a way out. The second one goes only so far, or deeper, and another play is required to try again.

The depths to which Kennedy travels primarily affect the characters' language. Like Gertrude Stein, Kennedy is an obsessive writer, able to dramatize that obsessiveness in the rhythms of her language, the dense weave of her structure, and the singlemindedness of her characters. And, as with Stein's, Kennedy's dialogue is composed of repetitions and minute variations on set themes – among the more distinctive traits of Kennedy's theater, and reasons often cited by those who dislike her work. A woman in one of Kennedy's plays will speak a sentence, then return and speak it again a few minutes later, then recapitulate it when linking it to others in another few minutes, then subtly rearrange its words, then grasp hold of just two or three fragments of the same sentence even later. Speaking becomes the way Kennedy's characters maneuver their way through their often painful memories. And the evolution of their language gives readers a way to gauge the effects of remembering.

Yet the driven quality of remembering and telling in Kennedy's plays does not make for consistency of tone, stability of characterization, or flatness of structure. Dialogue that sounded unremarkable at the start becomes, on repetition, more fraught with anxiety, as though each statement contained a world of experience growing more difficult to master. Memory, Kennedy reminds us, demands a rigor absent from mere nostalgia. Remembering is never wistful here – it is wracking and often nauseating. There is no swooning. The lucidity of these characters leads to fragmentation, as though the pressure to articulate emotions or the concentration required to remember events causes her characters to shatter. Many of Kennedy's scenes read as though their few words, repeated over and over, were all that survived a mysterious, scouring psychological torment, and from these words her characters go about trying to reassemble their lives. We are left with moments of dramatic life, large pieces of emotion, but not the connective tissue that would render Kennedy's dramatic action whole.

Kennedy provided much of that connective material twenty-three years after producing her first play, when she published her memoir, *People Who Led to My Plays*, in 1987. It is ironic, given the constant self-exploration of her theater, that it wasn't until the publication of this book that she gained wide attention. Many of the readers who bought *People* probably had never seen more than one of her plays – usually *Funnyhouse* – if that. Yet the memoir and the theater are best read together, each elaborating within the constraints of its form the same details of Kennedy's life.

Biographical criticism is often held in low regard, but with Kennedy's work, critics ignore the life at their peril. Her plays aren't interesting for their disclosures about her life, of course, yet they do have much to show about how one particular writer answered the recurrent urge toward self-discovery, about the expectations of epiphany writers load upon their work, and about the battle one goes through to make a work that manages to be both privately enlightening, even redemptive, and yet still publicly involving.

With any other writer, such self-centeredness would be tiresome. Why is Kennedy's so fascinating? Perhaps because Kennedy never contents herself with simply putting chapters of her life on display and leaving them alone. That's too complacent, certainly not appropriate for an art as dynamic as theater. Rather, she exploits the temporal aspect of theater in order to push into her autobiography so thoroughly that its tale of suffering, joy, or confusion becomes almost iconic. She reaches the essence of her life, beneath the outlines, the material details, the chronologies, and who-said-what-to-whom or I-did-this-here-and-there. Once she's able to expose the essence, her life becomes exemplary, not just curious; instructive, not just informative – theater, not just a good story. Kennedy already had all the elements of her theater before she wrote her first play; they had been steadily accruing since childhood and drifting through her consciousness. They simply wanted an arrangement that would reveal their fullest significance – a revelation available only in art. Looking for that perfect arrangement, Kennedy herself is the most commanding figure in the plays – the only full character, one could even say. We watch her in the self-consuming act of writing her plays – watch her more closely than we do the people she writes about.

One doesn't study Kennedy's memoir for the usual details of a life – date of birth, schooling, parents' occupations, marriages, and divorces. Information on those subjects is provided, but it remains in the background. More important to the development of the writer are all the peripheral activities, the passing acquaintances, the treasured items and remembered books – accumulated souvenirs of a private life lived parallel to the "official" one whose telling she leaves to conventional biographers. The story of *People* leads only as far as 1961, shortly after Kennedy finished a draft of her first major play, *Funnyhouse of a Negro*. Before then, her days, as she chooses to remember them, were filled with old movies – *The Red Shoes* and *The Invisible Man, The Best Years of Our Lives* and *Giant* – which sparked her lifelong fascination with celebrity. (The fascination ran in the family: Kennedy's mother named Adrienne after the movie star Adrienne Ames.) Like most girls, she devoured fairy tales and nursery rhymes but, unlike most children, never grew to dismiss their notions of pure goodness and absolute evil, or the way they enveloped their heroes in worlds full of fantasy and menace. The conventional religious upbringing that many middle-class girls receive was particularly intense in the Kennedy household. Pictures of Jesus were everywhere; the spirituals she sang, Kennedy says, put her "in touch with a mystery beyond my visible sight"; and every Sunday at church she heard a minister whose peculiar, galvanic way of sermonizing showed her that "there was a rage inside religion."[9] She never forgot the kinship between violence and purity.

The story of Jesus' suffering and redemption, the fairy tales, and the movies (especially horror movies, like *The Wolf Man* and *Frankenstein*) taught Kennedy the basics of her craft as a playwright. Each of these turned on the magic of transformation; identity was revealed as something malleable, never fully fathomed, always capable of surprise. There were other selves hidden behind public personas, Kennedy learned, and only at certain moments, usually under particularly taxing conditions, did they reveal themselves. When it came time to write her own first characters, Kennedy recalled these stories and movies from childhood. (Later in life, her enthusiasm shifted to the movies of Ridley Scott, famous for his own nightmare of transformation, *Alien*.) Her characters didn't have to follow a textbook idea of consistency. They could have double or triple identities that showed themselves all within the space of a single scene. The cast for *The Owl Answers* includes characters with metamorphosis built into their names: "She who is Clara Passmore who is the Virgin Mary who is the Bastard who is the Owl," "Goddam Father who is the Richest White Man in the Town who is the Dead White Father who is Reverend Passmore," and others. Kennedy would determine which face of her characters to reveal on the basis of the particular setting, the sequence of dramatic action, and the psychological weather of any given moment. (In an important essay comparing Kennedy and Sam Shepard, Herbert Blau defines Kennedy's creations as "apparations rather than characters.")[10] In all of her plays, characters are amalgams of numerous emotional states, each with a distinct appearance, tone of voice, manner and bearing: a layered characterization that literalizes, in a highly theatrical way, all the talk about inner and outer life and subtext that circulated among psychologically based Method-acting classes in the fifties and sixties. Acting students kept much of that layering hidden; Kennedy couldn't help exposing it all.

Kennedy's childhood also holds clues to the origin of her emotional courage as a playwright. She tells us that the most important aspects of her spiritual upbringing were the many evenings her mother read aloud from the Book of Psalms. The psalms showed Kennedy how a rigorous formal technique could help shape the most devastating emotional turmoil. In each psalm the speaker takes a single idea – usually fear of an absent God or, conversely, certainty that He is nearby – and works it over and over until, from continued, careful handling, its mysteries are known, if never solved. Kennedy came to cherish the hypnotic rhythms in the psalms, as well as their unaffected tone, and matched these qualities in her own work – until she was writing plays that could be described as theatrical psalms.

Herbert Blau suggests something similar when he describes Kennedy's authorial voice as "not so much crying out as crying within."[11] The most memorable passages of her plays have a cold, deliberate, slightly awkward bearing, yet also tremble with the awe that their speakers feel amid intoxicating passions and visions. The thrill of discovery always vies with the shame at talking about what has been discovered. A speech from *A Rat's Mass* (1966) is representative of Kennedy's troubled lyricism:

> BROTHER AND SISTER RAT: Now it is our rat's mass. *(From now on their voices sound more like gnaws.)* She said if you love me you will. It seemed so innocent. She said it was like a wedding. Now my sister Kay sends me gnawed petals from sunflowers at the State Hospital. She puts them in gray envelopes. Alone I go out to school and the movies. No more do I call by for Rosemary. She made me promise never to tell if you love me she screamed you'll never tell. And I do love her. I found my father's rifle in the attic. Winter time . . . gray time dark boys come laughing starting a game of horseshoes gnawing in the beams. The winter is a place of great gnawed sunflowers. I see

them in every street in every room of our house. I pick up gnawed great yellow petals and pray to be atoned.[12]

Reading the psalms, Kennedy also discovered ways to dramatize her spirituality, making it accessible to anyone who cares to enter her work. No longer did she feel constrained by the elaborate rituals of organized religious ceremony. The psalms presented the alternative: a small-scaled, humble, hushed approach to ideas and emotions overwhelmed in the everyday world.

The psalms returned Kennedy to herself. The writers of the psalms begin and end with their own spiritual longings. Theirs is not an art of external experiences, public places, historical events. When those matters do appear in a psalm, the writer usually makes clear how far from that world he is, and how alienated, how thrown back on himself. Kennedy's work is not just personal, the way all art is to some degree. Nor do her plays merely depict chapters from her autobiography, although many events in her theater can be easily traced back to what we know about her life. Kennedy's theater, as she says, presents "states of mind" more than events, and all of those states are essentially the same: self-doubt and self-loathing, mixed with the need to sort out the mysterious implications of one's presence in the world and survival of the adversities encountered in the course of a life. Entering each of her characters, Kennedy explores an aspect of this large murky condition, illuminates for just a moment one more corner, phrases her questions to herself slightly differently, or presses a point with a bit more force. The effect, and significance, of her plays come forward most impressively after they have *all* been read. For, like the psalms, the interrogation of the self is most intelligible in accumulation, each installment defining another facet of the writer. Hers is a drama of what she herself calls "becoming a self."

The process of becoming Adrienne Kennedy the writer accelerated as each year went by. She began to feel intensely the need to "make an imprint" with her life, as she put it. She yearned for a model family, along the lines of the Dick-and-Jane family in the storybooks she consumed in elementary school. More challenging books succeeded these in her affections, but no matter the level of sophistication of the writing, Kennedy always responded in the most naive of ways: total identification. Jane Eyre, Mary in *The Secret Garden,* Anne of Green Gables (and, of course, the icons in *Modern Screen* magazine) – Kennedy wanted to be each of her heroines; she wanted (as she said) "to be *in* books." And in plays: "Intensely I wanted my family on stage (like the family in *Our Town*)," Kennedy writes, "like Tom, Laura and Amanda in *The Glass Menagerie.*"[13]

Reading took her far from the predictable realities of growing up in suburban, middle-class Cleveland, daughter of a civil-servant father and housewife mother. Her neighborhood turns up very rarely in her memoir. It usually appears as a place to depart from (the rides in the family Plymouth every Sunday; the trips to Dad's office at the Y downtown), or arrive at after a journey from a more enchanting place, usually Georgia, where Mrs. Kennedy's family lived. The Kennedy family seems to close in on itself in the pages of the memoir – Mother, Father, Brother, Sister – a world unto itself, touched by all the detritus of American life in the 1940s, conversant in all the current events, but in the end inviolate, still unfathomed, an unseen place, an unfamiliar family. It was only when Kennedy eventually left home for college that she could see her family whole (and thus possibly consider writing about it, writing about its inwardness).

College also introduced Kennedy to a different kind of gulf between people: segregation. "A darkness would surface that had not been seen before," she writes in the memoir.[14] Ohio State University in 1949 was hardly a welcoming place for a bright black woman, and for four long years Kennedy felt lost and despised. Even though she lived in dormitories with white students, the dividing lines remained clear. Few white students concealed their suspicion of Kennedy; teachers often wouldn't credit Kennedy with her usually outstanding work (thinking it plagiarized); her aspiration to major in English was dashed on the basis of a barely disguised Jim Crow law. She read all the books anyway – Pound, Faulkner, Richard Wright, Fitzgerald, Shelley. Studying T. S. Eliot, she changed her idea "as to what could be accomplished in poetry." And the work of Lorca became her constant companion: His *Poet in New York* somehow explained (and dignified) her anomie at Ohio State; no matter how lonely she would get, "Lorca's dark, complex vision was thrilling and comforting." Along with all the other favorite writers, he taught that "tragedy was the nature of life . . . a crosscurrent that moved across football games, dances, clothes, worries over our possible silver patterns and wedding dresses." Kennedy would return to Lorca again and again as she began to teach herself playwriting, drawing themes and techniques from his fevered work. His poetry, she said, showed her that "imagery comes from recovering connections long ago lost and buried."[15] When Kennedy was 59, she did just that – returning in her imagination to Ohio State to write *The Ohio State Murders*, a play that finally confronted the most trying period of her life.

Suffocating loneliness also marked her marriage and life in New York in the 1950s. Her husband, Joe Kennedy, was a doctoral student at Columbia, and so was often absent. Her newborn son, Joe Jr., kept her home, allowing her only the most fleeting of encounters with other young writers. The people she did meet never knew she wrote; she was only a mother and wife to them. Just as she had done at Ohio State, Kennedy turned inward to draw her greatest stimulation from art and from the memories that began crowding her mind, now that she was far from home.

The "Marriage and Motherhood" chapter of *People* is filled more with names of artists, writers, books, paintings, and songs than with details of domestic life. She grew to admire Emily Dickinson's devotion to solitude, Chekhov's restraint, the clash of visions in *Rashomon,* Emma Bovary's courage in the face of alienation. She attended to Thornton Wilder and O'Neill, probed Dostoyevsky's understanding of trauma, underlined Wordsworth's lesson that "memory and longing for the past are with us daily." She returned to Chekhov, this time to memorize Nina's frustration, her inability to say what she means. She studied Beethoven's quartets, and received from them sanction for her own obsessiveness, her determination to alchemize her unhappiness into beautiful art. The music makes its influence felt in all of her plays: Like the quartets, each play turns introspection into a process more molelike and painstaking than it ever had been in American drama.

Every piece of art Kennedy encountered seemed to carry advice. *Guernica* demonstrated the secrets of turning dreams into dreamscapes. Virginia Woolf's novels have the knack of capturing evanescent states of being, making their tranquillity somehow charged, dramatic. Duke Ellington's music explained that "there was immense poetry inside her life as a Negro." The "density" in Monet, Emerson's inspirations about self-reliance and the fluidity of life, Jackson Pollock's refusal to be figurative: All these sightings filtered through her consciousness until they stimulated her imagination and provoked her own urge to make art. And again and again, under it all, the psalms, always the psalms and the memory of her mother reading them, leaning across a porcelain counter.

Kennedy was writing constantly during these years, but nothing was coming of it. Stories made the rounds and came back in the mail, writing classes provided company but no real instruction, agents and editors were encouraging but, ultimately, powerless. Something was blocking Kennedy's development as a writer; something prevented her from turning all the memories of her family, all the lessons in technique, and all the inspiration she received from other art into art of her own. It was only when she submitted herself to yet another uprooting and relocation that she began to write her most serious work. She traveled to Africa with Joe, lived in Ghana for several months, and returned completely transformed. It was as if this, her first trip abroad, shook from her all the unessential material cluttering her mind, severing unimportant attachments while clarifying the ones that really mattered. Kennedy was liberated in Africa, but she was also more alone than ever before: This solitude was so thorough that only by writing her past back into her life could she find solace.

Naturally the African sojourn strengthened Kennedy's consciousness of her race – instilling pride in a history that she had barely known before her trip, offering an alternative to the self-hatred she developed at Ohio State. She couldn't help but learn the political significance of her blackness in freshly independent Ghana, with Kwame Nkrumah the new leader, and in the

Congo, where she met Patrice Lumumba, its president until his assassination in 1961. Kennedy set her impressions of these men alongside her memories of Count Basie, Sarah Vaughan, James Baldwin, and Mary Bethune, and drew sustenance from their example. But she never thought in purely racial terms. Blackness and Africanness were abstractions to her; "Black Pride" meant nothing if she couldn't identify who possessed it. African history, likewise, was only as important as the individuals who shaped it. Kennedy's plays are filled with images from African history; they draw on the distortions of identity possible with African masks; her characters struggle with the meaning of their blackness, but Kennedy should never be thought of as a "black playwright" or a writer speaking for her race or somehow putting a generalized black heritage on stage. Even when iconic figures from that heritage do appear in her plays, they are thoroughly transformed by the needs, confusions, and conflicted attractions of the highly individual, idiosyncratic character who remembers them. Perhaps this refusal to speak impersonally about black history explains Kennedy's isolation from other black writers; politics in her work, and in her life, has been simply one force among many affecting the consciousness of a character also assailed by the implications of a place, an upbringing, a family, and a lifetime of mundane, quotidian obligations.

Kennedy was 29 when she returned to New York. In her suitcase was the manuscript of *Funnyhouse of a Negro* – not her first play (there were others that never left her desk drawer), but the one that seemed best to express years of relentless meditation. Kennedy knew that she had finally succeeded in devising a theatrical space to accommodate her emotions and a technique to anchor something as intangible and fleeting as memory. She had also managed to represent *herself* – an unexpected dividend. The shock of seeing her reflection nearly kept her from ever writing again.

Early in 1963, Kennedy brought *Funnyhouse* to a writing workshop led by Edward Albee, and the play was scheduled to be produced later that year, under Michael Kahn's direction. Midway through the series of classes, Kennedy decided to withdraw; she felt embarrassed, she told Albee, because she had written such a personal play. The exposure would be humiliating. Albee consented, but not without explaining that her courage was precisely what made her work so enthralling. Baffled, Kennedy stayed in the class, and *Funnyhouse* was eventually produced in 1964, going on to win an Obie Award and putting its author in the pages of *Vogue* and Leonard Lyons's gossip column. Celebrity, of a sort, was hers at last.

One can recount the plot of *Funnyhouse* and still be no closer to understanding its mysteries. The play's action occurs on several levels at once; only one contains a conventional story, a melodramatic one, which is the least important aspect of the play. At the center of *Funnyhouse* is Negro-Sarah, a young woman who was conceived after her black father raped her white mother. During the course of the play, Sarah confronts the implications of her mixed heritage and the violence that engendered her, striving to learn which parts of her identity have been shaped by European culture and which by African history. She finds such a task daunting; the pressure to reconcile the contradictions in her character only fragments her even more. Her hair falls out; she's tormented by a vision of her father as a dead man, an axe through his head; her mother's whiteness seems a constant reproach. She pleads to Jesus, hoping to take strength from his example of suffering. Nothing soothes the pain of her memories; no one helps to place her in a history all her own; no experience or encounter clarifies her identity or answers her yearning for a fresh beginning, an erasing of her past. That's only possible in death; and so Sarah escapes her funnyhouse by hanging herself.

As befits a funhouse, a swirl of other images engulfs this story, complicating its unfolding, confusing a reader's sense of space, time, and the relationships among characters. "*Funnyhouse of a Negro* is perhaps clearest and most explicit," writes Kennedy in a stage direction, "when the play is placed in the girl Sarah's room . . . . Then the director is free to let the rest of the play happen around her."[16] The rest of the play is really an extension of Sarah's consciousness; there are seven other characters in the play, but four of them are each described as "one of herselves," the other three have life only when Sarah chooses to remember them or confront them in her dreaming.

Those "selves" come in the shape of Queen Victoria and the Duchess of Hapsburg, Jesus and Patrice Lumumba. The Queen and the Duchess aspire to be epitomes of whiteness, although here they are of mixed race. Patrice Lumumba celebrates blackness, yet he appears with a bludgeoned head, victim of his assassin. Kennedy's Jesus is a yellow-skinned, hunchbacked dwarf – an altogether disappointing savior. When Sarah is able to shut out the tauntings of these figures, she describes a quiet, isolated life in her small room on the top floor of a New York City brownstone, spent reading old books and daydreaming in front of photographs of castles and a plaster statue of Queen Victoria. Sarah is beguiled by the statue – "a thing of astonishing whiteness" – and longs to rid herself of all traces of blackness. "Black is evil," she says, "Black diseases." She treasures white things and wants only white friends, sure that they will function as an "embankment to keep me from reflecting too much upon the fact that I am a Negro." But Sarah's idea of whiteness transcends race. She doesn't merely long to be white. She seeks complete invisibility, a blinding whiteness that burns away all trace of her tortured birth. She wants to be "soulless," to "possess no moral value." "I want not to be."[17]

Like Sarah, denied the luxury of completeness, Kennedy's play seems to exist in a state of constant agitation, as scenes and images and snatches of dialogue keep darting toward each other, hoping to link up, only invariably to fail. Yet for all the disjointed action and rootless imagery, *Funnyhouse* is held together by the logic of self-interrogation, by Sarah's determination to plumb her own depths – to retrieve, name, and decode her secrets. She conducts this task while at the same time believing that she must "maintain a stark fortress against recognition of myself."[18] This tension – between the compulsion to understand oneself and the fear of what one might find – gives *Funnyhouse* its manic energy. Sarah's highly charged consciousness prevents her from relaxing enough to make connections and put thoughts in order.

> SARAH (Negro): The rooms are my rooms; a Hapsburg chamber, a chamber in a Victorian castle, the hotel where I killed my father, the jungle. These are the places myselves exist in. I know no places. That is, I cannot believe in places. To believe in places is to know hope and to know the emotion of hope is to know beauty. It links us across a horizon and connects us to the world. I find there are no places only my funnyhouse. Streets are rooms, cities are rooms, eternal rooms. I try to create a space for myselves in cities, New York, the midwest, a southern town, but it becomes a lie. I try to give myselves a logical relationship but that too is a lie. For relationships was one of my last religions. I clung loyally to the lie of relationships, again and again seeking to establish a connection between my characters. Jesus is Victoria's son. Mother loved my father before her hair fell out. A loving relationship exists between myself and Queen Victoria, a love between myself and Jesus but they are lies.[19]

Funnyhouse moves in spasms, exhaling long passages of confession then subsiding into a low rumble, as the characters consider and work over everything that has just been said, and test out images about to come forward in the next spasm of language. A character will mention that her hair is falling out, or a figure will cross the stage holding a bald head, but it's only in a subsequent speech that we'll learn the reasons for this affliction: "If I did not despise myself," says Sarah in the voice of Patrice Lumumba, "then my hair would not have fallen."[20] Images don't merely come and go in *Funnyhouse;* like the ravens that flit around the stage in the opening scene, they return over and over, growing in significance, becoming harder to ignore, haunting and hounding Sarah. The words "black" and "white" are sounded over and over, growing more oppressive each time. Kennedy doesn't employ this technique of repetition only with dialogue: Hair is everywhere, frizzy and so unlike the mother's straight hair, littering the stage, lying on furniture, fussed with, covered up with headpieces, falling to the floor like snow.

The memory of Sarah's father is just as omnipresent. He doesn't leave her alone, returning from "the dead," making a knocking sound that runs under all the action, seeking acknowledgment from a daughter who despises him. The more she tries to banish him from her mind, the more persistent he becomes, asking only that Sarah forgive him his blackness. Sarah can't accept him, though, for by now she has learned to distrust relationships of any kind. Even though she is bound to her father by circumstance, she strives for a liberating suspension, just as her mother did, taking refuge in madness and fleeing to an asylum. That psychological need also lies behind the theatrical decision to eschew a tidier dramatic structure. A seamless whole – a nice story, with all its parts effortlessly connecting – would be just another lie, another sham testament to "relationships."

Funnyhouse is strangely positioned between public and private life. It partakes of history and politics that anyone would understand: Victorian England, the Hapsburg Empire, colonialism in Africa. Yet it is also a hermetic play, contained within Sarah's consciousness. The autonomy of that consciousness is always in question: Who is Sarah without borrowed images from white and black culture? Kennedy deliberately doesn't give Sarah the chance to have an identity of her own; instead Sarah must rely on "herselves" to speak for her. Neither does she have a context, a place she alone defines. She drifts through many rooms – Hapsburg chambers, hotels, Victorian castles – but none are really home. Her room on the Upper West Side is barely seen before she clutters it with her dreams of European antiques, Oriental carpets, a piano. Her funnyhouse, home to memories, anxieties, and nightmares, is always open to her, yet that place, as one might imagine, is overwhelming: As orchestrated by a landlady figure and her boyfriend Raymond, who each take on the role as funhouse manager, Kennedy's play never pauses long enough to let Sarah study the dimensions of even her mental space.

In reflecting many things, and each thing many times over, the funnyhouse actually shows Sarah nothing, provides no reliable testimony about her, can't help explain where she is. It only teases. The "hope" and "beauty" that Sarah expects to discover once she creates "a space for myselves in cities" are, like her other goals, elusive. Sarah knows herself, and is known by others, only by what she reacts against and longs for – never by who she *is*. She is a noncharacter in a nonplace, a void within a void. Her suicide, then, is something of a redundancy. Yet it is also the only gesture truly her own. Anonymity is finally hers; she gathers up all her fragments of identity, lashes them together, obliterates them – and is at last complete.

The image of Sarah's hanging body at the end of *Funnyhouse* is more than just emotionally disruptive; it is also tonally jarring – an intrusion of realism into the midst of a dream world. "The poor bitch has hung herself," says the landlady, her coarse diction itself shattering the incantatory tone of the rest of the play.[21] Sarah's death is something final and unequivocal in a play where the dead keep returning to life, where characters cross the stage holding their heads in their hands. All of *Funnyhouse* resembles a ritual, a slow, painful reenactment of past suffering, but here the ritual comes to a sudden stop, and Kennedy leaves her audience with a vision no ceremony can accommodate. In terms of the play's sense of time, it is the only thing that happens in the present.

The suicide brings to a close Sarah's search for grace, purifying her more effectively than the rituals of remembering had done. Just before her suicide, the scene had shifted to an African jungle, where all the characters have nimbuses over their heads, suggesting (Kennedy says) that they will be Sarah's saviors. But these visions are no more to be trusted than Sarah's father. He, too, was supposed to be a god to her, Sarah says, but turned out "only" to be a black man. "Christ would not rape anyone," she says to him, refusing to forgive him. Her own purity will have to be restored through violence, as though that will offset the violence that destroyed Sarah's mother, "killed [her] light." In the funnyhouse, one can only be assured of one's purity if one dies.

By writing *Funnyhouse,* Kennedy cleansed herself as well. Through Sarah, she faced her own ambivalent feelings about her race, sorting through the attractions and curses of European culture and African history. She voiced her pain of rootlessness and showed how alone she was. She let herself be attracted to violence, and she played out persistent fantasies. By welcoming such imagery, she inoculated herself, in a way, ensuring that she wouldn't be overwhelmed again by the darkest products of her imagination: They could be let loose and seen whole. She also learned what she was *not:* neither Queen Victoria nor Patrice Lumumba, neither mother nor father. Writing *Funnyhouse*, she learned she didn't have to choose one aspect of her identity over another – the student enthralled by *Jane Eyre* or the woman transfixed by the mysteries of African masks. Ambivalence was not just an option; it would become a necessity if Kennedy was to mature as a playwright. No "pure statements" – Sarah's father's wish – for this writer, only the constant working and reworking of pressing concerns: a writing life in which constant dissatisfaction, constant feelings of inadequacy, bear fruit.

Kennedy killed off Sarah, and in a sense killed off the self she knew up to 1963. From now on, she wouldn't have to worry about losing herself in the no-man's-land of marriage or motherhood, Cleveland or the Congo, the unsatisfying identities of "black writer" or "woman writer" or, worse, no writer at all. She was no longer the Sarah who couldn't confront her demons, who couldn't face her past, who had to run into worlds of illusion lest the pain of remembering destroy her. Kennedy would return to the themes of

Funnyhouse – they weren't killed off with Sarah's suicide – but now she knew that the obsession had a purpose: Only by writing could she achieve what Sarah could not – familiarity with her life's patterns, a sense of connection and of placement, and all the hope that is its reward.

Kennedy had begun several other plays before the success of *Funnyhouse,* the most significant of which are *The Owl Answers, A Rat's Mass,* and *A Beast Story.* Produced intermittently in the years after the New York production of *Funnyhouse,* these plays could be loosely termed her animal trilogy, although such a category sounds too charming for plays more violent than anything she had shown before. Dormant pains and fantasies had been roused. In these new plays, she returned to many of the concerns of *Funnyhouse* with a stronger, more resolute temperament.

The life of the child again was Kennedy's inexhaustible theme. Each young protagonist in these three plays finds herself in the center of a storm of competing demands and attractions: importunate fathers, reproachful mothers, siblings who shift nervously between loyalty and animosity, a threatening dogma of religious virtue and the attendant horrific vision of judgment. Kennedy is one of the few contemporary writers for whom the idea of sin retains its power. In such a climate of fear, all the characters behave as though they await certain apocalypse. Indeed, inward cataclysms occur all the time, as one character after another collapses under the pressure to domesticate their demons.

Those demons always brandish memories of sex. In *The Owl Answers,* Clara confronts the implications of being the illegitimate mulatto daughter of the "Richest White Man in the Town and somebody that cooked for him." Brother and Sister Rat in *A Rat's Mass* can't dodge the pain of their incest. *A Beast Story* is filled with images of rape. Kennedy paces carefully through the maze of violent sexuality in each play, varying the details, but not the emotional atmosphere. She never emerges: These plays aren't the kind of trial that, once endured, delivers her to a safer place, where she can feel purged. The cathartic illumination is forever withheld.

Kennedy is not alone in dismissing happy endings, of course. But she is that rare playwright who denies audiences and characters the moment of supreme awareness that ends even the bleakest play. There's no sigh of resignation, as might close a play by her beloved Chekhov. Nor do her characters ever pause to take stock of where they have arrived. Even when there's a murder or a suicide, there is no release, only confirmation of the condition we've long suspected and now have seen.

The desperation at the core of Kennedy's plays marks a thrilling rejuvenation of psychological theater. Most drama aspiring to the term lacks a palpable vision of the psyche. "Psychological," in these cases, means the mere presentation of hazy "feelings," the outward signs of distress or thoughtfulness without any substance behind them, a mechanical plod through the stations of a breakdown, without any detours that might upset our expectations. Kennedy doesn't approach psychology so programmatically. Inspired by Tennessee Williams to embrace the muddled emotions of her characters rather than try to streamline them, she goes Williams one better. She explores a brand of primitivism. Her theater is based in elemental drives, physical turmoil, tangible evidence of mental disarray: menstruation in *A Lesson in Dead Language* (1970), the falling hair in *Funnyhouse,* the insistent sounds of vermin gnawing in *A Rat's Mass.* From one perspective, her plays cling to solid old-fashioned topics: virtue and evil, childhood and motherhood, faith and deferred expectations of redemption. Yet in her imagination, the old-fashioned becomes the primordial, the human becomes the animal – and what was once known as "psychology" becomes an unfamiliar journey into regions of brutal passion.

The play that brings Kennedy furthest from the above-ground, everyday world is *A Beast Story* (1965). Only ten pages long in the published version, it nonetheless manages to evoke masterfully a complicated domestic history and the dimensions of four tormented psyches. *A Beast Story* is set in a mid-western house, seemingly far from all other human life, presided over by a granite-souled minister (Beast Man). His wife and daughter also live there, and in the attic lingers the ghost of the Dead Human, the daughter's husband. All except the Dead Human are now "beasts": They are real black people, not furry creatures, Kennedy notes in warning to literal-minded directors. Their speech is sometimes distorted, she continues, their appearance maybe slightly askew, they can even move in a slightly animallike way (hunted-looking, perhaps) – but the play probably works best if the bestiality is considered psychological rather than physiological, a condition of degradation or submission to hidden urges, with all the consciousness of that condition a human might have. For all the characters in *A Beast Story* are consumed with disgust at their desires and actions, the manifold ways in which their bodies manage to elude the surveillance of their morality and so humiliate them.

There is little action in *A Beast Story:* The most flamboyant gesture comes at the end, as the Beast Girl swings an axe at all those pursuing her. But even that is a recollected image, a return to an event we heard described earlier in the play. As far as *dramatic* action goes – the movement through ideas or emotional patterns – that, too, is minimal. *A Beast Story* is a portrait of an arrested moment in the life of a family. As she often does, Kennedy dramatizes the brooding that follows a catastrophic event, knowing that only as the tragedy is reenacted in the mind does the true disaster show itself. And only then, too, can the damage be measured and the pain felt.

The unseen catastrophe unfolded when the Dead Human raped the Beast Girl on their wedding night; a child was conceived; the Beast Girl's mother (Beast Woman) insisted that it be aborted with quinine and whiskey. The Beast Girl also kills the Dead Human. During the course of the play, the Dead Human wanders the attic, holding his dead child, appearing from time to time to beckon his lost wife. Meanwhile, the Beast Man tries to reach out to his daughter, but he only reminds her of her ruined marriage, for he had raped his own wife, too. The Beast Woman sits alone during most of the play, slumped over her vanity table in tears or staring out the window, hoping for some relief. Her prayers are never answered. The Beast family ends the play as they began – in darkness, trapped within their beast house. The final words – "Now the sky above our house is blue, three robins with red chests appear on the horizon. All is warm and sunlit" – are mocking, a sham image of healing.[22] The light is too sudden to be real, too strong to endure. The darkness that follows has the final word.

As the title indicates, *A Beast Story* is populated with primitive life. Some of the animal life remains confined by memory. Characters speak of toads that hop on bedposts, of jackals and mice gladdened when the Beast Girl has sex and again when her child dies. The mother describes how she cut the throat of a pigeon poult and poured the blood on her bedsheets as a way of preserving her own innocence. The entire family waits to hear once more the wolves and bears just outside its door.

At other times, elemental things and energies make themselves visible. A dead blue crow and a dead toad float above the house, like warnings of further tragedy, or reminders of irrevocable damage already done. The sun turns black, another reproach. The family's faces grow steadily yellower and more ravaged as the play moves on. The boy accosts the girl, pushing her on the bed. Finally, the girl swings her axe, wildly venting rage no longer able to be contained by human civility.

The tension between purity and sinfulness that characterizes many of Kennedy's plays is tautest in *A Beast Story*. Purity can be protected only in the most violent ways. The mother says she keeps an axe to maintain her daughter's innocence; the abortion is ordered, as though that could restore lost virtue; the girl tries to smother the boy. An awareness of death runs under all the gestures and dialogue; it was present even at the Beast Girl's birth, for the mother went into labor at a funeral. And earlier: The Beast Man "spoke of death at our wedding," according to the Beast Woman. "Was I speaking of death or was it God?"[23]

Death and God. Both are external forces to which the Beast family submits, seeking death beneath the portraits of the Virgin Mary hanging above their beds. Death is the more persuasive, the more reliable of the two forces. Faith in *A Beast Story* becomes a yearning for oblivion, not transcendence.

The God who sanctioned marriage also remained silent when both men in the Beast family raped their wives. The women keep calling to their God, but know how useless are their prayers, how abandoned they are. After all, the Beast Woman's husband is a minister – only one mockery among many in the play. A savage God creates savage marriages. Marriage turns them into beasts, and it is as beasts that the Beast Girl and her mother seek retribution. The three levels of being in *A Beast Story* – God, Human, and Beast – are not merely united in their baseness and indifference to life. The entire hierarchy is reversed: In God's place floats a dead toad, like some ersatz martyr, one who, with the wolves, jackals, and mice, is the sole object of the Beast family's entreaties.

All of *A Beast Story* is an entreaty: the family's anguished remembering of past sins in an effort to name them at last and set them aside so that room can be made for thoughts about other experiences. As with any entreaty, great care is taken in saying the prayer. The influence of the psalms is nowhere more vivid than in *A Beast Story.* At one point, the father speaks the same words that the girl spoke at the beginning, saying he too was "revealed" to himself after his daughter's marriage. The allure of revelation drives all of the speaking in *A Beast Story:* If only we could learn the *reasons* for our pain, they seem to say, then the pain would be easier to withstand. They also seem to believe that if they speak enough about a subject it may begin to look smaller, something distant that has long since lost its fascination, a vision that they have been offered to take or leave rather than an experience they have had to endure. The act of incantation, however, can often make the fear only more vivid. Almost from the beginning, we know the bare facts of what happened, but as the play moves on, those events magnify in importance, tightening their hold on the characters. Even for those who read rather than see and hear *A Beast Story*, the horror is made irrefutably present through language alone. The following passage is spoken on a still stage, lit only by candles.

> BEAST GIRL: *(Staring at Beast Man)* My father comes toward me, saying something I do not comprehend. His face exudes a yellow light. The sky turns black. He catches my hand. He begins to sing, no particular melody yet the tone is unwavering and free. No words are distinct. Silence. He goes to the window, looks out, continues to sing. He sings a beast song. Our hair has grown, our eyes turned yellow. We are trapped in this beast house singing beast songs.[24]

Although the impressiveness of her lyricism seems self-sufficient, Kennedy is not shy about exploiting the means of performance. The Beast family lives in three dimensions, and light, space, and sound convey their own "texts." The linguistic repetitions are matched with gestural ones: The mother, for instance, follows a pattern of set movements, among them staring out the window, looking up to the ceiling, letting her head fall to a table, bursting out in tears – the choreography of desperation. The Dead Human rocks the baby over and over. The father stands in the same beseeching attitude by the threshold of his daughter's room several times during the play. (Bachelard writes of the "sacred properties" and "magic" of the threshold, and of how a simple door can suggest "images of hesitation, temptation, desire, security, welcome, and respect.")[25] All the characters wander the halls and meet each other in choreographed cycles; each encounter raises the emotional level a notch.

Kennedy sets these anxious characters in an equally anxious landscape. The house itself appears fairly ordinary – the walls and furniture suggest any number of realistic plays – but the light and sound that filter through it transform an external world into an internal, private one. Each scene ends in sudden darkness, plunging the characters into such depths that it is always fairly astonishing to see them alive and well in the next scene. The gaps allow Kennedy to make sudden startling transitions, the way dreams and obsessive thinking do. One moment the Beast Girl will be wearing an organdy dress, the next, a torn, stained wedding gown, pulling us back in time with her. The luxury of darkness helps Kennedy pare away everything but key images from the characters' condition. Different qualities of light help intensify the scenes that remain. At one point, the father is caught in a burst of golden light that seems to be both annunciation and accusation – an acknowledgment of his power, but also a reminder of his responsibility. The light brightens and burns him at the same time, before subsiding to a flatness that makes everyone look worn and forgotten. Only rarely does that flatness change.

The violence with which the Dead Human hums a lullaby seems like a protest against this desolation. His rough voice is heard in the interstices of *A Beast Story,* filling the darkness between scenes, seeming to comment on the action in other rooms, rebuking those who try to forget the child. At times, the Beast Man and the Beast Woman sing as well, just as corrosively and usually tunelessly. They sing when their language breaks down, and one more repetition doesn't seem possible – voicing their anguish and anger in the only way they know how, and preventing us from being hypnotized by the "mood" of the memory play.

Occasionally, all speech and song give way to snatches of organ music, returning us to the wedding ceremony, or the funeral, or simply conferring a ceremonial air on these proceedings. But the ceremony is skewed: The organ music sounds distant, as though these are scavenged notes, the only bits of music that managed to drift this far – a sad replica of the stately organ music that would grace more monumental settings or nobler occasions – no consolation.

The patterns of music, gestures, and light, like the repetitions in language, weave this family together – tightly together, to the point of claustrophobia. "I am the accomplice to your fate," says the Beast Man to his daughter.[26] In fact, all the characters are implicated in each other's fate. As they begin to share one another's language, then their light, and echo each other's music with singing of their own, their world grows smaller and smaller. Each character in *A Beast Story* has a room of his or her own, but the rooms constrain them, just as the house as a whole seems inescapable. Unlike Sarah's room in *Funnyhouse*, these are not spaces for liberating fantasy, or for the unfolding of identities forbidden in the outside world. One character's simple gesture triggers gestures in the other three. Nothing happens independently. The Beast Girl's explosion of violence at the end speaks to these frustrations, even though her act "really" takes place before the play begins. Unfortunately, these four don't have any recourse this time; they seem bound to an endless cycle of mutual recrimination. As the play goes on, the air seems to get thinner, the voices more strained, the rooms smaller. The family Kennedy puts onstage this time lets none of its members ever leave – even when they die. If only they were truly capable of devouring themselves, like the family in any good horror movie or well-meaning, "serious" family drama, at least that would bring a sense of relief.

As though she herself needed relief from the same claustrophobia, Kennedy fled to Europe shortly after completing *A Beast Story,* settling in London in 1966. She had been in London before, stopovers on either end of her stay in Africa (brief visits that influenced her most sustained play about her attraction to England – *The Owl Answers*). It was on one of those first trips that she realized London was capable of unlocking something in her that had lain low at home. In her room on Old Brompton Road, on a dark February evening, she could sense that "just beyond that darkness was a completed person, a completed writer, a completed life . . . . The city held a key to my psyche."[27] It was also the source of much of the writing Kennedy loved – the Victorian novels, the modern British poetry – and by coming back again in 1966, Kennedy was taking up residence in a once-forbidden literary history as much as in a city.

In her own writing during these years, Kennedy encountered numerous frustrations. A long play, *Cities in Bezique,* was turned down by the New York Shakespeare Festival. (The producer, Joseph Papp, persuaded Kennedy to use that title for a double bill of *The Owl Answers* and *A Beast Story* instead.) A play she wrote with John Lennon, *The Lennon Play: In His Own Write,* based on his nonsense stories for children, nearly fell apart over artistic differences. (It eventually was produced at the National Theatre in 1968.) *Sun,* also from 1968, is perhaps Kennedy's oddest, most abstract, least personal play; it had a short, forgettable run at the Royal Court Theatre. And she wrote several mystery stories, none of which saw publication. (In 1990, she did publish *Deadly Triplets,* a short mystery novel about her London years.)

The European sojourn was hardly lost time, though. For the first time, Kennedy came to acknowledge the consequences of her constant urge to escape. In her diary of these London years, "A Theatre Journal," Kennedy describes a lunch with the playwright Michael Weller in London shortly after her arrival, during which she complained that wherever she is, she never feels that she belongs. "But is it worth belonging to?" said Weller. Over a year later, another playwright, David Mercer, asked her why she was still in London, especially in 1968, when the American civil-rights movement was at its most exciting. (She couldn't answer.) Finally, she tells of how she listened to the rantings of her deranged next-door neighbor, who kept telling her to "go back to India where you belong." "Perhaps I should go home," she concludes. "And I did."[28]

Kennedy's idea of home, however, was not the comforting nest celebrated in so much American culture. She remembered the entrapment that she felt before leaving for Europe. The London years taught Kennedy to treat all homes as provisional. The only truly comforting place was on the margins, hidden from view. Anything grander left one vulnerable to the claustrophobia of *A Beast Story*. Kennedy dramatized this attraction to the margins, and the unfolding of character possible only there, in *A Movie Star Has to Star in Black and White,* itself a play written in the margins, for Kennedy had been a silent presence in the American theater for the eight years before *Movie Star* opened in 1976.

Movie Star is Kennedy's most openly autobiographical play, but it is also a portrait of Kennedy in flight from herself. Clara, the central character, is a playwright from Ohio, now living in New York and separated from her husband Eddie. (Kennedy had divorced Joe shortly after coming back to the States.) As *Movie Star* opens, Clara has returned to Ohio, because her brother, Wally, has been in a serious car accident and is in a coma. Kennedy's own brother, Cornell, died in a car accident. In many other details, especially the stories of her youth in Ohio and her parents' marriage, Clara's life is almost identical to Kennedy's.

Yet Clara herself doesn't tell us these stories. Kennedy subverts expectations about her autobiographical drama by incorporating movie stars into her play. Actors who look like Bette Davis, Paul Henreid, Jean Peters, Marlon Brando, Montgomery Clift, and Shelley Winters take centerstage and seem to reenact their roles in *Now, Voyager, Viva Zapata,* and *A Place in the Sun*. Behind them, in the shadows, Clara's family enacts its own story: a vigil at Wally's hospital room, awaiting the news from the doctor about possible brain damage. But they rarely tell their own stories, either. As Kennedy notes in a stage direction, "Clara lets her movie stars star in her life."[29]

The stars never actually deliver dialogue from their movies. Instead they take over Clara's ideas and memories, articulating them with the stylishness Clara felt she lacked and often scorned. According to a heroic-looking woman who opens the play (the same figure who appears bathed in light at the start of movies from Columbia Pictures), Clara plays only a bit part. Even this woman, visible again at the end, stands in for Clara, and begins *Movie Star* by describing Kennedy's own experiences in the New York literary set.

Kennedy had experimented with multiple identities before, and here she follows these impulses to their logical conclusion. Clara's identity dilates so much that she nearly vanishes: Her body is rarely present, but her state of mind fills the stage, voiced by all the leading players. Clara escapes her world, but also presides over it. Only by scattering her identity around the stage, projecting herself onto others, is Clara able to see herself. Kennedy makes literal the process every writer goes through – inventing surrogates who reveal the patterns of one's life. "My diaries make me a spectator watching my life," Clara says.[30] Indeed, Clara writes continuously in *Movie Star.* When she reads aloud from her pages, we hear long passages from Kennedy's earlier play, *The Owl Answers.* Not incidentally, that play too presents an image of transformed identity: The girl leaves her troubled life to become an owl, symbol of her mixed parentage, and sits in seclusion, calling "Ow – oww," the only language left to her. The only home available to Clara is writing – her *own* writing.

Perhaps the heaviness of Clara's language – and the story of family strife, divorce, violence – makes it near-impossible for Clara herself to speak it. But at least she can listen. Unburdened of the need to tell her own story, Clara also seems able to move freely through her play. While Jean Peters describes Clara's marriage to Eddie, for instance, Clara herself attends to her brother in the hospital, urging him to get well. Space also opens up – the stage is both hospital lobby and the deck of *Now, Voyager,* Wally's room and a bedroom in *Viva Zapata,* Clara's childhood room and a rowboat from *A Place in the Sun.* There is little actual separation between these spaces; Clara travels between them as though they occupied the same context, as indeed they do – the context of the imagination. "The rooms besiege me," Jean Peters says at one point, voicing the pain of remembering her childhood house.[31] Yet Clara doesn't have to stay anywhere for long in *Movie Star.* Finally, categories of time are also collapsed: Clara takes us to New York in 1955 and Ohio in 1963, to her marriage, her miscarriage, her mother's childhood, and her vigil at her brother's bedside. *Movie Star* contains numerous images of escape or withdrawal – the voyage out in *Now, Voyager,* Clara's divorce, the inward escape of Wally's coma, Dad's talk of suicide, Shelley Winters's drowning in *A Place in the Sun,* and the escapism of the movies themselves, whose romantic music should pervade any production of this play, in ironic counterpoint to its themes. (Like Maria Irene Fornes, Kennedy acknowledges the appeal of romantic experiences, but isn't a romantic herself.) The best demonstration of this hunger for release is *Movie Star*'s very structure: Kennedy frees her entire play from responsibility, lets it escape definitions of place, time, and character soon after it offers them.

In fact, *Movie Star* dramatizes nothing so effectively as the act of writing itself. The loosened context, the multiplicity of voices all emanating from a single consciousness, Clara observing the telling of stories from her life, the sudden leaps from one image to another – all these are familiar characteristics of the composing mind at work. Moreover, *Movie Star* makes explicit the writer's susceptibility to influence, showing how Clara the playwright accepts and transforms her inheritance of other works of art, making them serve her own needs. And when we see Clara scribbling in her notebook, *Movie Star* seems to shape itself in the moment we watch it: Its only plot is the story of its composition.

Kennedy is too thoughtful a writer ever to limit her examination of the writing life to only the formal level, though. Every structural choice in *Movie Star* has an emotional reason. "I get very jealous of you Eddie," Bette Davis says early in the play. "You're doing something with your life."[32] If Clara could do what she wanted with her life, she would spend all her time writing. But, as she says to her mother, Eddie doesn't understand her. If she is to write, she has to leave him and all the enclosed spaces, rigid schedules, and circumscribing contexts for her behavior. Kennedy's liquid dramatic structure offers a way out (and also saves Kennedy from having to make her points in a preachy, mawkish way). As further testament to Clara's success at devising space for her own expression, the male movie stars here are all silent.

Kennedy deflects the drama of *Movie Star* away from the expected places and characters. We hear only secondhand about Eddie's time in Korea or the Father's attempted suicide, but we are *shown* Clara's thoughts about them. The heroic scenes of *Viva Zapata* are passed over in favor of the quiet ones, such as Jean Peters's teaching Zapata to speak English. Most tellingly, Wally's suffering is muted, held in the background, even though he is the pretext that the family uses to gather and go over the past. Wally himself is only visible for part of the second scene before retreating into darkness.

Set among immobile, mute men, Clara testifies to the constant dodge from distraction and the hunt for privacy that characterize Kennedy's own writing life. Wally, Clara tells us, never felt at home anywhere, and so he compulsively changed professions, dropping out and reenrolling at numerous colleges, joining the army, leaving the army, finally working in a hospital, having long abandoned his dream of an athletic career. By writing an image of herself writing, Kennedy staves off that transient fate for herself, and insists on the permanence and hard reality of her own vocation – the only stable aspect of a continuously mutating play.

The slow-moving Kennedy autobiography reaches another chapter by the end of *Movie Star.* Until this play, the character standing in for Kennedy had always been a child. The young Kennedy appears again in *Movie Star,* resurrected in the stories her mother tells, but this is a valedictory visit: Now we are also introduced to Kennedy the adult, the writer. This Kennedy closes the play. Even her last surrogate, Shelley Winters, dies, leaving Clara to confront her grieving mother alone. With Winters gone, the play's world contracts, after being wide and malleable, encompassing many places and people.

In the same way, the store of materials from which Kennedy stocks her theater has gradually been shrinking – with provocative consequences. In the early plays, Kennedy staged her characters' encounters with large segments of history. Sarah shares the stage with Patrice Lumumba and Queen Victoria, "She," from *The Owl Answers,* with Anne Boleyn and William the Conqueror. In *A Lesson in Dead Language,* the students suffer under the stony eyes of Jesus, Mary, and Joseph and the Roman emperors. *An Evening with Dead Essex* (1973), tries (and fails) to stage an event from the news, the police's killing of Mark Essex, a disaffected black ex-sailor who lay siege to a New Orleans Howard Johnson's in 1972. *A Rat's Mass* mixes an intensely private drama – incest – with a horribly public one, the Nazi reign of terror.

In each of these plays, Kennedy's writing and reading self also encounters other artists, and assesses the power of their art – Shakespeare and Chaucer in *The Owl Answers;* Edith Sitwell (whose poetry Sarah tries to emulate) in *Funnyhouse,* and, of course, the seductive cinema actors in *Movie Star.* But *Movie Star* also limits the frame of reference. Outside history isn't present at all. When Winters drowns and the lights go down on the other characters, all other art disappears as well. The only writing present in *Movie Star* is Kennedy's own.

For readers and spectators who have been following Kennedy's work in sequence, some images in *Movie Star* no longer even refer to Kennedy's childhood, but instead connect this play only to her others, emphasizing the other modes of contraction in Kennedy's theater. When Jean Peters stains her clothes with blood and Marlon Brando pulls black sheets out from under her, we're reminded of *A Lesson in Dead Language,* in which schoolgirls stain their white dresses with menstrual blood. As in all of Kennedy's plays, the chain of linked images in *Movie Star* is extensive: Jean's bleeding (and Clara's miscarriage) echo Wally's own bleeding; these in turn echo Dad's longing for death, and all join up finally with the death in *A Place in the Sun.* But instead of expanding the play's reach, here such a chain circumscribes it, intensifying our attention on one event alone: Kennedy writing the play, forging the links in the chain, then hooking them together. The "Black and White" in the title is really the black ink on the white typing paper.

The events described on those pages, after all, are never the point, not even the most enthralling, the most dramatic in themselves, like Clara's experience of rape or Sarah's suicide. Kennedy's theatricality resides in the process of telling and showing, not in the things told or shown. We are meant to ask, How does this process of speaking affect the characters? What parts of the story seem difficult to tell? What parts do they breeze through so easily that we're left doubting the story's completeness or veracity, wondering what is withheld? These kinds of questions preoccupy careful viewers and readers of Kennedy's drama, not What will happen next? or Can you believe she went through that?

This inversion of expectation is best demonstrated in Kennedy's variation on the mystery story: *The Ohio State Murders* (1991), her next major play. Here, a writing woman occupies even more imaginative space than in *Movie Star,* no longer confined to the margins, and at times this play is as harrowing as anything Kennedy has written to date. It is the only one of Kennedy's plays that actually tells a story: Suzanne Alexander is a successful playwright invited back to her alma mater, Ohio State University, to lecture on "the violent imagery in my work." In the course of preparing for her speech, she recalls her unhappy years as a student and her eventual withdrawal. It seems that she had an affair with her white English professor, Robert Hampshire; much anxiety and twin girls had resulted. One day, one of the girls was kidnapped; her corpse was later found in a ravine on campus. A hunt for the killer ensued, leading nowhere until he struck again, breaking into Suzanne's home, killing the other twin and himself. The newspapers never let on that it was Hampshire himself who murdered his own children.

My telling of the story is far more melodramatic than Kennedy's. I waited until the end to reveal the killer's identity, like any decent whodunit writer. Kennedy names him relatively early, midway through the play and before we've even heard all the details of the kidnapping. The *new* mystery now asks how the recollection, forty years later, will affect Suzanne. We watch a younger incarnation of Suzanne – college age – flicker through the play, reenacting the stories, but the dramatic focus is not on her alone nor on her action. Kennedy directs us to the relationship between the older and younger Suzanne. Her true subject is the tension of facing yourself.

Kennedy also leaves out the expected scenes of confrontation between Suzanne and Hampshire, thus scorning another source of ready-made drama. We never see scenes of mutual recrimination, Hampshire urging Suzanne to give up the children, say, or Suzanne asking for assistance, Hampshire and Suzanne calling it off, and all the other staples of affairs gone wrong. Their lives rarely intersect, and Kennedy refuses to emphasize the few points of contact they do have. (We learn after the fact about their intimacy.) Far from muting the drama of the play, however, Kennedy's choice makes the anxiety all the more oppressive, for it lacks an escape valve. The ordeal remains private, sunk deep within the characters.

The Ohio State Murders is literally sunk underground. Suzanne prepares for her lecture in the "O" level of the campus library, several stories beneath street level. On this winter night, the library feels like a tomb, no one here but Suzanne. Once again, a Kennedy character occupies a world of literature, embraces the security of books. But at crucial moments in the narrative, the books seem to recede, leaving Suzanne with only her notes to clutch and study over and over.

This gothic setting is only one of several locations in Suzanne's story that carry considerable emotional power and meanings beyond their apparent ones. Places allude to customs, modes of behavior, rules and regulations, history and morality. "When I visited Ohio State last year," Suzanne says at the opening, "it struck me as a series of disparate dark landscapes . . . . The geography made me anxious."[33] *The Ohio State Murders* is as much about the attempt to master that geography and assuage that anxiety as it is about the tragic events that took place there. In this respect, Kennedy's play extends her powerful theatricalization of Bachelard's ideas. He concludes *The Poetics of Space* with a discussion of what he calls "intimate immensity" – how vast exterior spaces can help map comparably uncharted internal spaces: "The exterior spectacle," he writes, "helps intimate grandeur unfold."[34] Kennedy has said that the idea for *The Ohio State Murders* came to her when she happened to be in San Francisco during the 1989 earthquake. The ruined landscape led her to consider disrupted psychological space, to ask "where am I?" in interior as well as exterior sites.

Like a wanderer lost in an enormous desert, a person engaged in the intense consideration of a recollected or dreamed image eventually suffers a merging of psychological and geographical space. The spirit "drifts," Bachelard suggests. The mind "loses its geometrical homeland." In language that perfectly describes the phantasmagoric quality of Kennedy's theater, Bachelard quotes Henri Michaux's definition of geographical space experienced under these conditions as a "horrible inside-outside."[35] As in the more desolate paintings of Giorgio de Chirico, whose spirit informs much of *The Ohio State Murders,* the huge scale of a place forces one to acknowledge shadings of panic or despair that may never before have made themselves felt. The vulnerable figures in de Chirico's paintings seem to run from more than just the large abandoned piazzas. They also seek cover from the onrush of all the buried memories of abandonment, exposure, and humiliation in various other, unrelated contexts, from childhood on. The arcades in which they hide reveal new fears, though, and elicit a range of memories (of other hunted states, of forced furtiveness) and an accompanying psychological terror that have their own considerable force. Eventually, as Bachelard concludes, one must try to "put all space outside, in order that meditating being might be free to think."[36] Perhaps this conviction helps explain why Suzanne takes refuge in the bowels of the library, far beneath the walkways and buildings that once tormented her.

In the 1950s, place was often defined by race: Suzanne recalls the "lawn behind the dorm where the white girls sunned"; Mrs. Tyler's boardinghouse in the Negro District; High Street, where black students didn't dare walk; the segregated dining room; the English department, where an unspoken law kept away black students. Before *The Ohio State Murders,* the submerged meanings of places in Kennedy's plays have usually been just familial: the room where father died, the house of insistent adolescent memories. Now, place acquires social, political value as well. In *The Ohio State Murders,* the younger Suzanne finds a passage in one of her schoolbooks that articulates the operating ethic of the play and the life within it: "A city should have a sacred geography never arbitrary but planned in strict accord with the dictates of a doctrine that the society upholds."[37]

Sacred isn't too strong a word. The places through which this play moves – never literally, of course – all seem consecrated, as though Kennedy and her surrogate narrator were preserving them from misuse by those ignorant or cavalier about the landscape's history, or from the certain decay that follows neglect. Like all sacred territories, they are resistant to efforts at habitation, no matter how dogged. But they also have secular uses: Ordinary-looking knolls, parking lots, and classrooms have become *evidence.* Suzanne finds images of personal dilemmas in the very landscape. The horizons overwhelm her with their air of conspiracy, as though they possessed essential information about herself that has long been withheld. When Suzanne seeks relief from this taunting, or some kind of wisdom in hindsight about her youth, she addresses her inquiries to the places themselves, as though they could explain the significance of events they enclosed. Suzanne at one point refers to the "language of the landscape."[38] *The Ohio State Murders* shows the course of learning to speak that language.

The effort is full of frustration. Just as a fiercely classifying archeologist never succeeds in recapturing a lost city's spirit with his immense grids, so too with Suzanne. Yet her knowledge of her limitations doesn't dissuade her from trying: She maps her remembered campus with language, recreating all the dimensions of her life, the lines connecting and separating people, the distances spanned to achieve a goal or flee a fear. Suzanne retraces for us the route she took to English class, then the look of the quonset hut in which it took place. We learn where her dorm is, the names of the other dorms, and what route someone could take to get to campus from the train station. Even though she may never understand the secrets of individual places, she defines those relationships with great care, as though an accurate orientation would steel her against the disorienting process of remembering – and against the pain. Our awareness of that pain makes her craze for details seem less mindless, less gratuitous. By mapping the world and placing herself in the map, public spaces that were once painful to visit, carrying with them restrictions or prejudices, are at last made familiar, if never hers.

Suzanne's sense of the charged meanings of landscape is confirmed by the books she reads, or rather remembers reading as a student. Hampshire teaches *Tess of the d'Urbervilles,* and the lyrical places of Wessex excite young Suzanne with visions of romantic intrigue. The *Tale of King Arthur* introduces her to the "Abyss" – and the landscape of death. All of these become alternative environments for Suzanne. Even though they are no more open to her than those of Ohio State, and in the end no more decipherable, they nonetheless serve as a kind of guide to her own world. As Hampshire takes his class through the symbolism of places in fiction, Suzanne is able to assign symbols to her own world. The quonset hut is lost virtue, the dorm room is guilt, the campus Oval suggests Hampshire's denial of responsibility. If such symbolic readings do not ease the pain, they at least make it nobler.

Young Suzanne is often getting lost in Ohio State's maze of streets and impersonal, cookie-cutter buildings. That confusion has its own symbolic electricity. Although it is never mentioned, the text beneath all of *The Ohio State Murders* is *The Scarlet Letter.* Hawthorne's drear forest, where Dimmesdale and Hester lose their way, becomes Kennedy's wintry campus. As in Hawthorne, the panic of getting lost underscores psychic confusion, as characters move deeper and deeper into the consequences of their own actions. Each step forward and each attempt to leave only confirms the imprisonment in their own history of behavior.

Suzanne's monologue resembles nothing so much as a long journey into that forest. She eventually emerges, of course, but is not renewed in any way. She's exhausted more than healed. The pain doesn't subside, even forty years later; if anything, Suzanne demonstrates, it spreads itself over everything she touches and everywhere she goes, leaving among other traces the violent imagery in her writing. Kennedy's writing style changes substantially in *The Ohio State Murders* to express this pervasiveness. Identity no longer fragments as inventively as it did in her earlier plays: The two Suzannes are merely young and older versions of the same realistically conceived woman. Moreover, the point of view is held insistently on Suzanne alone. Despite the flashbacks, we never lose sight of the adult Suzanne sitting centerstage, describing what we're seeing behind her, or thinking about what to say next. Suzanne's fascination with the minute aspects of her life (at one point she speaks of examining her pores in a magnifying glass) becomes ours.

In performance, the intensity of that focus is especially strong. Kennedy's structural formality constantly vies with her character's emotional turmoil – in a manner that reminds one of French neoclassical tragedy. The proscenium catches and frames Suzanne; the monologue seems to stretch on and on; the burden of telling seems impossible to sustain; the endurance of the actor, with no activity to distract her from the sole task of sitting before us and speaking her history, challenges spectators to maintain their own attentiveness. Only rarely does the long leisurely line of Kennedy's style break off – replaced with a shocking staccato when the pressure of events overwhelms her reportorial control: One sentence ends with "rooms, stains, color, skin" – a telegraphic message encompassing the entire play.[39] And occasionally Kennedy shows Suzanne unable to stop herself from getting ahead of the story – referring to the murders in the first minutes of the play, then forcing herself back to the orderly schedule of telling, Suzanne saying simply, "that was later," in order to regain control – harnessing time for fear of getting trampled by it. But most of the time Suzanne maintains a generous detachment – generous with details, sincerely wanting to communicate, but protecting herself from new anguish with deliberate detachment. *The Ohio State Murders* is so disturbing in performance precisely because of this disjunction: Suzanne's tone remains muted, unsurprised, despite the awfulness of what she describes, just as the college setting is tranquil and stately, at odds with the atrocity it witnessed.

The question remains, Why speak about these trips at all? Why does Suzanne return to the past and so exhaustively describe it? The ostensible reason – she was asked to explain the source of the violent imagery in her work – doesn't explain anything, for the experiences she describes are unanswerable, immured against interpretation, just like the haunted sites of Ohio State University. One feels that Suzanne would have felt compulsion to speak whether or not she was asked; after all, she has been addressing these experiences in her writing ever since she left college. But Kennedy, perhaps unintentionally, does show another reason for her own autobiographical writing. By linking the murders at Ohio State with her subsequent plays, Suzanne assuages her pain: The murders now belong to the history of her *writing,* not just the history of her *life.* The murders cut off Suzanne's identity as a mother, but they also led to the creation of her writing identity. *The Ohio State Murders* begins and ends with a reference to Suzanne's vocation, and it's an investigation into vocation that Suzanne conducts before us: what lay behind the work, not what lay behind the life. Suzanne composes a biography of writing, not an autobiography of self. Sometimes one can only stand to talk about the writing, letting it lead the way back to the life.

Kennedy has published fifteen plays in all, but only a handful of those are as richly imagined as the four I've discussed here. Some of the others are earnest failures, exchanging the probing examination of the private life for a vague look at bigger fields. Kennedy's one foray into openly political theater – *An Evening with Dead Essex* – is little more than a brisk mourning ceremony, with boilerplate paeans to "freedom" filling space better used for a more specific show of grief. Kennedy's *Sun* shares the technique of character fragmentation with her other plays, but here the environment is a meaningless outer space, the character a mere everyman. The play seems more a demonstration of technique than an evoked state of mind. Kennedy's adaptations from the early 1980s – *Electra* and *Orestes* – testify to her fascination with families under siege and suggest other lines of literary influence; but, again, they lack the urgency that would make them memorable theater.

Kennedy's best work, work that makes it easy to overlook her lapses, never strives to reach a world larger than her own. (It invariably does reach far, because of that restraint.) Kennedy has spoken of how long it takes her to write a play, and how persistent are the habits formed during the many years she was censoring her own work. Her natural self-effacement – and a real fear of the outside world – also conspire to limit the work she's able to complete. She has spoken about how important have been the long stretches of not working in the theater at all: time spent taking notes and writing in her diary, reading, and letting ideas accrue until she has enough material to begin sculpting a new play. That process is every writer's, of course, but with Kennedy the schedule is stretched even longer, the gaps even wider between experiencing something, then recognizing the experience, and finally feeling ready to transform the experience and all the emotion attending it into theater. The stillness between periods of writing is as important to Kennedy as the stillness between utterances in her plays.

Despite Kennedy's announced discomfort under the glare of light – the public world of theater – she seems even more afraid of the dark. The plays she finishes, at least those that come from the deepest personal zones of her imagination, are safe harbors. Each signifies one more battle won, one more fear addressed, another part of her upsetting private history vanquished, at least for a while longer. In her best plays, she's able to enclose and organize all the images contending for attention during those long spells of darkness. An admirer of Wordsworth, Kennedy is nonetheless unable to "recollect in tranquillity" – but, like Suzanne Alexander, when she displays what has been gathered, she demonstrates preternatural calm.

Kennedy's *Sun,* despite its flaws, does end with a chilling image that suggests this balancing act. A man's body breaks apart; limbs fly through the air; planets go into crazed orbit; blood pours from the sky; the light intensifies in great blinding flashes; and finally the man disappears entirely. Just before the darkness, after his body has already vanished, we hear his voice:

> And a castle on a hill
> flowering rushes.
> I still[40]

It's a strange blossoming of lyricism in the midst of apocalypse; even stranger is the last line. Two meanings of "I still" seem apt: "I *am* still," quiet at last; and "I endure" – I am still here. The tranquillity comes as a relief, but it doesn't seem trustworthy. At any moment, another explosion could rock the stage. In fact, the stillness appears the most terrifying thing about the play: the intimation of turmoil as yet unseen, causing more anxiety than the sound-and-light show just ended. But the vision of endurance is also persuasive – I am still here. Not only still here, but able to make a simple, touching lyric, too: the castle on the hill, the rushes. The body may disperse, but the voice survives it, as does the imagination. The voice carries over the din of cataclysm, as if reluctant to stop sounding. (It surely isn't accidental that Kennedy withheld the period from the last line.)

The voice also returns us to Kennedy's stillness, her endurance. Quietly writing, she, too, is still here, making quiet spaces after the cacophony in her mind has subsided. Nothing sentimental in such survival, Kennedy warns: Only in that stillness is her endurance possible. Perhaps she wouldn't be able to see herself, her sole subject, as clearly were she not so neglected by the theater community. "The rooms are my rooms," says Sarah in *Funnyhouse,* "I try to create a space for myselves in cities." And Kennedy creates a space for herself in our culture. We read and watch Kennedy's plays knowing that she barely needs our company. Her plays serve her purposes well even without an audience. We are like passersby who stop to press our faces up against the windows of her house and look at the goings-on indoors without anyone noticing we're there. Few theater experiences are so compelling for being so humbling.

6

RICHARD FOREMAN

AMONG ADMIRERS OF RICHARD FOREMAN, there have long been a proud, possessive few who resist letting critics call him a playwright. A "play" is too ordinary or convenient a label, they say, for the kind of measured frenzy Foreman creates on stage. How can an event that mixes relentlessly philosophic dialogue, sudden bursts of noise and light, constant music, and the quirkiest of movement – all set within a densely decorated room and presided over by the man who wrote, directed, and designed it – be blithely summed up as a mere drama? Thornton Wilder wrote "dramas," August Wilson and Marsha Norman write them; but Richard Foreman? Foreman creates "pieces," they insist, "works" that have wound up in the theater almost by accident.

The protective admirers have a point. After all, Foreman *is* different, is that rare theater artist who carries on a lively dialogue with the other arts, and also with theology, literary criticism, and art theory; and his work does challenge a spectator's attention to a degree unknown in other quarters of the contemporary theater. But he is a writer, too, even a writer first and foremost, in spite of all the mesmerizing splendor of his productions. His texts can be read and reread; they can be analyzed; they can even be staged by other enterprising directors (and some have already tried).

In fact, when the twenty-six plays Foreman has published are read together, they constitute a long, often anxious investigation into writing itself. Few playwrights are as concerned with the dynamics and implications of the writing act, few as ready to conduct such ruthless self-assessment, as is Foreman. The events of his plays, the obscure doings of the even more obscure characters, are primarily instruments with which he can work his way into what really interests him: how the vague propositions of the imagination garb themselves in language and travel onto the page, assuming permanent shape as writing. The staging that comes later, as he has said, is really an extension of the writing process. When he sits in rehearsal and observes his actors take tentative first steps through the text, speaking what he has written, he's able to revisit the original site of writing, where he first heard these words in his mind and shaped them into drama. Speaking, writing, listening, and all the physical movement and activity of the senses associated with using language – these are the "subjects" of Foreman's drama, if subjects need to be named. Which is to say that a play by Foreman is a play *of* Foreman, about him and his idiosyncratic way of perceiving – a mirror held up not to life, but to himself.

The Foreman persona is worn by all his characters, so that to watch or read his plays is to feel enveloped by the author and the spectacle of him at work, rather than by any story he might tell or fictive world he might be able to conjure. That persona is neurotic, erudite, self-conscious, dry; those wearing it find their pleasure in toying with intellectual conundrums, savoring random perceptions or sensations, or allowing themselves lazily to follow the wanderings of their minds. Foreman's plays are really maps of the perambulations taken by his own mind, records of how it absorbed and obeyed the injunction to write yet another play.

One might expect that such self-absorption would lead to myopic, mustily hermetic theater. Admittedly, there is a cloistered feeling to even his most ebullient work, and in recent years he has pushed closer to chamber theater; but Foreman remains a humanist at heart, and readers who allow themselves to be lured into his perceiving mind shouldn't feel claustrophobic. Curious and restless, Foreman often resembles a great field of sensation, a receiver of data from the outside world, a magnetic pole, a sponge or vessel. He's also a human being in that field, tuning that receiver, and his fallible humanity always comes through stronger than any mechanical aspect of his work. Reading him, we ponder the myriad things he ponders and then deliberately get a long view of him pondering them, a dividend only unconsciously acquired when reading most other drama, and rarely so revelatory. For all its seeming intellectuality, Foreman's theater is among the most personal ever made – almost excruciatingly personal, which may account for the difficulties it has had in achieving broad recognition.

As a hovering presence in all his plays, Foreman makes sure that his discourse about writing is never *just* about writing. Foreman's plays aren't position papers, despite their theoretical richness; they are portraits of an artist, and so can be exemplary, instructive. Foreman shows us how he lives his life, and he expects us to examine our own lives in return. He spends his days writing, and reflecting on writing – but that vocation brings him face to face with large questions about his place in the world and the style in which he has chosen to travel through it. When Foreman speaks critically of "narrative," for instance, he hopes we'll think about similar notions such as control, or our relationship to time, or the dangers of streamlining a complicated world. When he meditates on "character," we shouldn't need nudging to look at "personality" and the roles played by fate, choice, and our relationships with others in the forming of our sense of self. The fun he has meddling with stage space, breaking up our field of view and clogging it with disparate objects, will seem only whimsical unless we let ourselves speculate on questions of home, of passivity, of the pleasure and good health that can come from alertness. Foreman's plays can be rewarding even if such connections are not made, for they do carry on a marvelously witty argument with art history. But one of Foreman's sovereign subjects is interpretation – the ways in which we imprint our identity on the experience passing through us – and we cheat ourselves of his plays' full impressiveness if we think about them only in formal terms and don't carry them with us out of the theater.

One's first encounter with a play by Richard Foreman is bound to be dizzying and infuriating, depositing one either in exhilaration or depression. On the page, Foreman's plays appear conventional enough. There are speakers with names; they talk in complete sentences, and the sentences are invariably intelligible. "I'm dizzy," someone might say, or "All I can think about is her body." As these two snippets show, the dialogue often calls up precise psychological states – fear, sexual desire, joy, anger. *Speakers,* in other words, have the makings of *characters.* And characters have the wherewithal to participate in stories: They often arrange themselves in couples, romantic or merely friendly; and in rivalries, too. For the first moments of a typical Foreman play, the mélange of dialogue and movement seems on the verge of coalescing into narrative. A character named Rhoda sidles up to Sophia, seeking her guidance. Leo and Ben commiserate about their sufferings under Hannah's seductions. Max sits still amid his friends' swirling flirtations and imprecations, proud of his despair. At first glance, the figures are so distinctive that it seems but a matter of minutes before they will lead the way through their beguiling world, pointing out the shape of mysteries, teaching their language, their shared codes of conduct. For a few early moments, they seem knowable – difficult and mercurial, but knowable.

Foreman even is generous with his stage directions, providing us with all those accoutrements that should reassure us of his text's essential playness. He notes where speakers pause, or where they laugh. He establishes the look of the room; he explains how figures move through it; he breaks acts up into scenes, and scores those scenes with considerable sensitivity to such textbook notions as the "arc" of a scene, "conflict," and "denouement." So why doesn't all of this add up to what we've come to call a "play"?

The flip, but true, answer is that Foreman won't add. The individual pieces of his texts are intelligible to anyone, but read in sequence or followed in the enforced linear time of performance, they refuse to correspond to accepted ideas of the completed work. The arrangements of narrative elements seem too random; there are so many details to notice that making even a plot summary is a daunting task; the tangents proliferate too much; ideas are raised, but never followed through, or at least not where we expect to find them; characters don't "grow" or "change" in readily apparent ways, if at all. In *Total Recall,* for instance, a scene of some twenty lines filling half a page addresses the following matters and displays the following events, in blithe succession: Sophia's body disappears into air; Sophia falls out of bed, because the bed tilted; she pretends to have a "real" body; Hannah detects perfume; Hannah hears music; Leo presents his lamp; Leo gets shot but doesn't get frightened; Sophia rebukes Leo for trying to touch her; Leo tries to understand just how Sophia's body could be like her mind; Leo decides to get dressed, then, finally, he is thrown out the window.[1]

Each event or utterance in this scene dislocates the one that precedes it; each sentence or gesture asserts its own priority, rearranges the scene around itself, directs our attention onto itself as strongly as it can, and radiates with an intensity that can only be achieved by an artist willing to dispose of the image or phrase after it has appeared. Foreman doesn't use lines of dialogue as linking devices, cogs in a plot machine that are meaningful only when they keep the story going. He prizes the shape and sensuality of each item on his dramatic list, and gives each a place all its own. Then he lets them go, unsentimental about their passing, elated, in fact, that he has fashioned a theater where nothing lasts because everything has been thoroughly present – one at a time, for one moment only – spoken and enacted with such commitment that we eventually learn to listen and watch with equal diligence. When Foreman is at his best, each moment of his plays is importunate but also confident, gracefully showing off with savage insistence.

The pleasures of such passionate encounters with the text have their price. Even the most experienced readers of Foreman have trouble remembering his plays as specifically as, say, they might recall *The Glass Menagerie* or even looser assemblages like Sam Shepard's *The Tooth of Crime* or Robert Wilson's *Einstein on the Beach.* The general "feel" of Foreman's world stays with us – the aggrieved weariness in *Total Recall;* the sexual intemperance in *Rhoda in Potatoland;* the lonesome, pensive reticence of *What Did He See?* – but, except for one or two residual moments, all the actions and conversations that created those moods float out of our consciousness, before we learn how to hold them down. Foreman is delighted, he has said, by our forgetfulness. For such dissolution is proof of our rapt attention in the moment of enactment and of the utter, totally expended presence of each delicately designed minute of his play. Foreman infuriates some of his readers for precisely this kind of disappearing act: They feel that they're not getting their money's worth, or not being treated well in exchange for putting in such strenuous time with the work – it doesn't let them get intimate as quickly as they're used to with other plays. Foreman makes it hard even for those who have the text in front of them to become involved in the traumas and triumphs of individual characters, to follow everyone's trajectory through the play to the end, or even to grow accustomed to the tenor of a speaker's language. Scenes sometimes pass into oblivion just at the point of their greatest fascination, where they've perfected their special allure, and readers are left with only their own raised expectations. Foreman keeps deferring conventional ideas of coherence in the hope that spectators will move past their confusion, past even their rage at the confusion, and start looking toward themselves for satisfaction.

A night at Foreman's theater or with his texts is always somewhat somber and, no matter how busy or funny his scenes may be, a little lonely. Those who do the work needed to assess each theatrical moment as it passes often find themselves narrowing and sharpening their senses so radically that much detritus of the world outside the play fades away. Foreman's theater – which began as an interrogation with himself, about his writing – urges its viewers and readers toward their own self-interrogations. He creates sanctioned ground for his mind's work, and as we read or watch, we enter into our own quarantine. The experience of his theater at its most potent, most crystalline, is gloriously solitary, a communion between art and auditor, a rigorously spiritual, private dalliance.

The religious overtones may sound out of place when discussing a writer so closely identified with the ironic, disillusioned avant-garde; and any hint of a spiritual dimension may disappoint those audiences bewitched by his theater's baroque splendor, its obsessive materialism. Encountering a skeptical interviewer, Foreman has said he has *always* been a closet religious writer, but until lately he wouldn't admit it out of shyness and an understanding of how easily such private impulses are cheapened.[2] As one reads more and more Foreman, however, it gets harder to set aside the mystical qualities of his theater. In fact, it may be easier for resistant readers to enter his dramatic world in the same state of mind they would bring to an evening spent reading philosophy or gnomic aphorisms, a sacred text like the Cabala, or, preeminently, a poem; that is, to open his book of plays with a cleared mind, the special talent for patience that all contemplation requires, a limber imagination able to make associations when they are called for (and not to force them when simple beholding is more appropriate), an ear for the rhythms beneath rhythms, and an ease in achieving an essential paradox: detached intimacy with the object of one's affection.

Foreman has long encouraged readers to bring to his theater an understanding of modern poetry; when asked about influences he refers to Wallace Stevens, the "Language" poets, or esoteric recent enthusiasms like Zanzotto from Italy, Sweden's Ekelund, and the Rumanian Lucian Blaga. Gertrude

Stein is one of the few playwrights still on his list (and here, we'll see, the relationship is long and profound); he confesses to not going to the current theater much. The difficulty in placing Foreman in a theatrical landscape is vexing to many readers, especially those charged with explicating him: How can we account for him, it's often said, if we cannot compare him to a colleague? How else to anchor him, to make his theater conform to a pattern, or consciously depart from one; how else, finally, to make it *mean* something other than itself? But it's precisely this self-sufficiency that defines Foreman's drama: He writes willful, marooned plays, plays that turn in on themselves, and then inward once more.

For all his contemplativeness, Foreman doesn't eschew everything in the outside world. On the contrary, it's a continuously fascinating place whose temptations and pressures he often engages, if only to battle them more seriously. But he has his priorities straight: Before addressing the world, he addresses himself. How do *I* function when all external influences are stripped away? he asks, only later asking how he might function in a variety of contexts.

In *The Art of Poetry*, Paul Valéry envisions a type of poet who uncannily resembles Richard Foreman:

> I imagined myself as a swimmer, cut off from all that is solid, let loose in the fullness of the water, and surrounded by an absence of obstacles, who thus acquires a sense of the forms and limits of his strength, from the center of his defined powers to their farthest reach. All I desired was the ability to act, not its exercise in the world.[3]

Foreman's theater is his swimming pool, where each play is an occasion to flex his muscles and test his ability to stay afloat in consciousness, moving through its density. Foreman doesn't learn about himself only, though. As he swims, he discovers much about the qualities of art. He's able to separate his own notions of playwriting from those of others, and to speculate on what might be the essential aspects of the form. He's also able to turn those elements to his own peculiar uses, and not worry about the propriety of what he's doing. "Propriety," and its cousins "relevance" and "verisimilitude," no longer matter to a swimmer "cut off from all that is solid" other than himself.

Foreman is in pursuit of an understanding of theater akin to Valéry's definition of "pure" poetry:

> Every time words show a *certain deviation* from the most direct, that is, the most *insensible* expression of thought, every time these deviations foreshadow, as it were, a world of relationships distinct from the purely practical world, we conceive more or less precisely the possibility of enlarging this exceptional domain . . . .[4]

Elsewhere, Valéry describes the poetic universe as a place where "resonance triumphs over causality, and 'form,' far from dissolving into its effects, is as it were *recalled* by them. The Idea claims its voice."[5] Prose, he insists, always enforces the utilitarian aspects of language, the ways in which words have to stick to things; ideas must be planted at the scene of events; sentences are always marshaled into the service of subject matter. But poetry is free of all such responsibility (if it chooses), and so can delve deeper and span further. Language in "pure" poetry isn't ruled by exigencies of logic or history or other coercive narratives; it can linger over moments of experience, probe obscure regions of behavior, landscape, or emotion without worrying about impatient riders of one's plot; or it can stay on the surface, enamored of designs, assonances, rhythms, tones that are rich or flat, sharp or supple.

Foreman's language isn't especially poetic, as such – there's little of the exquisite shapeliness of line that we come to expect from a poem. But Foreman does have a poetic temperament, and he makes liberal use of the privileges it affords him. He embraces Valéry's idea of "uselessness" and insists that his language won't be just a means to a more responsible end, meriting praise only for its unobtrusiveness. He lets his writing mind lounge amid his speakers and their setting, and toys with ideas and subjects, considering them from all sides, writing down whatever most interests him, even if it wouldn't seem particularly important or symbolic to an outsider. Theories of poetry give Foreman the luxury of starting from scratch as a writer; he can return to essentials – language, gestures, silences, conditions, the very aura or glow of a play – and ponder them as obsessively as he wishes. By aligning himself with poets rather than dramatists he is able to make a theater of his own, shaped to his own needs, desires, and peculiarities, a theater that moves at his own pace. "I wish that when you went to the theater and something interested you, you could just call out, 'Wait a minute! Let me go out for a drink and think about that for a while, and then I'll come back and you can continue.' Or even better," Foreman goes on, "I wish I could figure out a way to make a play that you could just have in your house, so you could relate to it as to a book."[6]

Foreman's taste and principles left him with little choice but to make a theater of his own. He had attended the Yale Drama School in the late fifties where, under the guidance of John Gassner, he learned how to turn out the suave, droll plays that occupied his energies for much of the sixties – what Foreman calls his "Murray Schisgal period."[7] But few of those plays were ever produced, and he spent most of his early years in New York out of the theater and rarely in the company of playwrights or directors. Foreman took up residence in the avant-garde film world, loitering around the director Jonas Mekas and helping him establish the Cinematheque, a center for alternative film. His friendships with underground filmmakers led him to painters and sculptors, choreographers and composers, and before long he was breathing the hothouse atmosphere of the late-sixties New York art world – a world that was fiercely theoretical, charged with the desire to break with the past, serious about reassessing the capacities of each medium, finding the "truth" of paint or steel, sound or celluloid, the human body in motion. It didn't take long for Foreman to break decisively with his theatrical inheritance and begin writing more independently, letting himself be affected only by nontheatrical forces. When his plays were ready, he didn't seek out producers by knocking on Off-Broadway doors; he asked Mekas to let him use the Cinematheque for a few nights, and in 1968 Foreman's private theater was born. He ended up having to do almost everything himself – designing, directing, producing, composing, choreographing, rustling up the nonactors (who were more malleable than professionals), being the technical man and the house manager. Immediately he realized he preferred things that way.

Foreman called his self-made, one-man organization the Ontological-Hysteric Theater, a name that in itself suggests how far he had moved from the rest of the theater world. Here, the name trumpeted, was drama that meditates on matters philosophical and psychological, drama concerned with fundamentals of being and feeling more than mere characters or intrigues. Another recurring concern – the yen for alternative worlds more attuned to the spiritual dimension – found voice in the title of Foreman's inaugural Ontological-Hysteric play: *Angelface,* a play in which, according to Foreman, the seeds of all his later work can be found.

Since poets take care with the selection of each word, since filmmakers study behavior in terms of individual frames, and since dancers worry about the precise arching of their backs and angling of their arms as they follow an immutable pace, shouldn't a playwright then also begin with small units of dramaturgy, building his play up from basics, as though language and styles of movement were suddenly new and unfamiliar to him? Foreman has likened himself to Kaspar Hauser, confronted with an art form about which he suddenly knows nothing, exploring it sometimes tentatively, sometimes clumsily, getting oriented. "I didn't want to write in a language that reflected all the cotton candy, the sweets I'd inherited from my culture, including all the art I'd been exposed to in the theater. I wanted to go back . . . to the beginning cells of consciousness."[8]

Angelface became a thoroughgoing exploration of the original element in any theatrical event: the body. Foreman uses the dramatic form to ask a deceptively simple question: What is presence? What does it feel like to be onstage? To look at someone on a stage? To be next to someone on a stage? What happens when you move on that stage – or when you speak from it, or touch someone else standing near you? Foreman has traced this fascination with physicality to his own ambivalence about his school-taught ability to make characters glide through stories as though on clouds, free of bones and flesh and inhibitions. The strange surreality of characters speaking without hesitation, moving without awkwardness, feeling without thinking first, thinking without battling emotion – all this Foreman set aside, and chose instead to "radicalize my personal stress," as he put it, "to reground the language, only registering what was physically present to my consciousness as I was writing it." He broke the habit of falling into reverence to ideas and put himself in the service of the "sensations going on in the body."[9]

Foreman's attitude recalls Rilke's definition of the "sayable" in *The Sonnets to Orpheus*:

> Praise this world to the angel, not the unsayable one,
> you can't impress *him* with glorious emotion; in the universe
> where he feels more powerfully, you are a novice. So show him
> something simple which, formed over generations,
> lives as our own, near our hand and within our gaze
> Tell him of Things.[10]

Writing about the *Sonnets* to a friend, Rilke explained his search for purity in utterance: "Any 'allusion,' I am convinced, would contradict the indescribable *presence* of the poem."[11] In *Angelface,* Foreman begins his search for the same elusive presence.

Angelface begins by refusing to begin. True to his word, Foreman takes nothing for granted about the theatrical event, and starts his play by analyzing the dynamics of the simplest action – the entrance. Max is sitting onstage alone. A door opens, revealing Walter, who stands at the threshold unable to come into the room.

> MAX: (*Finally he laughs once.*) The door opens. I don't even turn my head.
> WALTER: Does it turn?
> MAX: What?
> WALTER: (*Laughs once*) Heads turn.
> MAX: Heads turn. My head is a head. Therefore: my head turns. (*Silence. He smiles.*) Open the door a second time.
> WALTER: Why?
> MAX: Find out if my head turns.
> WALTER: I can't.
> MAX: What?
> WALTER: An opened door cannot be opened.
> MAX: All doors can be opened!
> WALTER: (*After a pause. No one moves a muscle.*) All right. I'm staring at it. Staring at it is opening it a second time.

MAX: (*Low.*) What is: opening it a third time.
WALTER: (*Turns his head once. Pause.*) . . . A third time, a fourth time, a fifth time – [12]

The scene goes on much like this for several pages, as Walter and Max scrutinize their encounter, figuring out just what changes when solitude must give way to companionship. They engage in hearty self-narration, announcing the way they feel and the things they see. They argue themselves into place, as though they believe that speech makes being there real at last. Walter tells about his "flexible eyes"; Max says his own are "beautiful," as are (he assures us) his hands and ears. Walter describes how his head can turn in all directions, and how he could walk backwards, if he wanted to. They speak of trembling hands and extended legs, vibrating ears and beating hearts; they begin to understand the differences between holding and gripping, kicking and pushing, seeing and visualizing, entering and intruding. Soon characters named Agatha and Rhoda, Weinstein and Karl, and a double for Walter (Walter II) join in, and Foreman expands his spoken choreography among numerous combinations of body parts. The stage is quickly filled with the sound of people talking about bodies that quiver, droop, shudder, jolt, thud, flop, sag, explode, freeze, jiggle, pant, roll around, bang together, stumble, wheeze, rise up, and gently laugh. The characters don't always do the things they talk about; and that's precisely Foreman's point. The body that *does* things is often at loggerheads with the body that thinks about that doing or that talks about it afterward.

In several crucial respects, the correspondences between this approach and Gertrude Stein's are manifold. Stein's landscape plays, preeminently *Four Saints in Three Acts,* also are much obsessed with the placement and proximities of figures in space; the simplest movement of one character toward another sets off psychological and emotional ripples throughout her world. Stein establishes dramatic situations geometrically rather than narratively, trusting that relationships among people's bodies will tell her audiences more about their stories, their ambitions and misgivings, than any windy exegesis could. She, too, believed that the essences of dramatic life were endlessly fascinating, meriting renewed interest, continuous study, rigorous manipulation. And her notion of the "continuous present" finds new demonstration in Foreman's determined (and often repetitive) assertion of his characters' "being there."

Yet the bodies in Stein's landscapes seem more cohesive than those afflicted by Foreman's ontological hysteria. It's this perpetual skirmish between the bodies and minds of Foreman's theater that sets him apart from his artistic mother. Despite the ecstatic formal inventiveness of Stein's theater, the body of a speaker reveals her mind; the two aspects of a character's being serve each other, even if they don't always behave synchronously. A character's physical aspect – her posture, her distance from another character, her placement on the stage – is often meant to show something about her mental and emotional condition; similarly, an emotional or intellectual occurrence sent Stein looking for the most telling change in a character's physical behavior. Stein's work is never basely illustrative, but it does acknowledge a close collaboration among the triple vocations of dramatic figures: thinking, perceiving, acting.

In Foreman's theater, however, the mind works to second-guess or elude the demands of the body; bodies seem only obstacles or unfortunate baggage weighing down the fleet foraging of the intellect. It doesn't take long in *Angelface* before the characters are squabbling with their bodies, talking about them as though they were sheer matter, detached from themselves. "My body is imitating me," says Walter II, and his double later acknowledges, "I don't have a face."[13] The characters crave invisibility; they long to escape their own corporeality. Max dreams of "stomachs full of light"; Walter exults that he's "shining" through his "shell" at last. Will they get a chance to be angels? they seem to ask. Foreman's title points to a constant challenge: Can the angel in each of them break free of its face – the dull, merely personality-oriented aspects of identity?

Almost in spite of himself, Foreman reveals that this longing for transcendence has its roots in real pain. In interviews and manifestos Foreman stresses his antipathy to emotionally manipulative theater: "I wanted to *purge* art of emotional habit," he has said, and explained that what looks like emotion in his plays is really just a cunning replica of the real thing, fabricated by Foreman using models from conventional art so that he (and we) may be able to study how such states of feeling work upon us. Actually feeling the feeling, he warns, is prohibited: "The experience of emotion erases the awareness of how it was technically produced."[14]

Seeing, though, does lead to believing; and Foreman's theater can't escape presenting a spectacle of deep emotional authenticity: Foreman's *own* longings, frustrations, and delights come into view, filling the space he cleared when he purged his *characters* of affect. The feeling is deflected, though, often made antic, exaggerated, or just clinical: In *Angelface,* Weinstein doubles over with pain; something's wrong with his leg; Max feels dizzy; Walter II worries that Max will step on his head or his hands; several characters fall to the floor and can't get up; Karl's arms ache; later, his feet hurt; Max's hand is burning; Walter's shoulder is throbbing. None of these visions of suffering is particularly moving. They're not even pathetic: We're not "involved" with Foreman's characters in such a way that their well-being matters. But these notations of distress can be read as signals of a larger, *creative* dilemma that, once our attention is directed toward Foreman's true subject, cleanses *Angelface* of its sarcasm and makes it seem the product of genuine anguish.

This pain is psychic, the result of a mind at war with the objects in its path. All through *Angelface,* and many of the plays that followed it, Foreman all but confesses his helplessness in the face of things and people he's determined to describe. Not that he's unable to confront them or to find a place for them in his play; he can and does so. But he feels he can never describe them sufficiently. He can never draw them fully into his theatrical world. More than anything else, Foreman's early plays are spectacles of how anxious he is to be precise. His characters talk compulsively, gratingly, about the same configurations of the body; they note every slight variation in the dynamics of a group, always feeling it necessary to tell us how they feel, what they want now and what they want a minute later. His characters have the agitated energy of people chasing butterflies, determined not only to net one, but also to pin it onto a board and jot down all its stripes and colors. With such characters, Foreman again differs from Gertrude Stein, whose exuberant passages of description rarely betray frustration. She is always calm, fluid, effortlessly exact. Foreman is wired, stop-and-go, piling up approximation on top of approximation, never willing to believe he's done enough.

The pain caused by his needing to be precise eventually makes Foreman want to discard all the objects and characters in his way. The beginnings of that decision are visible even in *Angelface:* Characters bump into things; they can't leave the room, so they try to empty it of its furniture and clutter; they close their eyes or look away, hoping things will be gone and that they'll be in a freer place when they look again. Max, faced with an open door and a shattered window, can't leave, can't, like Walter, put on wings and fly away. Max's entrapment is Foreman's own despair at not yet being able to reach beyond this world, beyond these ideas and emotions, into something strange, challenging, renewing, truly overwhelming. (Foreman will return to this theme and explore it with more deliberate energy and the benefit of much experience twenty years later in the 1988 play, *What Did He See?*) In *Angelface,* Foreman the artist is poised on the edge of a crisis, balancing like Max at the end of the play, unable to touch the things around him, unable even to move, suspended in his difficulty, and unsure how to voice his distress properly, much less resolve it. The next several plays Foreman wrote became, by his own definition, a form of therapy, addressing this self-made, sought-for, remarkably theatrical and lyrical neurasthenia.

Only two plays overtly refer to psychoanalysis – *Total Recall* and *Classical Therapy (or) A Week Under the Influence . . .* – but Foreman conducts sessions of psychic investigation in each of his efforts. And "efforts" they are, in the truest sense: dynamic demonstrations of how he pursues self-knowledge, with all the frustrations showing. It's a pursuit that forces him to acknowledge the tendencies and aversions of his mind, expand the reach of his curiosity to places he wouldn't go outside of art, clarify for himself the consequences of his thoughts and actions. Writing plays is his method of gaining self-mastery; it's his own prescription. Such a complicated endeavor seems daunting, requiring considerable intellectual exertion. Foreman meets the challenge; but like the best analysands, he knows that true discovery comes only from the mind's utter relaxation. The problem is in achieving that delighted, alert laziness.

"It's been very difficult for me to reach the point where I'm willing to admit that I write like taking dictation – that all the best things that come through me I don't control."[15] That's the ideal (it was Rilke's, too: He called the *Sonnets to Orpheus* the "most mysterious, most enigmatic dictation I have ever endured and achieved").[16] Unfortunately, if the evidence of Foreman's plays are to be trusted, the reality is more strenuous. Foreman quests for unclogged, ecstatic freedom in all his work, but usually he doesn't achieve it; when he fails, he stages the difficult saga of trying to maintain the flow of inspiration, of seeking to replicate the epiphanies over and over again. He's often his own worst enemy: The initial impulse to start a play may come unbeckoned – divine dictation – but Foreman then works over the received wisdom, unwraps the gift, takes it apart, fingers and disarranges the components so relentlessly that there's no hope of putting it back together. We get the parts as *our* gift. "The critique of the play," he has said, "is the body and flesh of the play – the critique of a play that isn't there."[17]

Foreman has produced almost as many articles about playwriting as he has plays; he's often his own best exegete, eager to trace the history of a play, point out its resonances, decode its puns and riddles, and brighten up its subtleties, if asked by an interviewer. For Foreman, there's no division between writing plays and writing theory – his plays are theory animated; his theory originates in and always retains a sophisticated sense of play. Articles and plays both have the same purpose: to unveil the secrets of writing.

Thanks to those articles and interviews, there's no secret about the way that Foreman spends his writing days. Cherished myths about him fall away rudely: He *doesn't* sit at a desk poring over abstruse theory, working to turn it into theatrical gold. He may devour more literature and philosophy than most playwrights, but when he sets out to write he pushes that all aside. It's as though Foreman takes a long hot bath in theory, then gets out, and lets the theory evaporate before sitting down to work. Foreman has said that he often lies about his apartment, drifting in and out of sleep, waiting until images and their kin, ideas, begin to surface. All is not blissful, though. Anxiety begins along with art, and Foreman is quickly overtaken with qualms: What is it I'm seeing? What does it sound like? Where should it go in the text? What is it *really*? The questions proliferate, but Foreman doesn't try merely to answer them. Rather, he incorporates the questions in the text as though they were caesuras, moments of doubt, and moves on, letting his consciousness expand. Foreman welcomes distraction, and deliberately makes himself vulnerable to digression.

In recent years, Foreman has described the actor in his theater as "someone trying to do psychic work upon himself in front of an audience."[18] At this stage of his evolution, however, the performers enact *Foreman's* psychic work, his consuming passion to get at sources of feeling, of memory, of ideas. The world of his plays spreads out before him as he writes, and he encourages conversations among characters to radiate as widely as they can, making their own structure. "My plays should not be *experienced*," he tells audiences, prepping them for action, "they should be discovered." "Write the meandering," Foreman says to himself; the art will come of "accretion."[19]

For a long time after *Angelface*, Foreman made idiosyncratic use of a favored writing crutch – the outline. Rather than follow it obediently, Foreman says he "de-writes . . . keeping the outline in mind, but saying 'Hah, look how I can show the antiuniverse to this universe that I'm supposed to be writing.'"[20] Foreman writes like a particularly inspired, dreamy delinquent, believing that if he goes against assumptions and relishes contradictions, he'll get to the only valid destination for art: a vision of oneself in action, vividly alive as a writer at last. For instance, Foreman may start with a trio of characters, two of whom are vying for the affections of the third – one of the standard bourgeois-comedy triangles for which Foreman has confessed his fondness – but he deliberately won't dramatize their conflict efficiently. He may dawdle around the fringes of the scene, letting characters hold forth on seemingly unimportant, undramatic matters like their suppers or their gardens (in *HcOhTiEnLa (or) Hotel China*), suitcases or day jobs (in *Sophia= (Wisdom) Part 3: The Cliffs*) or dressing nicely for one's Uncle Leo (*Classical Therapy*). When it comes to dramatic structure Foreman is capricious and intractable. He's confident that his mind is as reliable as a dowser, and will eventually lead him (and presumably us, too) to some kind of revelation, even if it means a long trek through stretches of seemingly unimpressive subject matter.

What is the point of such rambling? Foreman does have an ideological reason, although it's the very opposite of programmatic. His commitment to a method of digression is the result of his irritation with the theories of Bertolt Brecht. As a young writer, Foreman was much affected by Brecht's work, having first read about it, he says, when he was in high school. Brecht's desire to activate his spectators, to cajole them to draw conclusions about situations onstage and to reflect on their applications offstage, became Foreman's desire, too. Anyone who has seen a Foreman performance probably remembers more than any other element the web of strings that stretch from wall to wall, ceiling to floor, object to object. The strings break up the room into a particularly zany grid, diagraming the field of view and so helping us to see how one area of the stage relates spatially to the other. The strings also remind us that we are watching something happen: We can't help but track the movements of our eyes as they cross the borders of string. Foreman also shines blinding lights in our eyes from time to time and interrupts the dialogue with thuds and buzzers at the moment when we might be about to get lulled into a story or hypnotized by aimless chitchat. Along with the strings, these maneuvers keep us working – alert whether we want to be or not.

But Foreman makes use of our alertness in a radically different way than Brecht. Foreman never says so directly, but on the basis of his work it's apparent that he grew to resent Brecht's ulterior motives for activating audiences. Brecht's method of structuring plays so that a spectator would reach a predetermined conclusion seemed too coercive for Foreman, not to mention that Brecht hoped all the spectators would reach the same end. Such subjection was the very antithesis of the lively state Foreman wants his audiences to experience. Foreman doesn't care what conclusion you reach, as long as you think energetically in the first place. And he especially hopes that his plays provoke a multiplicity of responses, never a doctrine. A generous champion of individuality, Foreman encourages each of us to devise our own route through his plays. He packs a scene full of characters and actions, offers assertions and reflections, dangles riddles and red herrings – then leaves it up to us to pick up those of most interest and scrutinize them, proposing significances of our own, linking them to other aspects of the play as we see fit. We have to take more responsibility at a Foreman performance than we would at other plays, even at a Brecht performance. Foreman presents his patterns of thought as a way of spurring us to fashion (or at least acknowledge) our own, to enter our own systems of perception. The words his characters speak and the complicated paths they travel cajole us into making the play – the play that, in his irrepressible playing around, he teases us toward, then ultimately withholds.

Over the next stage of his writing life, Foreman slowly changed from an artist who wanted to pin down specifics of phenomena, one nodule at a time, into someone who wanted to know as much experience as possible, regardless of how precise he could be about it. It's as if he regretted having looked so microscopically at the elements of an experience or an individual, and now wished for a taste of infinity. Throughout his career, Foreman's plays sound a ringing defense of the pursuit of pleasure – whether it comes in the form of spiritual transcendence, exotic erotics, or chocolate cake (food is everywhere in Foreman). Each kind of stimulus is "delight fuel," as Foreman calls it; and despite the philosophic weightiness of his work, the ultimate purpose is essentially primal: the good life.

His next plays show him dashing from one sphere of activity to another, consuming sensations all the time, trying to fill himself to the brim. But Foreman is careful about what he emphasizes: These plays aren't going to display much splendor, as one might expect in, say, a picaresque novel. Foreman is writing his own eccentric variation on an esteemed form, the chronicle play, where the sufferings of the traveler command more interest than the passing sights.

Foreman has also attributed this reaction against his earlier work to a fear of idolatry. By paying too much attention to single objects or people, he risks letting his mind freeze. The imagination contracts when it should be expanding, goes limp when it should palpitate, and the artist as a whole approaches a kind of death. He is satisfied faster, questions less, prettifies the stage when he should be dissecting it. Rilke again:

> All Things want to fly. Only *we* are weighed down by desire,
> caught in ourselves and enthralled with our heaviness.[21]
>
> . . . .
>
> . . . fill out the dance-figure
> into the constellation of those bold
> dances in which dull, obsessive Nature
>
> is fleetingly surpassed. For she was stirred
> to total hearing just when Orpheus sang.[22]

Foreman is careful to imply that aesthetic death closely resembles the deadening of the soul that anyone can suffer – not just playwrights, but also those in the audience. And not just during their ninety minutes in the theater. Foreman worries over the dangers of idolatry as much to inspire us to seize the day as to keep himself creative. "Life can be lived according to a different rhythm," Foreman has said, "seen through changed eyes."[23] "Only by being a tourist," says an unnamed voice in *Rhoda in Potatoland (Her Fall-Starts)* (1974), "Can you experience. A place."[24] The aphorism turns much received wisdom on its head. Long stays don't really broaden your understanding; they only induce complacency, a familiarity that blinds you to the real texture of a setting. The senses are sharpest when they confront mysteries; they work harder to understand; one sees more, because one *needs* to see more; nothing is taken for granted.

Foreman fills these middle works with numerous obstructions to the journeys, but he also makes the characters more intrepid, readier for adventure. For Ben in *Total Recall,* just standing outside the window of his room is a revelation; the paralysis afflicting his cousins in *Angelface* lingers a bit, but there's also continuous talk of going out, of imagining other worlds, of being somehow *different.* Bodies may not move much in *Total Recall,* but as Leo says of Sophia, they "emanate." Treasures, and the more important epiphanies that come with finding them, seem nearby.

In *Hotel China, Sophia=(Wisdom) Part 3: The Cliffs, Classical Therapy,* and in most of the plays leading up to *Rhoda in Potatoland,* the characters are even more off kilter. They are figuratively and literally caught in a field of tension, buffeted about by each other's random-seeming impulses. Their trips through the plays consist of what Foreman calls multiple "false starts." Physical urges get stronger, but their goals are even less apparent. Speakers in *Classical Therapy* describe an uncanny knack appendages have for finding their way into orifices; the assortment of difficult tasks attempted by characters in *Sophia* turns the play into a maddened party game – Twister for the dysfunctional. (A typical stage direction reads, "Crew comes and holds pillow to Hannah's behind, as she opens suitcase and lets the top just hang down. Crew comes and ties a ribbon to Karl's penis, also sets a small screen with flower-shaped hole in front of him and runs ribbon through that hole and off.")[25] In these plays, the famous strings lashing Foreman's stage seem to imprison his characters, and so encourage them to resist entrapment. They also easily panic about loss and getting lost. Emotion in Foreman's work is the accumulated record of these bursts or swells of movement. And characters exist, Foreman asserts, primarily as "documents" of the "circulation of verbal and psychological energies which can be recombined in many different patterns, allowing that momentary arising and coagulation of traits known to us as 'character' – a most ephemeral and transitory thing."[26]

It was not until Foreman's most charming surrogate, Rhoda, headed to Potatoland that the full possibilities of travel were realized. Rhoda was always played by Kate Manheim, Foreman's longtime collaborator (and now wife), and the character acquired much of its memorable personality from her contribution. Manheim's triangular face always looked astonished – her cheekbones high and on the lookout, her eyes unblinking and often gravitating to corners. In many of Foreman's early plays, she ended up in some form of undress, but her body was always an instrument of her inquiring mind. "Thinking [happens] close to the surface of the body," Foreman once wrote.[27] (Did he feel he was exposing her mind, not her flesh?) In any case, nudity seemed the best, most appropriate form in which to explore her perplexing world, and expose *its* secrets. Her body, and the other characters when nude, also became additional obstacles for Foreman's inquiring mind to dodge; as played by Manheim, Rhoda symbolized the most vivid of the material world's temptations.

Manheim usually stood in profile and angled her head slightly outward, allowing us a three-quarter view of her features. The pose made her Rhoda look worried, as though she were caught up in a machine that was on the verge of running out of control, and she had no way of jumping off. She also seemed to solicit approval from some unspecified source in the audience or merely to gauge the degree to which her adventures were having an effect on us. At other moments she carried herself with the assurance that, alone among all the other characters, she knew the proper way through the hubbub surrounding her.

In all the Rhoda plays, language becomes an all-purpose aid to her endeavors: She swathes herself with lavish explanations of her own actions; binges on great heaps of description, enjoying the rush that comes from addressing everything in her path; and wields questions like rapiers, skewering a confusing moment and waving it around until it falls limp. She doles out admonitions and aphorisms to all comers, tosses off insults when they're least appropriate, allows herself a lyric, a lapse into doggerel, the odd, languid come-on. Lying in wait for the next jarring rearrangement of the scene, she may bide her time with sulky bits of self-mockery or exclamations of brash self-regard. Running beneath all her commentary are her own low conspiratorial hums and whistles, let out as though she were sounding the depths of the stage.

Rhoda is Foreman's savviest quester, willing and more than able to lead him out of suffocating quotidian life. From *Rhoda in Potatoland* to *Africanus Instructus* in 1986, she grows steadily more challenged, but also more resourceful about ways to "discover something magic," as she sings in *Africanus Instructus*, and "to be free / of emotional paralysis." These nine travel plays are not presented as a cycle, but if read in sequence, they can be considered one, for the tones and atmospheres of each play carry over to the next, bringing with them Rhoda, of course, and opening on to the next stage of her large project. The sameness of the plays seems deliberate, for they are in dialogue with one another: Dilemmas raised in one play are not fully solved until three plays later; Rhoda can accept the implications of her quest only after she has completed several legs of the journey. As each play runs its course (which is really running in place), we come to accept the essential fact of Rhoda's condition: She will always be in search of something else. Desire is more stimulating than satisfaction.

Rhoda in Potatoland is one of Foreman's most delightful plays, restlessly inventive and generous with its humor. (Foreman's highly developed whimsy is often overlooked by those put off by his theater's reputation for austerity.) Potatoland is a metaphor, of course, but that doesn't stop Foreman from having fun with it: His potatoes look real, massive, and mobile, poking their eyes in doorways and windows. "Everything up to now was Recognizable," says a voice after the potatoes have been spotted, "Now, however / The real potatoes are amongst us / And a different kind of understanding is possible."[28] Rhoda immediately feels like a potato.

The speed with which Rhoda accepts the strange intruders serves her well throughout the play. Rhoda says she wants to "be the place" where she lives, wherever that place may be, however often she may change locales. If she can vanish into the setting, she reasons, then she will be more various and free than she is, less bound by constricting ideas of "personality" – a more capacious receptacle for sensation.

Potato elixirs help Foreman escape his overfamiliar world and introduce him to other dimensions of life. But *Rhoda in Potatoland* only points the way: Foreman's knowledge, the voice says at the end, "only shows me the very tip of its wing," and so announces how much work is left to be done.[29] In subsequent stages of the cycle, Rhoda's quest acquires psychological, emotional dimensions – "Something that happened to her earlier, she longs to recapture," says a voice in *Book of Splendors, Part I.* "Her quest . . . is not a quest, but a need to express herself," says another voice.[30] In this play, its sequel *Book of Splendors, Part II (Book of Levers) (Action at a Distance)*, and in *Blvd de Paris,* Foreman also spells out an important change in direction of Rhoda's quest: Places, buildings, potatolands, even bodies (which the voice in *Rhoda in Potatoland* urged us to consider a "vast space" which we should "travel" in as in a "landscape") – all things that conventionally stimulate pleasure – now give way more openly to minds, imaginations, psyches. Of course, Foreman has long been devoted more to thoughts than to things, but now the protective metaphor is no longer necessary. In fact, only by confronting the imagination head-on can he test its potential to sustain him. Perhaps he has been taking the mind's pleasures for granted, never really examining what's inside there. Now he looks.

The old assumptions get a last hearing in *Book of Splendors, Part II,* when a voice on tape says, "EACH MOMENT IS AN EXIT DO YOU UNDERSTAND. EACH MOMENT IS A WAY *OUT*."[31] That decision is challenged and dismissed in the next play, *Blvd de Paris,* in which an unnamed speaker says, "what you thought was a way out, was really, a way *IN*" – a coming into the mind after being out in the cold world where senses take their pleasure. *Blvd de Paris* is the route taken by a "train of thought," and when Rhoda enters the city of mind, she moves more zealously than ever. She "penetrated deeper," says a voice, for "there are more decisions per square inch here than in any other city of the West."[32] The argument advances, and we advance into the argument. (The full title of the play perhaps best exemplifies its message of thought-travel: *Blvd de Paris (I've Got the Shakes) or Torture on a Train (Brain-Mechanisms of the Re-distributed French Virgin) or Certainly Not (A Torturous Train of Thought).* The homage to Duchamp aside, Foreman's title is a journey all by itself – amending itself, revising compulsively, moving back and forth to clarify its subtleties, adding links, swirling all its subjects together until it has built up enough steam to start the play going.)

Foreman's "cities" are more important for the impressions one registers passing through them than for the sights they contain. Rhoda exults: "Oh City, what I love are your implications." The city is no city, no "elsewhere," but a region of intellect, a space for choosing and for reflecting on the consequences of that choosing.

By *Egyptology (My Head Was a Sledgehammer)*, Rhoda is having a harder time finding a place for thought. Crash-landing into "Egypt," the nomad in her is severely tested: After wrangling with those who say she has really only fallen backward into time, she must face up to the confusing allure of numerous other distractions – darkened rooms, a house for rent, cubicles and beds, telephones to help her reach yet more places, radios to do the same, hallucinations of forests and airplanes, cabinets filled with books, which in turn are filled with promises of other worlds. Throughout the play, Foreman rings variations on the idea of enclosure: All these things and places threaten to root Rhoda in other people's versions of the world – and tempt her with idolatry all over again. She finally says, "I'm trying to go inside myself . . . . I try all the time. But I keep falling over real things."[33]

Later, Foreman clarifies: The path he seeks is "very close. Here. Present."[34] Once he (and Rhoda) fully install themselves in inner worlds, he can achieve the equanimity suggested at the end of the play: "I thought the world would / continue forever. Didn't it continue forever? / Or I don't care (proper response)?"[35] It *is* the proper response. Rhoda doesn't reject just the geographies of "Egypt," "Potatoland," "Paris," or "Café Amérique" (the title of another play in the cycle). That renunciation is only to be expected with a playwright who so cherishes the speculative life. More distressingly, Rhoda flees Foreman's own world, the dramatic landscape of possible paradises, sexy encounters, exotic treasures, where objects attracted wonder and remarkable feats of deliberation; where bodies presented themselves for scrutiny, a workout, tableau making, and, occasionally, eccentric violation. That world has emptied its mysteries entirely for Foreman; the time has come for something more challenging.

Africanus Instructus will rudely disillusion those who thought the answer lay in the mind's domain. Like *Egyptology,* the musical satirizes the Western fascination with unknown places, and pushes Foreman toward the jungle of his own intellect. But at the end, Rhoda exclaims, "the imagination doesn't work. It's not enough!"[36] The other characters try to excite Rhoda with music, antic dances, and roughhousing, hoping to cajole her to feeling once again the same wonder with which she started her long journey through Foreman's travel cycle, eight plays earlier. The band plays even more energetically; characters whoop it up, but Rhoda doesn't pay any attention; sequestered in her own quiet space, she stares with a mixture of desolation, thoroughgoing disillusionment, and perhaps a touch of new wisdom as the lights go out. Her journey has finally ended.

If the imagination isn't enough, what is? To find out, Foreman retrenched. In 1986 he devised his own version of chamber theater, and began writing quieter, more contemplative plays. With a muted tone came more somber subjects: Foreman's recent work is among his most frankly emotional and most searching. For some, this accessibility makes the work's profundity disreputable, as though Foreman hadn't earned it. For others (and for this critic), the lucidity is a sign of Foreman's continued generosity: After encouraging us to reflect when we go to theater, now he gives us the right tranquil space in which to really concentrate.

Foreman never neglected the moral dimension in his writing, but in these latest plays he has chosen more unequivocally to sustain a long, complex argument with himself on matters spiritual, psychological, and ethical. Like the journey plays, many of these recent works also form a cycle. Together they respond to the challenge implied at the end of *Africanus Instructus,* suggesting how Foreman should comport himself now that he has acknowledged the limits of the imagination. In these plays, Foreman inquires more deeply than before into the place of pleasure in his life, into the way he manages his need for control, into his misgivings about his isolation from the social world – finally, into ideas of artistic responsibility.

For *The Cure* (1986), Foreman brings together two men and a woman, sets them in a tight, hushed room rich in brocade and velvet, and lets them luxuriate in talk about writing, dreams, and fantasies. They tempt each other with their deepest secrets; they experiment with tentative divulgences. They play word games, pretend to be children, perform private rituals, pair off in different combinations to torment the one left out. Foreman has said that he wanted to set the play in a turn-of-the-century European salon favored by occult societies, circles of symbolist poets, or devotees of a particularly obscure religion. In his production, elements of these worlds remained visible, but Foreman eventually decided the only real and appropriate setting for *The Cure* would be his "private meditation chambers."[37]

Foreman refurbishes those chambers over the course of *The Cure,* cleaning out many of his cherished assumptions. He takes a new look at habits of thought, and decides to organize his perceptions differently. "Look at this jewel," the character named David (after the original actor) says at the opening of the play, sporting a gleaming ring on his finger. "A jewel of an idea. A jewel of an act. A jewel of an emotion."[38] Or, just as plausible, a jewel of a play or of an entire art, a state of consciousness and aroused creativity, sought for in all of Foreman's previous work. The delight at the discovery is certainly compelling but, coming after the conclusion of *Africanus Instructus,* it also seems arch, as though the speaker knows how difficult it will be to sustain such excitements, as though this were just another discovery, soon to go pale. David quickly changes the subject.

What Foreman realizes that he wants more than anything else is a sense of *possibility.* In the past, he has asked for increased awareness (in his earliest plays) or escape from enclosed, quotidian worlds (in the middle works) or powerful revelations of interior worlds (in the final travel plays). Inside his previous work he could feel self-possessed, wise, soothed by a paradise no one else would ever know or ever sully. Here, in *The Cure,* Foreman carries with him the wisdom of knowing that such bliss isn't sufficient. Great experiences aren't satisfying enough, self-made paradises soon grow dull, one more glamorous series of images or witty bit of writing that he produces tarnishes too easily.

Under Foreman's withering skepticism in *The Cure,* even his beloved pastime of writing about writing loses dignity. Kate (as the woman is called in the published version, for Manheim played her first) shows her companions how she can write a new version of *War and Peace* using cornflakes instead of ink – she affixes the flakes to a blackboard in strange patterns until, as the character named Jack says, "the psychological and spiritual content took precedence over external incident."[39] That, of course, has long been Foreman's aim, but it's only here that he fully acknowledges the impossibility of leaving behind "external incident" when one is still beholden to words and their inescapable tendency to refer to real things and experiences. Cornflakes can't *refer;* they simply *are.* Cornflakes, in this equation, are also free of meaning; they exist before and beyond meaning, and so, despite their materiality, symbolize the kind of freedom Foreman wants.

Foreman raises the stakes for himself: He wants the *ability* to achieve multiple goals, not to have to compromise on his potential by actually exercising that ability. *The Cure* and the plays that follow it celebrate what, for lack of a better word, might be called "verging." Verging is Foreman's ideal action – precisely because it is no action at all. Before he reached this stage, Foreman had been determined to transcribe the exact patterns of his mind onto the page, to let the writing go wherever it wanted, and to bring him into a world of language. It was as though he could confirm his existence only by writing; the traces on the page were all that testified to his roaming spirit. Now, in *The Cure,* he begins to feel his way to an even freer state. As early as 1977, in his essay "How I Write My (Plays: Self)," he had articulated this urge; only here, it seems, is he actually trying to find a dramatic equivalent. In the essay, he had described a state in which he "might write" – distinct from writing – in which the imaginative impulse stays active, alert, trembling, not yet domesticated by the injunction to choose a word, form a sentence, set it down on the page. "To 'MIGHT write' is to stay in the center of where writing arises. Where thinking arises. Where living arises. Only it's not a center . . . it's an everywhere."[40]

Throughout these recent plays, Foreman's characters are always finding themselves in this center, and he is loath to let them leave. In *Lava* (1989), he calls this place a "gap": Like the "center," it is outside of grounded, roofed, walled life, and so a place of intensely charged energy, danger – and, especially, of potential. "Writing is built out of such gaps," he notes in an essay on the play, illustrating his idea with the example of the metaphor, where a gap between literal meanings of words inspires a reader to make an imaginative leap. "You increase the size of the gaps," Foreman continues, "if you want more consciousness . . . . [The] gap is the field of all creativity."[41] The characters in *Lava* spend ninety minutes "wobblelike," as a voice says in the play; for wobbling, not letting oneself settle down or stand still, is another way to verge.

Gaps, wobbling, and the policy of might-writing all suggest a floating state, a condition where the mind is at its nimblest, where the imagination isn't pinned down by the things it might imagine. What Paul Valéry says (in dialogue form) about dance is similar to this ecstatic verging:

> PHAEDRUS: Let us enjoy the exquisitely delicate moment when [the dancer] is in the act of making up her mind! . . . As the bird which has reached the very edge of the roof, breaks away from the beauty of the marble and falls into flight . . .
>
> ERYXIMACHUS: I care for nothing so much as for what is on the point of occurring . . . .[42]

In these plays, Foreman is pulling himself back rather than forging ahead, contracting his consciousness after encountering (in the travel cycle) the perils of expanding it to the point of bloatedness and subsequent sterility. Pulled into himself, he is able to renew himself, erase the slate, start over – young again, all potential, on the verge. Not for nothing are these recent plays filled with images of childhood.

The characters of *The Cure* talk about so many different things because no one thing holds their interest; eventually they talk about *being interested* itself, and then they show the greatest mental fervor. Sometimes they quote others as a way of instructing themselves in their new priorities: "Music may come nearer it than words," says David, quoting Alfred North Whitehead as he seeks an elusive sense of artistic omnipotence. "The definite concepts are there, in tones or phrases, but all around them hover the infinitudes of possibility – the *other* ways in which this vastness might have been expressed." As though in response to this desire, Kate immediately starts calling out a long list of dance steps, while music plays in the distance. Dances turn up in just about every Foreman piece, but here, where characters don't want to settle into only one great experience, everything comes in multiples: "Do the uptown. Do the zip. Do the dum-dum. Do the waltz . . . ."[43] And so on, through samba, rumba, the stovepipe, the hat trick, the I-don't-know, and the derrick. Of course, they don't actually dance all these dances. They *verge* on dancing, measuring their potential but not draining it away. It's as if they stood on their toes, ready to step out, but never relaxing enough to actually do so.

Whitehead again: Jack likes his celebration of excess and his disappointment with those who "ignore many things in order to proceed with one thing." Joanna Field, another philosopher, is also a beloved source of new wisdom: Kate quotes her suggestion to try out many different attitudes and gestures, and to give up the anxiety that comes from "striving with whips to make my thoughts follow the path I had chosen."[44] Foreman is really calling into question the foundations of art making: While he has long been an advocate of artistic drifting, relishing the wanderings of the consciousness, he invariably selected material from what he saw, committed certain favored images to paper, and transferred those to the stage. But now he's wondering aloud even if that work is too much, too damaging for the artist within the fabricator, the selector: "Don't guess, don't analyze, don't do anything!" Kate declares. She could be rebuking Foreman himself, a compulsive analyzer and doer if ever there was one. "You expect results?" Jack asks next, and later makes fun of "a man that spends too much time watching the private pictures it paints on the back side of the brain" – a man, in other words, remarkably like Richard Foreman, whose brain and its flashing pictures have occupied so much of our time. "No more graven images!" David says at last – decisively closing down a chapter of Foreman's history, denying him one of his most reliable distractions from the arduous work of knowing himself.[45] He won't find that self, David implies, in the beautiful plays he makes.

The Cure ends with a short list of deferred prospects: "I could have been one of the most famous amateur horseback riders of the 1980s," says Kate. "I could have pleased people in ways that are not trivial," David adds. Jack: "I could have taken wealth and added the idea of perspective." Kate: "I could have shifted certain centers of gravity." *Could have, could have*: Foreman speaks about ambitions, not acts; worlds that are anticipated and unknown – not inhabited, not even imagined. What *might be* is liberating in a way that even the most fanciful inner world is not – cannot be.

"Twisted. Touched. Turned. Perceived. Prepare. Possibly. Certainly. Absolutely." This sequence, spoken like a fugue by all three actors, could fairly well describe elements of Richard Foreman's standard artistic process: Things (or ideas or experiences) that are perceived are then touched by Foreman's writing self, turned, twisted, prepared to serve another function, reflect another world. Possibility hangs in the air throughout these artistic manipulations, until the play's text and performance renders the original image or impulse certain and absolute: *there*, to be seen, read, heard. That, at least, was how things usually went. But in the stage directions Foreman asks that Kate hold a plastic globe in her hands during this passage, and that once the speaking subsides, she hesitate for a moment, then finally toss the globe away, letting it roll out of sight. What was "certain" or "absolute" – *contained* the way a globe is – is now returned to flux, uncertainty – the realm of the possible. The world – of theater, imagination, writing – is lost to him once more, and he's happy about it. He has returned to a childhood state and can begin again.

The Cure is Foreman's favorite play, and whether or not readers agree, it certainly is among his more courageous. Foreman initiates an intimate examination of his own need for control – artistic control, certainly, but also psychic control, intellectual control, the sense of acute awareness that had become so important to him. That anxiousness has never abated, despite years of indulging in the "meanderings" and "driftings" of his consciousness. Even when he can give himself up to the flow, he still wants to get the experience down on paper, give it all a name.

The alternative to control isn't chaos, nor is it a kind of flaccid inattentiveness. In the preface to *Symphony of Rats* (1988), he raises the notion of ambiguity – but makes it clear that ambiguity is a condition of life that needs to be "sustained," not merely accepted or, worse, wallowed in. There are those who are up to this task, says Foreman, and there are those who "reduce every issue to clearly defined choices, either black or white, and so become conservative reactionaries."[46] (The President in *Symphony* is among the latter until a visit to "Tornadoville," where nothing stands still long enough to be classified, shows him the merits of uncertainty.) Foreman sees how vulnerable he is: Anyone as steeped in theory, art making, and manifesto writing knows the temptation to say, *This is how I feel; this is what this play is about; this is how I see the world* and, finally, *this is what the world IS.* In other words, by acknowledging the dangers of control in art and the difficulties of accepting ambiguity, Foreman is revealing the uncomfortable proximity of art and power. How different, he might very well be asking, is the artist who lords over a dramatic world from the politician who lords over a social world? If one can learn to accept ambiguity in life, can learn to savor contradictions in behavior rather than attempt to resolve them, then one will have a clearer understanding of the realities of human life – and perhaps be more humane.

Such a discovery has a dark side: An acceptance of ambiguity, like a life spent verging, may mean the end of theater. Indeed, Foreman's recent plays speed him toward a renunciation of his art. *Film Is Evil: Radio Is Good* (1986) presses for uncertainty in more limited terms, but the consequences are just as far-reaching as in *The Cure.* Film is evil because, among other reasons, it provides images – a service that less charitably could be described as spoon-feeding us with colorful pabulum – and so utterly smothers any inventive urges we might develop on our own. (Foreman leaves it up to us to make the inevitable connection to theater.) Radio, on the other hand, offers only stimuli – words – and encourages listeners to devise a visual, gestural world to go with them. The words tickle the imagination into action, whereas cinematic images reduce it to a stupor.

But words, in Foreman's subsequent plays, are just as numbing. *Lava* presents characters in flight from language. Like the trio in *The Cure* with their cornflakes, they yearn for a reprieve from representability. Only when one gets off the "talk-a-lot bus" (a voice says) is one "hot" – really living, in other words, able at last to "notice with no verbal excess," and so really seeing.

When all of Foreman's work is taken together, it looks like a long sequence of denials – an ongoing assertion of what he won't let his theater become. Images insult our intelligence, Foreman posits in *Film Is Evil.* Words betray their weakness with every syllable, he adds in *Lava.* In *The Cure,* he insists that an action, once executed, prohibits you from doing something else during that time or in that space; better to have the *capacity* to do something than actually to do it. Further back in Foreman's writing life, he voiced his impatience with other assumptions of the artistic world: One cannot keep looking for new subjects or sensations, he concluded in the midst of the travel plays; the inner world deserves one's explorations more. Yet, in *Africanus Instructus,* he decided that imaginative journeys were also unsatisfying. And, before that, of course, Foreman had rejected narrative as being too emotionally manipulative. Underneath all these rejections have been successive calls for freedom, growing ever more desperate as Foreman grows more obsessed with questions of control and ambiguity.

Where has all of this spirited intolerance been leading? In *What Did He See?* (1988), one of the characters mentions "a great silence." Silence is a flickering, animated condition in Foreman's world. Like ambiguity, it does not come easily or automatically after some brave renunciation: It must be shaped, moderated, maintained, just as someone treading water has to muster concerted energy simply to stay in one place. To withhold action and keep mute in Foreman's exceedingly active and verbal world is more demanding than even the most athletic doing or most voluble, idea-saturated speaking.

Foreman experiences this kind of silence, or floating, after coming to what Will, in *What Did He See?*, calls the "conclusion that self-realization, the desirable goal, . . . cannot be achieved."[47] Up till now, Foreman had been using the theater to attempt just that: Each play was one more description of his progress toward artistic maturity, a state where all the missteps of youth (and youthful creativity) would be behind him, scorned. Here, Foreman turns around, looks back at what he passed through, and wonders about what he might have missed. *What Did He See?* is full of longing for return, for a time when all things still wore their mysteries. "Let's stop throwing words around like cream pies," Will says, "and let them kinda FLY BACK to whatever home base thay have as a real home base. How about it?"[48]

In *What Did He See?* Foreman proposes that the ideal theater would be a nontheater, where every gesture or word was held in abeyance. If *The Cure* showed Foreman that he was most happy with a vast sense of possibility, if *Symphony of Rats* instructed him in the uses of ambiguity and the dangers of too much control, if *Film Is Evil* urged him to give the spirit wider berth, then it no longer makes sense to continue creating tangible, audible artifacts of his imagination. Speaking through Will, Foreman suggests there is "no value in letting the impulse . . . COAGULATE . . . into an artifact, into a thing, a task accomplished, or an adventure" – in other words, into a play. To make theater, in fact, is to be corrupted, to fall. The alternative: "Perhaps it would be better," Foreman writes in the play's preface, "to invest my energy, as Duchamp said in a late interview, in the simple joys of breathing!"[49]

It's difficult to imagine what the next stage of Foreman's artistic life will look like once it's over, for the conclusions of *Lava* and *What Did He See?* are so powerful that they make any further deliberation superfluous. One wonders if Foreman will ever make good on his oft-repeated threat to leave the theater entirely. He has all but said outright that his plays wouldn't be there if they didn't have to be, if there were another way of expressing his yen for preexpression. Foreman's goal dooms him to failure – and he knows it. The famous Schiller quotation about the soul is apt here: "Once the soul speaks it is not the soul speaking." Taking Foreman at his word, one might see his plays as mere accidents, collections of detritus that slipped out inadvertently while Foreman was working to resist the gravitational plunge of his ideas. His plays, in this view, are the only traces left behind as Foreman runs away from the theater: They are the froth in his wake.

Perhaps Foreman has been disingenuous: After all, he continues to write plays (although they are even more preoccupied with death), and in 1992 installed himself in a permanent performing space in New York City – about as "coagulated" as one can get in the theater. If Foreman's intentions aren't as renunciatory as he'd have us believe, if theater still exerts its seductions, perhaps his recent plays are what his plays have always been (which makes them no less fascinating): the dust kicked up as he tromps around from one vision of his life to another, among multiple worlds of things, from one person and his offer of entanglement to the next and the next – looking for some calm place to settle. In the absence of such a place, these plays present an enduring picture of an artist in the act of choosing a shape for his ideas. Most artists give us art – artifacts; Foreman gives us the search for, the aversion to, and the constant dissatisfaction with art. Throughout his writing life, his drama is never quite there; it is always about to gather itself together.

Something beyond our sight and hearing promises real pleasure, but Foreman keeps us in our place (with those strings!). We "verge" along with him. Foreman's plays are addictive: We're teased into them, then bumped out, then reeled in again, then pushed out once and for all, challenged to make something new after he has scoured away old ideas of the creative life.

AFTERWORD: NEW DIRECTIONS

IN HIS EARLY POEM "CLEPSYDRA," John Ashbery writes of "a moment that gave not only itself, but / Also the means of keeping it."[1] The lines point to the source of the notorious difficulty of Ashbery's poetry. His phrases – linguistic "moments" – give themselves over to the reader so briskly that "keeping" them in the memory becomes almost impossible. Words shorn of rhetorical or narrative context cluster in unexpected combinations; a perception takes shape for a spell, then dissolves under the pressure of new lines; an isolated image contains its own inner logic, and may even correspond to something known, but surrounded by rival images no longer looks familiar. At times, the actual experience of reading itself seems to distract from the subjects one reads about. Ashbery envisions a watery flow of language, in which the experience of passage makes as strong an impression as the sights passed by. But something *is* arrested in Ashbery's work: The poems represent time itself, and so hold it up for inspection, even as it continues moving. A reader is encouraged to attend to independent sensations as they succeed one another in the poem, and to hold off wondering what they add up to.

The same impulses, as I hope these essays have shown, have been felt by some of the most challenging American playwrights since Gertrude Stein established an alternative to Eugene O'Neill. Although these writers recognize that, for many critics and audiences, the ideal play is a perfect whole, each part fitting together seamlessly – like a lovely sonnet or sculpture, or an intricate mystery story where all is explained at the end – still, they have been in perpetual search for the means of drawing a spectator's attention away from stories and onto moments of perception and speech.

With her mischievous plays, Gertrude Stein reminds audiences that theater exists in time, and so can never be looked to for exquisite objects. Nothing ever stands still in her work; a play is a collection of verbal turns occurring in what she famously calls "the continuous present." Tennessee Williams inadvertently adapts this approach to his interest in the emotional life, and creates drama structured around character rather than narrative or instruction. Williams cherishes the changeability of a character, her contradictory urges always vying with one another, and her passions threatening to disable her. His plays demand audiences prepared to go where an unpredictable character might wander, and able to enjoy cascades of language that rarely advance a plot but always deepen our understanding of the speaker.

In the 1960s, Sam Shepard, Maria Irene Fornes, Adrienne Kennedy, and, as the decade ended, Richard Foreman began to extend these innovations. Using diverse subjects as pretexts, they created (and continue to create) a supercharged gestural vocabulary in which a single move takes precedence over an entire action. They isolate the quiet aspects of behavior that often go unnoticed in the rush to climactic events. Rather than make generalizations about "psychology," they concentrate on limited, highly private zones of memory and thought. And, finally, they follow the instincts of the imagination, even when the intellect is demanding more orderliness.

But more than aesthetic strategies unites these six writers. They also share a temperament. Each of their plays seems a testimony to self-doubt, wearing openly the questions other writers conceal or never bother asking: Have I seen enough? Felt enough? Written too little or too much? Have I done my subject justice? Stein keeps hunting down unheard connotations in an utterance and unseen shifts of gravity in a movement. Williams lets his characters talk around and about their neuroses, even though mastery of them is impossible. Shepard and Kennedy break down the elements of identity into ever more discrete pieces, returning over and over to the emotions meant to bind people together. Fornes works tirelessly to transcribe the smallest grace note in a character's voice. And Foreman can't write fast enough, can't keep up with the ways his mind challenges his senses: Like the five other playwrights, he is bound on a circular journey.

What is most apparent in Foreman's theater is true, to varying degrees, of all these writers. Burdened with a sense of responsibility toward their themes, they stitch into their work the worrying, the dissatisfaction, the addictions and brooding patience of perfectionists. Even as we read or see one of their plays, we can sense that the writer hasn't quite loosened his grip, that the play is only on loan for our brief encounter – then back it will go onto his desk for more tinkering. Each writes as though his prey is always escaping: A character's emotions shift under new pressure and lose their familiar shapes; one view of a situation isn't sufficient, for its revelations wear off too quickly, and the impressions it conveys only spark more questions. Yet, early on, these writers learn that they will never see something from all sides. Their own curiosity keeps creating more facets to consider in a character, event, or emotion. Moreover, time keeps passing, relentlessly, and what they knew about their subjects a minute ago no longer holds. The light cast on their plays has changed, and so they must start over.

The anxiety is an occupational hazard for those who scorn the hospital corners of standard drama in order to be more attuned to moments of play. Since there are an infinite number of parts to any dramatic sequence, such playwrights never find that ordinary dramatic structures are capacious enough, nor do they feel confident that they will ever understand what they are writing about. Even Maria Irene Fornes, delicately paring away at her scenes, does so in order to see more, to see all the subtleties usually obscured by unnecessary apparatus. Perhaps the most enduring contribution of this group of theater artists is their idea of a writer's purpose: Writing should be an act of looking for, they remind us, not a showing off of what has been seen. (Even in such overt memory plays as Adrienne Kennedy's, memory is an unknown, unvisited territory; the writer ventures into it as nervously as one who has never experienced these events before.)

As with each play, so too with an entire phase of American theater. The restlessness and renewal of attention do not end with Richard Foreman. The extreme despair in his work does mark a crisis of sorts for American playwriting, but, far from capping the century-long discussion, he opens up new avenues of inquiry. It's difficult, in fact, to sum up the importance of these six writers, to propose any conclusions about how they have changed the theater – for the change is ongoing. One can't look back just yet. Their project continues, not least of all because four of them are still writing and, in their best new work, challenging our assumptions about them; but also because expansion and change are built into their very philosophy of theater. "Boredom dropped once we dropped our interest in climaxes," wrote John Cage about his music.[2] The maxim applies equally to the plays I've discussed, and to this entire era of writing. New writers share the aversion to climaxes, refining techniques to avoid them while expanding the possibilities open to their plays if they succeed, ingeniously complicating the process of writing, and thus extending the Stein tradition one generation further.

As Foreman wonders in his recent plays whether or not the very act of writing prevents him from achieving genuine energy in the theater, these newer writers are proposing answers. They seem to share Foreman's worry that words on a page can freeze the original impulses of the imagination, that little of substance stays alive and mutable once the writing is completed, and that the performance is merely the trace of what had been a wild turmoil in the artist's mind, when images fought to be acknowledged and a finished play was seen only as a distant, somewhat disappointing stillness. Along with Foreman, they find the battle thrilling, and ask how one can maintain that experience and still make art.

One way to address this dilemma, several younger writers suggest, is to concentrate once again on the act of speech. For the writer who embraces his or her own obsessiveness, plays in which speaking takes precedence over the other aspects of drama – even, at times, over the very substance of what is spoken – could not be more attractive. Speech is linked inexorably with the present, acquiring life at the moment it expends itself, renewing its energies with every utterance. Only in speech is the presence of time felt so closely – time giving ground for language to be heard, guiding its course, and efficiently erasing it once spoken. Speech, moreover, is variable – defined by an enormous number of tones, cadences, and pitches, many degrees of volume and pacing. Writing, on the other hand, is cemented into place. The words look the same every time one reads them. After a while, they seem (to a particular kind of writer) like relics.

Any discussion of this new direction must be tentative, for it is just that: new, not yet familiar, and only a direction, not yet a destination. In considering several writers who are exploring the possibilities of speech, I'm also compromising with the breadth of activity now enlivening the theater. Many critics have said that these are good days for American theater – in particular, that more exciting *writing* is going on now than at any time in recent memory – and I'm inclined to agree. I've chosen four who are representative of a crowded field: Wallace Shawn (who began working in the seventies, but who didn't write his most significant plays until the mid-eighties), David Greenspan, Suzan-Lori Parks, and Mac Wellman. This disparate quartet by no means sees itself as a group. Each one stimulates in idiosyncratic ways and provides pleasures unknown in other quarters. But they are all artists whose work I find myself returning to out of my frustration (an enjoyable frustration), bringing along nagging questions about what they are trying to do, about how they fit in with what I already know, and – when they don't fit, as is often the case – about how I can learn the language necessary to engage with them. Their strongest work has the kind of vitality that encourages audiences to match it with equally vital attention.

Despite the diversity of their concerns – openly political in the case of Shawn, for instance, or rhythmically experimental in the case of Parks – they share a desire to preserve the intensity of dramatic "moments." And they believe that the best way to do that is by recharging dramatic language: making the writing come to life. The "life" of writing is something to take literally. Dramatic language in their work is not inert or inviolate; it hums, parries, bobs, and dances. Words assume the dynamic forms of argument (Shawn), incantation (Parks), oratory (Wellman), or persistently elude form altogether, as in the tentative utterances of David Greenspan. In a passage about Wallace Stevens that inadvertently has much to say about this kind of drama, R. P. Blackmur writes: "There is a kind of close roistering in the syllables, with such yelping at the heels of meaning and such a hullabaloo of meaning in the sound, which prevents one from knowing what is going on except in such a double and darting image as drunkards delight to see."[3]

As Blackmur suggests, the liveliest act of speaking brings with it a sense of discovery. As a character speaks, something inchoate is slowly clarified. An emotion evolves into an idea; an idea deepens into a belief. Or, conversely, a belief crumbles under the weight of doubt; an abstraction retrieves the emotional urgency that engendered it. Regardless of the outcome, in this brand of dramatic speech nothing is ever settled; there is always another dark recess for language to explore. For a spectator, the experience of listening to such talk can be thrilling: We no longer feel preached to; rather, we travel with the characters to the places speech brings us. We probably don't know where we're going, and so can share with the speaker the same sense of discovery.

As a counterexample, Wendy Wasserstein's *The Heidi Chronicles* typifies what a play *without* a sense of discovery is like. The title suggests the presence of time, and the play's structure – each scene set in a different year between 1965 and 1989 – requires characters to get older and reconsider their past selves. Wasserstein encourages us to cast an affectionate, satirical look at the passions that animated the sixties, rethink the ambitions of the seventies, and nod compassionately at the shocks of living in the eighties. Heidi's change from a headstrong radical to a thoughtful single mother and art historian is carefully plotted in a series of vivid, snapshotlike scenes, making the play compelling in the way time-lapse documentary footage might be, or titillating in the manner of before-and-after photo spreads. And that's precisely why the play is so lifeless: The presence of time is merely ceremonial. *The Heidi Chronicles* reads as if a thesis were being proved – a thesis about "change." Change doesn't really occur, though; it's only referred to. Everything in the play is concluded at the start; we merely witness the unfolding.

Nothing unfolds neatly in the work of Shawn and Wellman, Greenspan and Parks. Instead, these plays welcome obstacles to their action, digressions from their narrative course. They grow steadily more layered; the density, in fact, seems part of a strategy to envelop the spectator in a world of language. "Involvement" is redefined as a total, often disorienting experience, not the temporary visitation it is in many other plays. Finally, as with their predecessors, nothing is final in their work: One never leaves these plays believing an idea has been definitively dissected or a passion fully spent. The dance of language seems ready to continue, and the arguments remain open to skepticism. As Gertrude Stein wrote (in *The Geographical History of America*), "In writing not any one finishes anything. That is what makes a master-piece what it is that there is no finishing."[4] Or, responding to Ashbery, the only way to preserve the life of the moment is never to acknowledge that it has passed.

All four of these playwrights have been accused of self-indulgence, so there is a danger in reinforcing that false impression by valuing Stein's idea of incompletion or Ashbery's of the preservation of moments only for the ways they advance our sense of theatrical *form*. For Stein and Ashbery, as for the best formally inventive playwrights, such ideas are most important for how they help illuminate larger matters of human conduct. In ways never apparent to critics who recognize moral significance only when it's announced, these playwrights experiment with the social dimensions of language. Indeed, once writing becomes speech, it inevitably absorbs social pressures. There's no such thing as "pure" language in this work (much as admirers of Wellman, in particular, would like us to believe). Instead, language is impelled by circumstance and returns to address facts of life visible to all – racial identity in some plays by Parks; sexual and religious identity, in the work of Greenspan; the allure of immoral thought, in some of Shawn's writing; the equally dangerous joys of demagoguery (and its roots in fear), as seen in many of Wellman's plays.

Yet the ramifications of these writers' works go further than specific issues. When David Greenspan encourages us to listen patiently to a character's painstaking revision of a single sentence, he is also cajoling us to engage critically with our own experience. As Suzan-Lori Parks's characters return to a key situation, enacting it repeatedly, she may also be suggesting that one's social contract requires constant maintenance, that the fullest lives are those attended to with the greatest self-consciousness. The perils of complacency also concern Shawn and Wellman. When a character in Shawn follows a line of reasoning as far as it will take him, or when one in Wellman weaves an enormous network of linguistic and aural correspondences, it is not possible glibly to sum up and dispense with the action. All four of these writers resist simplifications and urge spectators to reconsider even the most basic assumptions – the smallest units of thought and speech.

How is such a reexamination accomplished in practical terms? Furthermore, how can a writer take up Stein's injunction and show that a play is always spinning, that it still continues after the last lines are spoken? All but improvisatory plays are finished products, aren't they? How then can a play convey the energy of making discoveries? Finally, how can one tell the difference between lively and inert speech?

Wallace Shawn proposes one approach when he writes out the act of inquiry. Such characters as Aunt Dan in *Aunt Dan and Lemon* (1985) and, especially, the unnamed speaker in *The Fever* (1991) seize an idea at the start of their plays and then probe it relentlessly for the rest of their time before us. For Shawn, the "means of keeping moments" of thought is the endless questioning of them.

Any playwright hoping to explore moral concerns eventually comes to terms with the risk of seeming pompous. The least convincing moral art is invariably the most pithy; quotable observations rarely contain the substance needed to be accurate. Shawn recognizes these dangers at the outset, and in his most provocative work he addresses them as much as he speculates on larger political questions. For in fact there is no separation: "Morality" or "political commitment" have particular lives in language, and the way we talk about them reveals the deeper significance of what one truly thinks.

Such a premise should be obvious, but when *Aunt Dan and Lemon* and *The Fever* first appeared they were greeted in some quarters with a disdain that only someone uninterested in discourse could feel. Both plays contain ugly ideas – a "just" genocide of the Vietnamese defended in *Aunt Dan*; the "nuisance" of the poor lamented in *The Fever* – but Shawn's subject isn't so much the ideas as the manner of speaking that leads one to embrace them. Shawn explores how one thinks one's way to disgusting thoughts, and does so by entering gingerly into the thoughts himself – trying them out so as to resist them better. The experimental nature of his endeavor seems to have been lost on those who dismiss him.

Shawn's notion of "experimental," in fact, is crucial to understanding him. He takes nothing for granted about the ideas that concern him. Rather, he starts from scratch, analyzing their smallest components, the words themselves. Throughout his plays, characters are always puzzling out the meaning of individual words, as though they believe that only by first nailing them down can one ever stand securely on an argument. For Lemon, the dangerously vague word is "compassion." "I remember my mother screaming all the time, 'Compassion! Compassion! You have to have compassion for other people! You have to have compassion for other human beings!' And I must admit, there's something I find refreshing about the Nazis . . . . because they sort of had the nerve to say, 'Well, what *is* this compassion?' "[5] Lemon may never convince us of her humanity, but by observing her we have an opportunity to question our own.

In *A Thought in Three Parts,* an early play whose title alone suggests the analytic impulse behind all of Shawn's writing, a couple is equally hard on the word "love." "Do you know what love means?" asks one character, only to find out that neither of them can adequately define it, nor explain what they're doing with each other. The lone speaker of *The Fever* is the most impatient with the words he hears and speaks. Shawn forces us to pay attention to the workings of an argument by stripping his play of all the trappings of "theater." The action consists mainly of a person sitting at a desk talking about his visit to Latin America, and the crisis of thought it provoked. In one passage, he tells of encountering a man throwing about terms he'd "encountered all of my life," although, till then, he'd "never met anyone who actually used them" – terms like "the ruling class," "the elite," "the rich." Later, he looks again at another term that he senses is important for his purposes, but that has also suddenly lost all its meaning: "commodity fetishism." Anxious about his privilege and tempted to join the poor he sees around him, Shawn's speaker drolly assumes he's guilty of this vice – but without first defining it, he can't hope to see his way toward penance.

From words Shawn moves to lines of reasoning, and from them to whole systems of belief. At each stage of his analysis, as he explains in the afterword to *Aunt Dan and Lemon,* he is determined to show how seductive a well-tooled thought can be. There's something captivating about logic, he knows – and also something numbing. One is so dazed by the workings of a sharp mind that one can easily overlook the substance of its pronouncements. They sound so plausible, so definitive – and they're witty, too! Shawn hopes to break the spell: not by sounding an alarm, but rather by letting us succumb to a character's charm and agree to one apparently sound proposition after another, so that eventually, on our own, we'll be appalled at where we've let ourselves be taken.

The crux of any Shawn play is that moment when the arguing mind suddenly crosses the line into a forbidden idea. "Take the uncomprehending poor out to be shot," says the speaker in *The Fever.* "If we hadn't bombed them . . . " says Aunt Dan, and then launches into a paean to Kissinger. By writing the outrageous thought, Shawn forces himself to experience it from the inside. And only by holding himself to that moment of speech, not running past it or trying immediately to atone for it, will he understand how careless are all the daily uses of speech. Here, the simple act of making an assertion suddenly seems violent.

Shawn's theater succeeds at being "moral" because it doesn't attempt to convince us of anything. Rather, it works to unconvince us – of unexamined pieties, hoary assumptions, ideas that are vulnerable to misuse. If we recognize the dangers of rationalism, he suggests, we'll become more truly reasonable. If we observe the bullying and opportunism inside a well-crafted argument (as we see in Aunt Dan's tirades), we'll better resist it, and may even discover a way of arguing that is free of coercion. If we learn how close explanation is to self-justification, and how easily language prettifies real horror, we'll better be able to use language to penetrate the moral world. If first we doubt, maybe we'll eventually be able to believe with greater conviction.

The reactionaries, phonies, and well-heeled guilty in Shawn's plays aren't horrifying only for what they believe. If they were, his plays wouldn't be so troubling to all the people who never liked Kissinger in the first place, or who understood better the responsibility of their privilege. Instead, the greatest shock comes when a character, "good" or "bad," gives up the inquiry and settles for a conclusion. For then, nothing can be discovered anymore: He is trapped inside his own small world of thought. The speaker in *The Fever* argues himself into passivity – unable to give up privilege, no longer eager to act on his distaste for the poor, and skeptical of the value of charitable acts. His idleness doesn't come from despair or self-hatred; it's a condition of language – *his* language.

The character in *The Fever,* for all his pathos, had briefly suggested an alternative, which eventually he passed over. At one point he starts to shed all his opinions, even the nihilistic ones: "Dear God, what's happening to me? I feel like there's nothing left of me. I feel like I don't think anything – I don't remember – . . . . What are the things I always say? I believe that there are – . . . . I believe that – ."[6] The dashes of silence after his words are the most important moments of the speech, for they are full of potential. His process of losing his beliefs is painful, yet his pain also presents an opportunity – for criticism or silent empathy, perhaps also the steady evolution of new impulses into thoughts of greater complexity. That process, though, should never end, Shawn implies; one should always "feel like I don't think anything." Only by ceaselessly asking questions can one ever genuinely engage with one's world. The Gertrude Stein who saw the merits in incompletion would approve.

David Greenspan answers Stein by pushing even further back into the workings of consciousness, tirelessly analyzing instinct and emotion. His plays discuss gay identity, sex, family, death, loneliness, and ambition – but the overriding theme is always language. Using his ostensible subjects as raw material, he demonstrates the mechanics of speech, paying special attention to the act of revision. He refuses to edit out the false starts, warmups, and follow-ups that surround the rare moment when people say exactly what they intend. A typical Greenspan monologue consists of multiple versions of a single thought – lust for a fellow character, say, or despair over someone's illness – and allows a spectator to hear the speaker sift out all that might have been or that shouldn't have been thought. Even the most trivial thought, such as a writer's daydream of fame, comes fraught with the anxiety that it won't be expressed adequately:

> Well, I think it's – I think . . . . Right, well, I think it's a complex . . . . Right, well, I think it's complex, you know. Right, well . . . . Right, well, I think it's complex, you know. Right, well, being . . . . you know, being well-known, you know, being famous, whatever, has never been that important to me. I mean[7]

Greenspan writes like a pianist going over a progression of notes until he gets it right – or like a composer at work pushing through a particularly difficult passage, not sure of his direction. Before going on to a new bar of music, he goes back over what's achieved so far, revving himself up.

Greenspan's speeches of revision are never primarily important for what is said (much of the content is, in fact, banal), but they do offer a way to study how emotion evolves over the course of speaking. Moments of revision can reveal the encroachments of fear or egotism. They can allow one to see how self-doubt resolves into self-confidence, or how it escalates into rage. They can show characters still in the making, still open to suggestion – unpresentable, and therefore most affecting. Greenspan is drawn to moments of vulnerability, and his speakers are most vulnerable when they don't know what to say.

The endless revisions also encourage audiences to listen harder, for the changes in a line of speech are subtle, occurring usually in intonation or emphasis. But such a change – stressing the word "I" rather than "think," for instance – rearranges the distribution of emotional weight in an entire scene. Greenspan works on a minute scale: no panoramic tales, no Shawn-like moral debates, not even a simple love story. Discrete moments of feeling are more compelling. And when they are explored exhaustively they can be as overwhelming as an adventure-filled epic.

On the surface *2 Samuel 11, Etc.* (1989) is a study in idleness. A writer sits at his desk, blocked. One of his characters, a woman, stands before him, by her sheer presence goading him to get to work. Instead, the writer indulges in lurid sexual fantasies and masturbates. Later, having written almost nothing, he takes a long shower – and the play ends. Beneath this surface, however, is a vivid picture of consciousness – of the imagination at war with reason, and the separate regions of the imagination at war with themselves. Greenspan isolates numerous kinds of mental activity in order accurately to portray something hitherto only lazily explored in theater: psychology. In the first half, he further clarifies psychology by assigning all the words his writer would have spoken to the female character. Like us, the speechless writer observes the workings of his own mind. Each level of consciousness has its own language: the calm words of his created character (a version of Bathsheba); the overheated seduction monologue; the everyday self, answering the phone; and the thoughts that run beneath all of this, cajoling him to work harder. Id, ego, and superego are all given the floor.

Each of these kinds of speech is easily thwarted. Bathsheba's tale is shoved aside by the fantasy; the fantasy is interrupted by the phone ringing, or by the writer urging himself to "put this down on paper." Even the longest uninterrupted passages are full of spasmodic, unfinished language. An utterance is an attack on remote experience – a substitute for impossible contact, for instance, or an attempt at making an uncooperative character come to life. As he assembles all these attempts, Greenspan stages a picture of sheer hopefulness – and remarkable patience as the hopes are repeatedly dashed.

Music again provides an apt analogy: Greenspan's speakers are like the figure of Einstein in Robert Wilson's *Einstein on the Beach,* sitting at the front of the stage and sawing away at the violin for long stretches of time, repeating stoically the same few phrases of Philip Glass's score, not breaking his concentration and oblivious to the spectacle transpiring behind him. He's tremendously moving in his solitude. Continuing to play longer than one thought possible, he seems aware that even the smallest goal requires contant searching. Suturing himself in place with his music, he ensures that at least one thing will be known fully: his living presence.

Einstein's arms moving feverishly are as eloquent about his state as the music they play. And so it is with Greenspan's characters, who insist on restoring physicality to speech. Certainly, a lot of Greenspan's writing concerns sex, and many of his characters conduct their most rigorous linguistic explorations while in a condition that draws special attention to the body – in the shower, sitting on the john. But Greenspan also finds a way for speaking itself to seem kinetic. In his play *Jack* (1990), three characters speak about the death (from AIDS) of the title character, who sits quietly near them. Like the figures in urns from Beckett's *Play,* they talk in fractured sentences, pursuing their own paths until, amazingly, they link up with the others. Greenspan avoids sentimentality by breaking up the sentiment into pieces – and also achieves a more complex kind of theatrical emotion. Different memories of Jack collide and dispute with one another as they take shape in language; pain or indifference rushes into the gaps in speech; characters seem to use speech as an instrument to pare away layers of memory in search of the "true" Jack, or at least a true feeling about Jack.

Almost no one in *Jack* says how he or she feels, preferring instead simply to chronicle Jack's life and demise. But Greenspan does much with this self-imposed limitation: He modulates the pace of speech to suggest all the emotions withheld. As the characters begin to describe the onset of Jack's illness, for instance, the language jams up, loses its previous rhythm, and seems to swerve off course:

SPEAKER 1:	SPEAKER 2:	SPEAKER 3:
and so	I think it began; I think this is where it began.	 this is –
		no – no; this is not when it started long before but no one knew it no one knew what was going on.
it began. It it it began Jack began		 No. Christ! No.

<table>
<tr><td></td><td></td><td>Began (?!) as if it
  could
  begin.</td></tr>
<tr><td>began to</td><td></td><td></td></tr>
<tr><td></td><td>I</td><td></td></tr>
<tr><td> to get</td><td>think this is</td><td></td></tr>
<tr><td>it is where</td><td>when did Jack</td><td>Jack;</td></tr>
<tr><td>when</td><td>get sick?</td><td>no</td></tr>
<tr><td></td><td></td><td>no.[8]</td></tr>
</table>

And when description fails, speakers grind their wheels in a single ordinary word: "like like like like like like like like."

The word "like" gets harder to say the more it is repeated; moreover, it loses all shred of meaning. The coarse, open-ended sound of it alone expresses the largeness of the loss, and how hard it is to know it adequately. It can't be compared to anything – it's "like" . . . what? Yet *not* to speak would probably be more painful. Greenspan's characters have enduring faith that by using words they can pin down the mysteries of their lives – even if the words themselves are not, in the end, sufficient. The fear of losing experiences and emotions keeps them talking, even when, despite their best intentions, the talking isolates them.

"Hold it. Hold it. Hold it. Hold it. Hold it. Hold it. Hold it." All the characters in Suzan-Lori Parks's *The Death of the Last Black Man in the Whole Entire World* (1990) say "Hold it" seven times as the play ends. The lines capture the contradiction between fixity and flux that gives the play such energy. Her characters always try to mark the sensations and perceptions of their lives, but know too that nothing holds for more than a moment. The play is a portrait of the ensuing desperation. In these last lines, the characters reiterate their command as a way of resisting the inevitable. The title behaves the same way: It speaks of death, but as it stretches on, adding "entire" to "whole," it refuses to end.

Like David Greenspan, Parks is a fanatic reviser. Her plays, beginning with *Imperceptible Mutabilities in the Third Kingdom* in 1989, sound like fugues of language, always turning back on themselves in order to travel again through significant perceptions. On the surface, her writing seems too private, like a prayer never meaningful for those who overhear it. But Parks's repetitions – of key phrases, gestures, entire actions – move us deeper into tense situations and troubling thoughts; and when those thoughts concern racial identity, the uses of power, and the distortions of orthodox history writing, Parks's use of reiteration encourages us to be more skeptical of what we experience in and out of the theater.

The Death of the Last Black Man chronicles a succession of near-deaths of a character known only as Black Man with Watermelon – by electrocution, hanging, drowning, and sheer exhaustion. He doesn't die – or perhaps he has always been dead and yet continues to haunt the other characters (who also have names that play off black stereotypes: Lots of Grease and Lots of Pork, Black Woman with Fried Drumstick, among others). Parks's characters take great pride in eluding finality – Black Man is on the run for much of the play – much as the play itself shirks conventional ideas of character, narrative, and dramatic speech. "Some things is all thuh ways gonna be uh continuin sort of uh some thing," says the Black Man, using the propulsive, breath-filled way of speaking that for Parks carries more life than orthodox dialogue.[9]

The idea of "continuin" is vexing: These characters, for all their lively engagement with one another, spend most of their energy negotiating with time itself. On the one hand, they long for endlessness: "Before Columbus," says Queen-then-Pharaoh Hatshepsut, "thuh worl usta be roun. They put uh /d/ on thuh end of roun makin roun*d*. Thusly they set in motion thuh enduh. Without that /d/ we could uh gone on spinnin forever." But at the same time they hope to root themselves in history: "You should write it down," Yes and Greens says to Black Man, "because if you don't write it down then they will come along and tell the future that we did not exist."[10]

The contradiction isn't meant to be reconciled, only acknowledged. The spinning "worl" offers seemingly limitless possibility – no death, no vulnerability to entrapment. By letting the moments pass and shirking fixed identity, these characters keep alive and spiritually free. But with the passing of time comes pathos: It's all too easy to pass one by or be passed over. The politics of race underlies this entire rarefied discussion of time: As Alisa Solomon notes in an early essay on Parks, the "worl" in its spinning can also spin right past black experience, as though it never filled even a moment. So even as Parks's figures celebrate flight and the possibilities it offers, they seem equally serious about the need for the dignity that comes only with holding your ground. The Black Man, for instance, is eager to fix people in the present moment: "I: be. You: is. It: be . . . You: still is. They: be . . . You. Remember me."[11]

Time is made of language in *The Death of the Last Black Man*. Verbs alone indicate passage, anticipation, feeling. "There is uh Now and there is a uh Then. Ssall there is," says Black Man. "Thuh me-has-been sits in thuh beme; we sit on this porch."[12] As characters work over language this way, time ceases to be an abstraction. Rather, it can be manipulated as deftly as one can fiddle with grammar and syntax. By speaking, Parks suggests, one can arrest phenomena that would otherwise pass unnoticed: The utterance marks the spot. And by "continuin" to speak, one stands a chance of always being able to master history. One rides with time.

Parks's next major play literally digs into the past – it meditates upon archeology – and emerges with more strategies for preserving moments and regaining mastery over time. *The America Play* (1993) is set in a huge hole, where Lucy and her son Brazil are excavating objects from their own and the country's history. They retrieve documents, medals, wooden teeth – and by holding them they take hold of time. *The America Play* is both a story of a family (and its loss) and a nation (and *its* loss). Parks travels between the two zones, sifts the spiritual and historical dirt of both, contemplates the relics of one to learn about the other.

We also hear from Lucy's late husband, the Foundling Father, who had his own way of entering history: He impersonated Abraham Lincoln, and for a slight fee would reenact his assassination. *The America Play* echoes with his mimicry – always preceded by his lilting, confident spiel:

> The death of Lincoln: The year was way back when. The place: our nations capitol. Forescore, back in the olden days, and Mr. Lincolns great head. The the-a-ter was "Fords." The wife: "Mary Todd." Thuh freeing of thuh slaves and thuh great black hole that thuh fatal bullet bored. How that great head was bleedin. Thuh body stretched crossways acrosst thuh bed. Thuh last words. Thuh last breaths. And how thuh nation mourned.[13]

Every time the Foundling Father sits in "Lincoln's Chair" at "Ford's Theater" and "dies," he is doing more than merely returning to a legendary moment. He is also forcing the past back into the present, and thus enabling himself to revise history. By putting himself in the place of the Great Man, and laughing his laugh ("Haw, Haw, Haw") just before the shot, he experiences for a moment a kind of significance otherwise inaccessible. He speaks his way toward what he had been denied.

Whether they search for signs of the past, as Lucy and Brazil do, digging for relics, or make themselves into a sign of the past, as the Foundling Father does with acting, the characters of Parks's theater are always hoping better to understand their relation to their inheritance. Parks herself is intent on understanding all the forces that bring a character to life on stage, and takes almost nothing for granted about the apparatus of theater: speech, space, movement, presence. Watching her work, a spectator eventually comes to share this hyperawareness. At key points during *The America Play,* Parks urges us to pause and pay attention to everything surrounding her characters' activities. This is what one such passage looks like on the page:

> BRAZIL:
> LUCY:
> BRAZIL:
> LUCY:[14]

Lucy and Brazil aren't saying anything during these sections, but Parks wants to be sure a production (or a reader) doesn't just whip past, anxious about what's coming next. So she writes the silences into her text, like a composer. She frames them, and so tells us how much time we should spend listening. The effect is much like that of John Cage's *4′33″*: During the four minutes and 33 seconds in which no music is played, we learn to listen to all the sounds ordinarily passed over – air conditioning, the rustling of spectators, breathing, traffic in the distance. During Parks's measured silences, we start to perceive all the aspects of theater we would normally ignore – preeminently, the drama of time passing. During these passages, time no longer moves the way it does in other drama. It is now seen, heard, *felt* as it passes. With this radically simple gesture, Parks comes closest to answering Ashbery's challenge. Such moments of performance give of themselves only because Parks has given us the means of keeping them.

Wallace Shawn, David Greenspan, and Suzan-Lori Parks, for all their vast differences, share a belief that spectators will note the mechanics of speech if the focus narrows and the components of language are analyzed closely. Mac Wellman is just as serious about getting his listeners to really listen, but he tries a far more antic strategy. Wellman shares Gertrude Stein's partiality for a language in which "words have the liveliness of being constantly chosen." One may not immediately (or ever) understand what his characters are talking about, but the zeal with which they speak persuades us to keep trying.

Reading or watching Wellman's plays is like taking a roller coaster ride on tracks of speech. Many passages move so fast that they sound as if Wellman were anxious about being caught writing at all. His vocabulary is rich in hyperbole and neologisms; his diction tangles easily; anything that threatens the rapture of talking – like standard grammar or characterization – is discarded. Wellman seems to fear being parsed, for that would make his plays smaller than the spectator, and slower, too. He writes with the conviction that plays are animate, and so the writing keeps changing voices, contexts, and rhythms as a reminder of the unpredictability of all mortal creatures.

Wellman's most engaging characters are visionaries. They fix on an idea and launch themselves into lyrical flight. Readily going to extremes, they seem amazed at where language has taken them – out from under stifling ideas of proper dialogue, far from polite behavior, deep into a realm of big emotions. Wellman is fond of quoting Blackmur's phrase "language as gesture," and gives the concept a more concrete application than Blackmur, in his discussions of poetry, probably ever imagined. Wellman's language doesn't acquire its full shape, persuasiveness, and moral thrust until it is spoken. He is tuned to what Blackmur calls the "language beneath or beyond or alongside the language of words," and believes too that, as Blackmur puts it, "gesture is native to language, and if you cut it out you cut roots and get a sapless and gradually a rotting if indeed not a petrifying language."[15] But even more than Blackmur, Walt Whitman is Wellman's muse. Of his *Leaves of Grass,* Whitman wrote:

> It is a language experiment – an attempt to give the spirit, the body, the man new words, new potentialities of speech – an American range of self-expression. The new world, the new times, the new peoples, the new vistas need a tongue according – yes, what is more, will have such a tongue – will not be satisfied until it is evolved.[16]

Wellman's theater tries to show this "evolving" of the tongue. His plays rarely display well-crafted arguments or sparkling wit, and for all their linguistic dexterity, they share nothing with the work of other verbal wizards like Wilde or Shaw or even Mamet. The shagginess of Wellman's work is often used against him: He's overwriting, some say, or underclarifying; nothing coheres. What's the point? Where's it all going? The complaints are just, in many cases, but they also show exactly what's so invigorating about Wellman's best work. Those very qualities that seem frustrating can also open the way for a kind of alert engagement with the act of performance rarely available in the contemporary theater.

Many of Wellman's plays are generated by his disgust with phoniness, especially as it sustains the worlds of politics, commerce, and fashion. His popular 1990 play *Terminal Hip* depicts a solitary man raging at all manner of hucksterism. In *Bad Penny* (1989), Wellman's characters lash out at urban and moral decay. And *Murder of Crows* (1991) assails the ease with which genuine belief (in an idea, a morality, or a god) descends to mere posturing. In much of his work, Wellman uses speech as a scourge: As his characters tear away at falseness, they clear space for other kinds of speech – the free-ranging hypothesis, the careful inquiry, the prophesy, the giddy lyric – as in this passage from *Bad Penny*:

> I think the true sky must
> be a wonderful, wonderful place where
> all the lost things of the world assemble,
> are discovered, and are kept in safe-keeping.
> Forever. Safe forever. Lost hats, socks,
> thumbtacks; I think there is a separate place
> for solitary shoes and socks and other stuff,
> solitary stuff. I think there is a separate
> place for twisted paperclips, and too-short
> pencil stubs, and old newspapers, like big,
> dumb birds with broken wings, skittering
> across the pavement, the pavement of the sky . . . .[17]

The momentum of these speeches can be irresistible. Wellman's characters grow more fevered the more they say. Just as one vision clarifies, two, three, or ten more rise up over their imaginative horizons and demand acknowledgment. Listeners move through such passages moment to moment, not allowed to stop and linger. We're in thrall to a spectacle of speech. Each phrase obliterates the one before it, for each is fanciful on its own terms and is charged with so much passion that retaining them all is near impossible. Yet that passion holds Wellman's plays together. He writes about the unending struggle to find the words elastic enough to contain unruly experience.

An expectation of imminent apocalypse hangs over Wellman's recent work. Little can be done, he implies, to avoid ethical decadence and ecological ruin on a cosmic scale. But his plays also show impatience with this same fatalism: There's no excuse, he seems to say, for a what-me-worry lack of engagement, for not addressing the reasons behind the disaster and at least protesting its inevitability. (The anger in these plays makes it hard to understand why so many critics describe them as whimsical, and, in their cultish admiration for Wellman, turn him into a jester.) *The Land of Fog and Whistles* (1993) is typical of Wellman's outraged, cynical science fiction. The solitary speaker, one of the few creatures on Pluto (here a toxic-waste dump "destroyed by plutonium contamination nine times over"), is surrounded by her memories of the detritus of life as it once was known: gadgets, apparel, toys, foods, machines – junk meant to give shape to experience and substance to personality, but whose flimsiness wasn't apparent until it failed. The speaker catalogues the scraps, nevertheless, hoping to reassemble some notion of humanity. She could be any number of recent Wellman characters: Small, feisty voices in the midst of huge, entropic chaos, they share a driving interest in figuring out just where a human being belongs in such a despoiled world.

A man in *Bad Penny* is so terrified of the "senseless whirling" of the moon and stars and the "mad merry-go-round of comings and goings" that he interrogates the cosmos. A woman in the same play can't abide the standard mythology of her life anymore, not when evil is so everpresent and inexplicable. The three crows in *Murder of Crows* want even more answers – about "the basic issues of being . . . where we come from . . . whither we are headed." "You gotta think about these things, or you'll go crazy," a crow says as the play ends.[18]

The crow addresses a variety of audiences. Whenever a character speaks in one of Wellman's plays, one hears complete commitment to each word. *Terminal Hip,* for instance, is a long poem that, on the surface, seems like mere automatic writing, arcane wordplay. It *is* playful, certainly, but when spoken it also seems deadly serious, as though the character believes that his words are getting close to something no one has ever said. That commitment informs Wellman's entire sense of aesthetics. He has been mercilessly critical of theater that refuses to admit the existence of evil or moral disarray. Such plays are like proverbs: charmingly phrased, reassuring, and invariably insufficient. (*Bad Penny* contains a memorable chorus of such platitudes.) They hardly impress characters who doubt quick explanations and wonder at the meanings beneath appearances. And once those characters locate possible meanings for their experiences, a new challenge arises: What to believe? "Our sad, wretched unbelief," says a woman in *Bad Penny*, caught on the "Bow Bridge of our human unknowability."[19]

Wellman's plays implicitly ask what one needs to do to have faith. Does one follow the people in *Murder of Crows* and create private gods – a "black radio" for one, a light coming through a prism for another? Does one believe only in the most horrifying aspects of life – "asbestos, oily rags, power, mold," a man says in *Bad Penny*, as though he knows that anything purer would be soon ruined? Perhaps the inner worlds of fancy and instinct offer the only possibility for belief. No one can dispute the truth of what isn't shared, whether it be the conspiracy theories in so many of Wellman's plays or the sense of subterranean energies no one else feels. (Weather forecasting becomes an occult activity in *Murder of Crows*.) Still other characters are committed only to changeability: In a world of reductive thinking, the freedom of indeterminacy seems revolutionary – and eminently reliable.

But most of Wellman's characters have greater tenacity. They are certain that if they sustain an intense scrutiny of an idea, its importance will reveal itself and the quandary of belief will be solved. With their long speeches and high-pitched passions, Wellman's characters finally learn to have faith in their power to surround in speech what threatens to surround them.

Wellman joins Shawn, Greenspan, and Parks in insisting that one's belief in the power of imagination needs to be renegotiated at every juncture. They remind their audiences that the meanings assigned to ideas, and the systems by which one organizes and reflects on one's experiences, require constant vigilance. The moments pass too quickly and urge an endless renewal of our attentions. This exhausting task may be a reason why these writers have yet to find as wide an audience as they deserve. None of their plays feels final, none satisfies utterly. Rather, each seems to bode much for the one coming next, or looks most impressive when seen in relation to those it followed. In a sensitive and respectful discussion of *The Death of the Last Black Man,* Robert Brustein suggested that Parks's work will be even more exciting once she "clarifies her vision" – a sentiment that many critics have at one time or another echoed in assessments of the other three writers as well.

This lack of clarification, unsatisfaction, lack of completeness – hardly qualities one feels comfortable praising in a work of art. How difficult, too, to see the seriousness in a style that consciously tries for restlessness. Yet this work is praiseworthy and serious for exactly these qualities. These writers probably wouldn't mind being assailed for the evolving nature of their work. They argue against satisfaction and shapeliness (as they're commonly understood) in the theater, and warn that the decay of belief begins once one stops questioning the foundations of belief. These plays are always trying to shirk their knowability, always eluding categories. They are works in progress in the most spirited sense of the term: The writing is going on before our eyes; the seams are torn open so the work of inquiry can continue. Or, as Wellman puts it in *Terminal Hip*, "plod on, question, squirt, debamboozle . . . untranslate the square fable."[20]

This writing is easiest to discuss for its formal, "experimental" qualities. Even its ramifications for the conduct of life are accessible to those who seek them out. But the plays are perhaps most impressive for their often overlooked emotional stature. Each of these writers is determined to do whatever possible to get thought down on paper. "You should write it down," says Yes and Greens. "I've got to put this down," says the writer in *2 Samuel 11, Etc.* "Maybe we haven't looked into the question with sufficient rigor," says a crow in *Murder of Crows*. "Listen. I want to tell you something," says the speaker in *The Fever.*

They echo the similar calls of their predecessors – from the quiet assertiveness of Stein, asking "what happened?" before telling us in her first play, and Williams, whose Tom pledges a writer's loyalty to memory in *The Glass Menagerie,* to the more fevered pitch in later years: The inarticulate Lee crying "I gotta write somethin' out on paper!!" in Shepard's *True West;* Fornes's couple in *The Danube* hoping to master the coming nightmare by mastering its language; and Kennedy's Clara, her diaries in *A Movie Star Has to Star in Black and White* having made her "a spectator to her own life," vowing to "write a page a day," no matter how tired she is.

For all of these writers, no mere dutiful recording will do, though. The language must be as full, as vibrant, as complex as the experience itself – and have the resonance of speech. Foreman keeps reminding them that the enterprise may be doomed, of course: How lively is even the liveliest art when compared to life? Knowing that, these writers keep at it anyway. They dramatize only the attempt, and so achieve that rarity in the theater – poignancy unaccompanied by self-congratulation.

NOTES

INTRODUCTION

1 Gertrude Stein, *Lectures in America* (Boston: Beacon Press, 1985), pp. 118–19.
2 Quoted in Bert O. States, *The Shape of Paradox: An Essay on Waiting for Godot* (Berkeley: Univ. of California Press, 1978), epigraph preceding p. 1.
3 Robert Lowell, *Notebook* (New York: Farrar, Straus, & Giroux, 1970), p. 262.
4 Roland Barthes, *The Responsibility of Forms: Critical Essays on Music, Art, and Representation*, trans. Richard Howard (New York: Hill & Wang, 1986), p. 286.
5 Arthur C. Danto, "Dislocationary Art" (*Nation*, January 6/13, 1992), p. 30.

1. GERTRUDE STEIN

1 Gertrude Stein, *Lectures in America* (Boston: Beacon Press, 1985), p. 25.
2 Ibid., p. xi.
3 Ibid., p. 230.
4 Gertrude Stein, *Everybody's Autobiography* (London: Virago Press, 1985), p. 277.
5 *Lectures in America,* p. 84.
6 Ibid., pp. 118, 119.
7 Gertrude Stein, *Geography and Plays* (Boston: Four Seas Company, 1922), p. 205.
8 Ibid., pp. 207–8.
9 Ibid., p. 206.
10 Antonin Artaud, *The Theatre and Its Double,* trans. Mary Caroline Richards (New York: Grove Press, 1958), p. 108.
11 Gertrude Stein, *Operas and Plays* (Barrytown, N.Y.: Station Hill Press, 1987), p. 155.
12 Quoted in John Malcolm Brinnin, *The Third Rose: Gertrude Stein and Her World* (Reading, Mass.: Addison-Wesley, 1987), pp. 172–3, 185.

13 *Lectures in America,* p. 165.
14 Ibid., p. xiv.
15 Gertrude Stein, *Selected Writings* (New York: Vintage Books, 1990), p. 246.
16 *Lectures in America,* p. 183.
17 Ibid., p. 174.
18 *Geography and Plays,* pp. 327, 323.
19 Gertrude Stein, *Selected Operas and Plays of Gertrude Stein,* ed. John Malcolm Brinnin (Pittsburgh: Univ. of Pittsburgh Press, 1970), p. 275.
20 *Operas and Plays,* pp. 306, 181, 73.
21 Ibid., pp. 18–39.
22 *Lectures in America,* pp. 104–5.
23 Ibid., pp. 176–7.
24 Gertrude Stein, "A Translatlantic Interview 1946," in Robert B. Haas, ed., *A Primer for the Gradual Understanding of Gertrude Stein* (Santa Barbara, Calif.: Black Sparrow Press, 1971), p. 20.
25 *Operas and Plays,* p. 19.
26 *The Third Rose,* pp. 212–13.
27 *Selected Writings,* p. 262.
28 *Everybody's Autobiography,* p. 104.
29 Ibid., p. 50.
30 *Selected Operas and Plays,* p. 233.
31 Ibid., p. 181.
32 Ibid., p. 201.
33 Ibid., p. 202.
34 *Lectures in America,* p. 217.
35 *Selected Operas and Plays,* pp. 168–9.

2. TENNESSEE WILLIAMS

1 Tennessee Williams, *27 Wagons Full of Cotton and Other One-Act Plays* (New York: New Directions, 1966), p. 50.
2 Tennessee Williams, *Three by Tennessee* (New York: New American Library, 1976), p. 132.
3 Tennessee Williams, *Memoirs* (Garden City, N.Y.: Doubleday, 1975), p. 41.
4 Susan Sontag, "Going to Theater," *Partisan Review* 31, no. 1 (Winter 1964), pp. 95–102. The reference to Williams, in a section primarily about Edward Albee, is on p. 98.
5 Gore Vidal, Introduction to Tennessee Williams, *Collected Stories* (New York: New Directions, 1985), pp. xxiii–xxiv.
6 *Three by Tennessee,* pp. 130–1.
7 Tennessee Williams, *Four Plays* (New York: New American Library, 1976), p. 31.
8 Clive Barnes, quoted in Catherine M. Arnott, ed., *File on Tennessee Williams* (London: Methuen, 1985), p. 53.
9 Tennessee Williams, *The Glass Menagerie* (New York: New Directions, 1970), p. 50.

10 Ibid., p. 48.
11 Ibid., p. 52.
12 Tennessee Williams, *A Streetcar Named Desire* (New York: New American Library, 1947), pp. 81–3.
13 Ibid., p. 91.
14 Ibid., p. 96.
15 Ibid., p. 117.
16 Tennessee Williams, *Cat on a Hot Tin Roof* (New York: New Directions, 1975), p. 61.
17 *Cat on a Hot Tin Roof,* pp. 116–17.
18 Norman Mailer and Gore Vidal, "Mailer and Vidal" (a conversation), *Esquire,* May 1991, p. 110.
19 *Cat on a Hot Tin Roof,* p. 24.
20 Ibid., p. 173. The scene between Big Daddy and Big Mama occurs on p. 80.
21 Quoted in C. W. E. Bigsby, *A Critical Introduction to Twentieth-Century American Drama,* vol. 2 (Cambridge, U.K.: Cambridge Univ. Press, 1984), p. 91.
22 Tennessee Williams, *Clothes for a Summer Hotel* (New York: New Directions, 1983), p. 26.
23 *Four Plays,* p. 79.
24 *Memoirs,* p. 144.
25 Letters reprinted in *The Theatre of Tennessee Williams,* vol. 5 (New York: New Directions, 1990), p. 294.
26 Richard Gilman, "Williams Shocked American Theater into Maturity," *New York Times,* 29 April 1990, pp. 7, 32; "Tennessee Ascending," *Village Voice*, 3 Oct. 1989, pp. 103, 106.
27 Interview with Arthur Bell, *Village Voice,* 24 Feb. 1972 (quoted in *File on Tennessee Williams,* p. 74).

3. SAM SHEPARD

1 David Sylvester, *The Brutality of Fact: Interviews with Francis Bacon* (London: Thames and Hudson, 1987), p. 12. Discussion of paint throwing appears on pp. 90–6.
2 Sam Shepard, "Rip It Up," in *Hawk Moon* (New York: PAJ Publications, 1981), p. 55.
3 Sam Shepard, "Language, Visualization and the Inner Library," in Bonnie Marranca, ed. *American Dreams: The Imagination of Sam Shepard* (New York: PAJ Publications, 1981), pp. 216–17.
4 "Language, Visualization and the Inner Library," p. 215.
5 Sam Shepard, *Fool for Love and Other Plays* (New York: Bantam Books, 1984), p. 147.
6 *Fool for Love and Other Plays,* pp. 154–5.
7 Quoted on the book cover of Sam Shepard, *Motel Chronicles* (San Francisco: City Lights Books, 1982).
8 "Language, Visualization and the Inner Library," p. 217.

9 Robert Hughes, *Frank Auerbach* (New York: Thames & Hudson, 1990), p. 149.
10 Sam Shepard, *Seven Plays* (New York: Bantam Books, 1984), pp. 214–15.
11 Ibid., pp. 247, 225.
12 Ibid., p. 227.
13 *Motel Chronicles,* p. 42.
14 *Fool for Love and Other Plays,* p. 169.
15 Sam Shepard, *The Unseen Hand and Other Plays* (New York: Bantam Books, 1986), p. 268.
16 *Fool for Love and Other Plays,* p. 215.
17 Kenneth Chubb and the Editors of *Theatre Quarterly,* "Metaphors, Mad Dogs and Old Time Cowboys: Interview with Sam Shepard," in *American Dreams: The Imagination of Sam Shepard,* p. 208.
18 Ibid., p. 197.
19 *Fool for Love and Other Plays,* p. 77.
20 *The Unseen Hand and Other Plays,* p. 220.
21 Ibid., pp. 225–6.
22 *The Unseen Hand and Other Plays,* p. 236.
23 *Fool for Love and Other Plays,* p. 156.
24 *The Unseen Hand and Other Plays,* p. 226.
25 Ibid., p. 229.
26 Ibid., p. 53.
27 *The Unseen Hand and Other Plays,* p. 152.
28 Quoted in Don Shewey, *Sam Shepard* (New York: Dell, 1985), p. 175.
29 "Language, Visualization and the Inner Library," p. 217.
30 Quoted in *Sam Shepard,* p. 122.
31 Quoted in ibid., p. 47.
32 Bonnie Marranca, "Alphabetical Shepard: The Play of Words," in *American Dreams: The Imagination of Sam Shepard,* p. 30.
33 Joyce Aaron, "Clues in a Memory," in *American Dreams: The Imagination of Sam Shepard,* p. 174.
34 Interview with Michiko Kakutani, quoted in John Dugdale, ed., *File on Shepard* (London: Methuen, 1989), p. 62.
35 Jonathan Cott, "The *Rolling Stone* Interview: Sam Shepard," *Rolling Stone* (18 December 1986–1 January 1987), pp. 166–72, 198, 200.
36 *Motel Chronicles,* pp. 55–6. The photograph appears on p. 56.
37 *Seven Plays,* p. 130.
38 Ibid., p. 196.
39 Ibid., p. 167.
40 Sam Shepard, *A Lie of the Mind* (New York: New American Library, 1986), p. 57.

4. MARIA IRENE FORNES

1 Maria Irene Fornes, "I Write These Messages That Come," in *The Drama Review* 21, no. T76 (December 1977), p. 26.

2 Maria Irene Fornes, *Promenade and Other Plays* (New York: PAJ Publications, 1987), p. 132. In his interview with Fornes, "Seeing with Clarity: The Visions of Maria Irene Fornes" (*Theater,* Winter 1985), Scott Cummings first drew my attention to this passage.
3 Maria Irene Fornes, *Plays* (New York: PAJ Publications, 1986), p. 25.
4 *Promenade and Other Plays,* p. 74.
5 Ibid., pp. 83–6.
6 Ibid., p. 18.
7 Ibid., p. 37.
8 Ibid.
9 Ibid., p. 44.
10 Bonnie Marranca, *Theatrewritings* (New York: PAJ Publications, 1984), p. 72.
11 Maria Irene Fornes, *Abingdon Square,* in *American Theatre* 4, no. 11 (Feb. 1988), p. 8.
12 *Promenade and Other Plays,* pp. 129–35.
13 Ross Wetzsteon, "Irene Fornes: The Elements of Style," *Village Voice* (29 April 1986), p. 43.
14 *Theatrewritings,* p. 69. The quotation from Susan Sontag is from her preface to *Plays,* p. 8.
15 "Seeing with Clarity," p. 55.
16 Maria Irene Fornes, *Fefu and her Friends*, in *Word Plays* (New York: PAJ Publications, 1980), p. 13.
17 Maria Irene Fornes, "Creative Danger," in *American Theatre* 2, no. 5 (Sept. 1985), p. 15.
18 *Word Plays,* pp. 16–17.
19 Ibid., p. 12.
20 Ibid., p. 9.
21 Ibid., p. 19.
22 Ibid., p. 24.
23 Ibid., p. 20.
24 "Irene Fornes: The Elements of Style," p. 43.
25 Ibid., p. 44.
26 "Seeing with Clarity," p. 55.
27 Ibid., p. 55, and "Maria Irene Fornes" in David Savran, *In Their Own Words* (New York: Theatre Communications Group, 1988), p. 55.
28 *Plays,* p. 85.
29 Ibid., p. 39.
30 Ibid., p. 40.
31 Maria Irene Fornes, *Drowning,* in Anne Cattaneo, ed., *Orchards* (New York: Alfred A. Knopf, 1986), p. 61.
32 "Seeing with Clarity," p. 55.

5. ADRIENNE KENNEDY

1 Adrienne Kennedy, *People Who Led to My Plays* (New York: Theatre Communications Group, 1988), p. 59.

2 Adrienne Kennedy, *Adrienne Kennedy in One Act* (Minneapolis: Univ. of Minnesota Press, 1988), p. ix.

3 As far as I know, Kennedy has never discussed Bachelard, and it is unlikely that, if she has read *The Poetics of Space,* she would have done so before 1964, when the first English translation was published. Incidentally, in an unpublished, unproduced musical for which Kennedy wrote the book, *Film Festival: The Day Jean Seberg Died* (1984), a character mentions his admiration for Bachelard.

4 Adrienne Kennedy, "A Growth of Images," *The Drama Review* 21 (December 1977), p. 42.

5 Gaston Bachelard, *The Poetics of Space* (Boston: Beacon Press, 1969), p. 9.

6 Paul K. Bryant-Jackson, "An Interview with Gerald Freedman" in Paul K. Bryant-Jackson and Lois More Overbeck, eds., *Intersecting Boundaries: The Theatre of Adrienne Kennedy* (Minneapolis: Univ. of Minnesota Press, 1992), pp. 206–15; Elinor Fuchs, "Adrienne Kennedy and the First Avant-Garde," ibid., pp. 76–84; and Howard Stein, "An Interview with Gaby Rodgers," ibid., pp. 199–205.

7 Personal interview, March 1991.

8 *The Poetics of Space,* pp. 13–14.

9 *People Who Led to My Plays,* p. 14.

10 Herbert Blau, *The Eye of Prey: Subversions of the Postmodern* (Bloomington: Indiana Univ. Press, 1987), p. 60.

11 Ibid., p. 57.

12 *Adrienne Kennedy in One Act,* p. 63.

13 *People Who Led to My Plays,* p. 81.

14 Ibid., p. 69.

15 Ibid., pp. 72–3, 98.

16 *Adrienne Kennedy in One Act,* pp. 1–2.

17 Ibid., pp. 5–6.

18 Ibid., p. 6.

19 Ibid., p. 7.

20 Ibid., p. 13.

21 Ibid., p. 22.

22 Adrienne Kennedy, *Cities in Bezique* (New York: Samuel French, 1969), p. 42.

23 Ibid., p. 37.

24 Ibid., p. 39.

25 *The Poetics of Space,* pp. 223–4.

26 *Cities in Bezique,* p. 41.

27 Adrienne Kennedy, *Deadly Triplets* (Minneapolis: Univ. of Minnesota Press, 1990), p. 105.

28 Ibid., pp. 112, 124.

29 *Adrienne Kennedy in One Act,* p. 87.

30 Ibid., p. 99.

31 Ibid., p. 97.

32 Ibid., p. 88.

33 Adrienne Kennedy, *The Alexander Plays* (Minneapolis: Univ. of Minnesota Press, 1992), p. 27.
34 *The Poetics of Space,* p. 192.
35 Ibid., p. 216.
36 Ibid., p. 231.
37 *The Alexander Plays,* p. 38.
38 Ibid., p. 53.
39 Ibid., p. 61.
40 *Adrienne Kennedy in One Act,* p. 77.

6. RICHARD FOREMAN

1 Richard Foreman, *Plays and Manifestos* (New York: New York Univ. Press, 1976), pp. 48–9.
2 Personal interview, March 1991.
3 Paul Valéry, *The Art of Poetry*, trans. Denise Folliot (Princeton, N.J.: Princeton Univ. Press, 1985), pp. 115–16.
4 Ibid., pp. 184–5 (emphasis Valéry's).
5 Ibid., p. 146 (emphasis Valéry's).
6 Personal interview, March 1991. Quoted in Marc Robinson, "A Theater of One's Own," *Village Voice*, 23 April 1991, pp. 92, 94.
7 Michael Feingold, "An Interview with Richard Foreman," in *yale/theatre* 7, no. 1 (Fall 1975), p. 8.
8 Richard Foreman, *Unbalancing Acts: Foundations for a Theater* (New York: Pantheon Books, 1992), p. 68.
9 "An Interview with Richard Foreman," pp. 10–11.
10 Rainer Maria Rilke, *The Selected Poetry of Rainer Maria Rilke,* ed. and trans. Stephen Mitchell (New York: Vintage Books, 1984), p. xli.
11 Quoted in the notes to ibid., p. 338.
12 *Plays and Manifestos,* p. 1.
13 Ibid., pp. 18–19.
14 *Unbalancing Acts,* p. 69.
15 Personal interview, March 1991. Quoted in "A Theater of One's Own," p. 92.
16 *The Selected Poetry of Rainer Maria Rilke,* p. 336.
17 Richard Foreman, *Reverberation Machines: The Later Plays and Essays* (Barrytown, N.Y.: Station Hill Press, 1985), pp. 215–16.
18 *Unbalancing Acts*, p. 209.
19 *Reverberation Machines,* p. 193.
20 *Unbalancing Acts,* p. 77.
21 *The Selected Poetry of Rainer Maria Rilke,* p. 247.
22 Ibid., p. 253.
23 *Unbalancing Acts,* p. 4.
24 *Plays and Manifestos,* p. 207.
25 Ibid., p. 129.
26 *Reverberation Machines,* p. viii.

27 Ibid., p. 189.
28 *Plays and Manifestos*, p. 213.
29 Ibid., p. 223.
30 *Reverberation Machines*, pp. 21, 23.
31 Ibid., p. 40.
32 Ibid., pp. 51, 61.
33 Ibid., p. 177.
34 Ibid., p. 180.
35 Ibid., p. 184.
36 Richard Foreman, *Love and Science: Selected Music-Theatre Texts* (New York: Theatre Communications Group, 1991), p. 133.
37 *Unbalancing Acts*, p. 105.
38 Ibid., p. 114.
39 Ibid., p. 122.
40 *Reverberation Machines*, p. 239.
41 *Unbalancing Acts*, pp. 314–15.
42 Paul Valéry, *Selected Writings of Paul Valéry* (New York: New Directions, 1964), p. 190. This passage, from "Dance and the Soul," is translated by Dorothy Bussy.
43 *Unbalancing Acts*, pp. 123–4.
44 Ibid., p. 126.
45 Ibid., pp. 127–8, 131, 134.
46 Ibid., p. 206.
47 Ibid., p. 282.
48 Ibid., p. 293.
49 Ibid., p. 262.

AFTERWORD: NEW DIRECTIONS

1 John Ashbery, *Rivers and Mountains* (New York: Holt, Rinehart & Winston, 1967), p. 30.
2 John Cage, *M*, quoted in Natalie Crohn Schmitt, *Actors and Onlookers: Theater and Twentieth-Century Scientific Views of Nature* (Evanston, Ill.: Northwestern Univ. Press, 1990), p. 34.
3 R. P. Blackmur, *Language as Gesture* (New York: Harcourt, Brace & Co., 1952), p. 19.
4 Gertrude Stein, *The Geographical History of America or the Relation of Human Nature to the Human Mind* (New York: Random House, 1936), p. 194.
5 Wallace Shawn, *Aunt Dan and Lemon* (New York: Grove Press, 1985), p. 83.
6 Wallace Shawn, *The Fever* (New York: Farrar, Straus, & Giroux, 1991), p. 36.
7 David Greenspan, *The Home Show Pieces* (*Plays in Process* 13, no. 6) (New York: Theatre Communications Group, 1992), p. 3-1.
8 David Greenspan, *Jack*, in M. Elizabeth Osborn, ed., *The Way We Live Now: American Plays and the AIDS Crisis* (New York: Theatre Communications Group, 1990), p. 158.

9 Suzan-Lori Parks, *The Death of the Last Black Man in the Whole Entire World,* in *Theater* 21, no. 3 (Summer/Fall 1990), p. 86.
10 Ibid., p. 87.
11 Ibid., p. 92.
12 Ibid.
13 Suzan-Lori Parks, *The America Play* (unpublished MS, 1993), p. 62. As with *The Death of the Last Black Man,* the unconventional spelling and grammar are deliberate. (As this book went to press, *American Theatre* magazine announced plans to publish the play.)
14 *The America Play,* p. 66.
15 *Language as Gesture,* pp. 3–4.
16 Quoted in H. L. Mencken, *The American Language* (New York: Alfred A. Knopf, 1937), p. 73.
17 Mac Wellman, *Bad Penny* (unpublished MS, 1989), pp. 2–3.
18 Mac Wellman, *Murder of Crows* (*Plays in Process* 13, no. 3) (New York: Theatre Communications Group, 1991), pp. 9-35, 9-37.
19 *Bad Penny,* pp. 17, 19.
20 Mac Wellman, *Terminal Hip,* in *Performing Arts Journal* 14, no. 1 (Jan. 1992), p. 56.

BIBLIOGRAPHY

PRIMARY SOURCES

Foreman, Richard. *Eddie Goes to Poetry City, Part I.* Unpublished manuscript, 1991.

Eddie Goes to Poetry City, Part II. Unpublished manuscript, 1991.

Love & Science: Selected Music-Theatre Texts. New York: Theatre Communications Group, 1991.

Madame Adare. Theater 12, no. 3 (Summer 1981), pp. 4–15.

The Mind King. Unpublished manuscript, 1992.

Pandering to the Masses: A Misrepresentation. In *The Theatre of Images.* Edited by Bonnie Marranca. New York: Drama Book Specialists, 1977.

Plays and Manifestos. Edited by Kate Davy. New York: New York Univ. Press, 1976.

Reverberation Machines: Later Plays and Essays. Barrytown, N.Y.: Station Hill Press, 1985.

Unbalancing Acts: Foundations for a Theater. Edited by Ken Jordan. New York: Pantheon Books, 1992.

Fornes, Maria Irene. *Abingdon Square. American Theatre* 4, no. 11 (Feb. 1987), special insert.

And What of the Night. Unpublished manuscript, 1990.

Cap-a-Pie. Unpublished manuscript. 1975.

adapt. and trans. *Cold Air,* by Virgilio Pinera (*Plays in Process* 6, no. 10). New York: Theatre Communications Group, 1985.

"Creative Danger." *American Theatre* 2, no. 5 (Sept. 1985), pp. 13–15.

Drowning. In *Orchards.* Edited by Anne Cattaneo. New York: Alfred A. Knopf, 1986.

Evelyn Brown (A Diary). Unpublished manuscript, 1980.

Fefu and Her Friends. In *Word Plays.* Edited by Bonnie Marranca and Gautam Dasgupta. New York: PAJ Publications, 1980.

"I Write These Messages That Come." *The Drama Review* 21 (Dec. 1977), pp. 25–40.

adapt. and trans. *Life Is a Dream*, by Pedro Calderón de la Barca. Unpublished manuscript, 1981.

The Office. Unpublished manuscript, 1965.

Oscar and Bertha. In *Best of the West*. Edited by Murray Mednick, Bill Raden, and Cheryl Slean. Los Angeles: Padua Hills Press, 1991.

Plays. New York: PAJ Publications, 1986.

Promenade and Other Plays. New York: PAJ Publications, 1987.

The Red Burning Light. In *Promenade and Other Plays*. Edited by Michael Feingold. New York: Winter House, 1971.

A Visit. Unpublished manuscript, 1981.

Fornes, Maria Irene, Tito Puente, and Fernando Rivas. *Lovers and Keepers* (*Plays in Process* 7, no. 10). New York: Theatre Communications Group, 1987.

Greenspan, David. *The Home Show Pieces* (*Plays in Process* 13, no. 6). New York: Theatre Communications Group, 1992.

Jack. In *The Way We Live Now: American Plays and the AIDS Crisis*. Edited by M. Elizabeth Osborn. New York: Theatre Communications Group, 1990.

2 Samuel 11, Etc. (*Plays in Process* 11, no. 5). New York: Theatre Communications Group, 1990.

Kennedy, Adrienne. *Adrienne Kennedy in One Act*. Minneapolis: Univ. of Minnesota Press, 1988.

The Alexander Plays. Minneapolis: Univ. of Minnesota Press, 1992.

Cities in Bezique: The Owl Answers and A Beast Story. New York: Samuel French, 1969.

Deadly Triplets: A Theatre Mystery and Journal. Minneapolis: Univ. of Minnesota Press, 1990.

An Evening with Dead Essex. *Theater* 9, no. 2 (Spring 1978), pp. 66–78.

Film Festival. Unpublished manuscript, 1984.

"A Growth of Images." *The Drama Review* 21 (Dec. 1977), pp. 41–8.

People Who Led to My Plays. New York: Theatre Communications Group, 1987.

Kennedy, Adrienne, John Lennon, and Victor Spinetti. *The Lennon Play: In His Own Write*. In *Best Short Plays of the World Theatre 1968–1973*. Edited by Stanley Richards. New York: Crown Publishers, 1973.

Parks, Suzan-Lori. *The America Play*. Unpublished manuscript, 1993.

The Death of the Last Black Man in the Whole Entire World. *Theater* 21, no. 3, (Summer/Fall 1990), pp. 81–94.

Imperceptible Mutabilities in the Third Kingdom. Unpublished manuscript, 1989.

Shawn, Wallace. *Aunt Dan and Lemon*. New York: Grove Press, 1985.

The Fever. New York: Noonday Press / Farrar, Straus, & Giroux, 1991.

Marie and Bruce. New York: Grove Press, 1980.

A Thought in Three Parts. In *Word Plays 2*. New York: PAJ Publications, 1982.

Shepard, Sam. *Fool For Love and Other Plays*. New York: Bantam Books, 1984.

Fool For Love and *The Sad Lament of Pecos Bill on the Eve of Killing His Wife*. San Francisco: City Lights Books, 1983.

Hawk Moon: A Book of Short Stories, Poems, and Monologues. New York: PAJ Publications, 1981.

A Lie of the Mind and *The War in Heaven* (with Joseph Chaikin). New York: New American Library, 1986.

Motel Chronicles. San Francisco: City Lights Books, 1982.

Rolling Thunder Logbook. New York: Limelight Editions, 1987.

Seven Plays. New York: Bantam Books, 1984.

States of Shock; Far North; Silent Tongue. New York: Vintage Books, 1993.

The Unseen Hand and Other Plays. New York: Bantam Books, 1986.

Stein, Gertrude. *The Autobiography of Alice B. Toklas*. New York: Vintage Books, 1960.

Everybody's Autobiography. London: Virago Press, 1985.

Fernhurst, Q.E.D., and Other Early Writings. New York: Liveright, 1971.

The Geographical History of America or the Relation of Human Nature to the Human Mind. New York: Random House, 1936.

Geography and Plays. Boston: Four Seas Company, 1922.

Ida. New York: Vintage Books, 1972.

Last Operas and Plays. Edited by Carl Van Vechten. New York: Rinehart, 1949.

Lectures in America. Boston: Beacon Press, 1985.

Look at Me Now and Here I Am: Writings and Lectures 1909–45. Edited by Patricia Meyerowitz. Harmondsworth: Penguin Books, 1971.

The Making of Americans. New York: Harcourt, Brace & World, 1962.

Operas & Plays. Barrytown, N.Y.: Station Hill Press, 1987.

Paris France. New York: Liveright, 1970.

Selected Operas and Plays. Pittsburgh: Univ. of Pittsburgh Press, 1970.

Selected Writings of Gertrude Stein. Edited by Carl Van Vechten. New York: Vintage Books, 1990.

Three Lives. New York: Modern Library, 1933.

Useful Knowledge. Barrytown, N.Y.: Station Hill Press, 1988.

Wellman, Mac. *Bad Penny*. Unpublished manuscript, 1989.

The Land of Fog and Whistles. *Theater* 24, no. 1, 1993, pp. 52–8.

Murder of Crows. (*Plays in Process* 13, no. 3). New York: Theatre Communications Group, 1991.

Terminal Hip. *Performing Arts Journal* 14, no. 1 (1992), pp. 52–72.

"The Theatre of Good Intentions." In *Performing Arts Journal* 8, no. 3 (1984), pp. 59–70.

Williams, Tennessee. *Camino Real*. New York: New Directions, 1970.

Cat on a Hot Tin Roof. New York: New Directions, 1975.

Clothes for a Summer Hotel. New York: New Directions, 1983.

Collected Stories. Introduction by Gore Vidal. New York: New Directions, 1985.

Dragon Country. New York: New Directions, 1970.

Four Plays. New York: New American Library, 1976.

The Glass Menagerie. New York: New Directions, 1970.

A Lovely Summer for Creve Coeur. New York: New Directions, 1980.

Memoirs. Garden City, N.Y.: Doubleday, 1975.

The Red Devil Battery Sign. New York: New Directions, 1988.

A Streetcar Named Desire. New York: New American Library, 1947.

The Theatre of Tennessee Williams, vol. 5. New York: New Directions, 1990.

Three by Tennessee. New York: New American Library, 1976.

27 Wagons Full of Cotton and Other One-Act Plays. New York: New Directions, 1966.

Vieux Carré. New York: New Directions, 1979.

SECONDARY SOURCES

Arnott, Catherine M. *File on Tennessee Williams*. London: Methuen, 1987.

Artaud, Antonin. *The Theater and Its Double*. Translated by Mary Caroline Richards. New York: Grove Press, 1958.

Ashbery, John. *Rivers and Mountains*. New York: Holt, Rinehart & Winston, 1967.

Bachelard, Gaston. *The Poetics of Space.* Translated by Maria Jolas. Boston: Beacon Press, 1969.

Barthes, Roland. *The Responsibility of Forms: Critical Essays on Music, Art, and Representation.* Translated by Richard Howard. New York: Hill & Wang, 1986.

Bartow, Arthur. *The Director's Voice: Twenty-One Interviews*. New York: Theatre Communications Group, 1988.

Bentley, Eric. *What Is Theatre? (Incorporating The Dramatic Event)*. New York: Limelight Editions, 1984.

Betsko, Kathleen, and Rachel Koening. *Interviews with Contemporary Women Playwrights.* New York: Beech Tree Books, 1987.

Bigsby, C. W. E. *A Critical Introduction to Twentieth-Century American Drama* (3 vols.). Cambridge, U.K.: Cambridge Univ. Press, 1984.

Blackmur, R. P. *Language as Gesture: Essays in Poetry*. New York: Harcourt, Brace & Co., 1952.

Blau, Herbert. *The Eye of Prey: Subversions of the Postmodern*. Bloomington, Ind.: Indiana Univ. Press, 1987.

Bordman, Gerald. *The Oxford Companion to American Theatre.* Oxford: Oxford Univ. Press, 1992.

Brater, Enoch, ed. *Feminine Focus: The New Women Playwrights.* Oxford: Oxford Univ. Press, 1989.

Brinnin, John Malcolm. *The Third Rose: Gertrude Stein and Her World.* Reading, Mass.: Addison-Wesley, 1987.

Brustein, Robert. *Who Needs Theatre?* Boston: Atlantic Monthly Press, 1988.

Reimagining American Theatre. New York: Hill & Wang, 1991.

Bryant-Jackson, Paul K., and Lois More Overbeck, eds. *Intersecting Boundaries: The Theatre of Adrienne Kennedy*. Minneapolis: Univ. of Minnesota Press, 1992.

Chinoy, Helen Krich, and Linda Walsh Jenkins, eds. *Women in American Theatre.* New York: Theatre Communications Group, 1987.

Cott, Jonathan. "The *Rolling Stone* Interview: Sam Shepard." *Rolling Stone* (Dec. 18, 1986), pp. 166, 168, 170, 172, 198, 200.

Cummings, Scott. "Seeing with Clarity: The Visions of Maria Irene Fornes" (interview). *Theater* 17 (Winter 1985), pp. 51–6.

Danto, Arthur C. "Dislocationary Art." *The Nation* (Jan. 6/13, 1992), pp. 29–32.

Davy, Kate. *Richard Foreman and the Ontological-Hysteric Theatre.* Ann Arbor, Mich.: UMI Research Press, 1981.

Diamond, Elin. "An Interview with Adrienne Kennedy." In *Studies in American Drama, 1945–Present* 4 (1989), pp. 143–57.

Dolan, Jill. *The Feminist Spectator as Critic.* Ann Arbor, Mich: UMI Research Press, 1988.

Donoghue, Denis. *The Arts without Mystery.* Boston: Little, Brown, 1983.

Dugdale, John. *File on Shepard.* London: Methuen, 1989.

Feingold, Michael. "An Interview with Richard Foreman." In *yale/theatre* 7, no. 1 (Fall 1975), pp. 5–29.

Fuchs, Elinor. "Presence and the Revenge of Writing: Rethinking Theatre after Derrida." In *Performing Arts Journal* 9, nos. 2–3 (1985), pp. 163–73.

Gass, William H. "Gertrude Stein and the Geography of the Sentence." In Gass, *The World within the Word.* Boston: David R. Godine, 1979.

"Gertrude Stein: Her Escape from Protective Language." In Gass, *Fiction and the Figures of Life.* New York: Vintage Books, 1972.

Gilman, Richard. *Common and Uncommon Masks: Writings on Theatre 1961–1970.* New York: Vintage Books, 1972.

The Confusion of Realms. New York: Vintage Books, 1970.

Glore, John. "The Canonization of Mojo Rootforce: Sam Shepard Live at the Pantheon." *Theater* 12, no. 3 (Summer/Fall 1981), pp. 53–65.

Haas, Robert B., ed. *A Primer for the Gradual Understanding of Gertrude Stein.* Santa Barbara, Calif.: Black Sparrow, 1971.

Hardwick, Elizabeth. *A View of My Own: Essays in Literature and Society.* New York: Farrar, Straus, & Cudahy, 1962.

Harris, David. "The Original *Four Saints in Three Acts.*" *The Drama Review* 26, no. 1 (1982), pp. 102–30.

Hart, Lynda, ed. *Making a Spectacle: Feminist Essays on Contemporary Women's Theatre.* Ann Arbor, Mich.: Univ. of Michigan Press, 1989.

Hill, Errol, ed. *The Theatre of Black Americans: A Collection of Critical Essays.* New York: Applause Books, 1987.

Hobhouse, Janet. *Everybody Who Was Anybody: A Biography of Gertrude Stein.* New York: Anchor Books, 1989.

Hoffman, Michael J., ed. *Critical Essays on Gertrude Stein.* Boston: G. K. Hall, 1986.

Hughes, Robert. *Frank Auerbach.* New York: Thames & Hudson, 1990.

James, Henry. *The Figure in the Carpet and Other Stories.* London: Penguin Books, 1988.

Jones, David Richard. *Great Directors at Work: Stanislavsky, Brecht, Kazan, Brook.* Berkeley, Calif.: Univ. of California Press, 1986.

Kauffmann, Stanley. *Theater Criticisms.* New York: PAJ Publications, 1983.

Kolin, Philip C., ed. *American Playwrights Since 1945.* New York: Greenwood Press, 1989.

Leverett, James. "Richard Foreman and Some Uses of Cinema." In *Theater* 9, no. 2 (Spring 1978), pp. 10–14.

Marranca, Bonnie. *Theatrewritings.* New York: PAJ Publications, 1984.

ed. *American Dreams: The Imagination of Sam Shepard.* New York: PAJ Publications, 1981.

Mencken, H. L. *The American Language.* New York: Alfred A. Knopf, 1937.

Pascal, Blaise. *Pensées.* Translated by A. J. Krailsheimer. Baltimore: Penguin Books, 1968.

Rilke, Rainer Maria. *The Selected Poetry of Rainer Maria Rilke.* Edited and translated by Stephen Mitchell. New York: Vintage Books, 1984.

Robinson, Marc. "A Theater of One's Own." *Village Voice* (April 23, 1991), pp. 92, 94.

Rogoff, Gordon. *Theatre Is Not Safe: Theatre Criticism 1962–1986.* Evanston, Ill.: Northwestern Univ. Press, 1987.

Savran, David. *In Their Own Words: Contemporary American Playwrights.* New York: Theatre Communications Group, 1988.

Schmitt, Natalie Crohn. *Actors and Onlookers: Theater and Twentieth-Century Scientific Views of Nature.* Evanston, Ill.: Northwestern Univ. Press, 1990.

Shewey, Don. *Sam Shepard.* New York: Dell, 1985.

Solomon, Alisa. "Signifying on the Signifyin': The Plays of Suzan-Lori Parks." *Theater* 21, no. 3 (Summer/Fall 1990), pp. 73–80.

Sontag, Susan: "Going to Theater." *Partisan Review* 31, no. 1 (Winter 1964), pp. 95–102.

Spoto, Donald. *The Kindness of Strangers: The Life of Tennessee Williams.* Boston: Little, Brown, 1985.

States, Bert O. *The Shape of Paradox: An Essay on Waiting for Godot.* Berkeley, Calif.: Univ. of California Press, 1978.

Sylvester, David. *The Brutality of Fact: Interviews with Francis Bacon* (3rd enlarged ed.). London: Thames & Hudson, 1987.

Treadwell, Sophie. *Machinal.* In *Plays by American Women: The Early Years.* Edited by Judith E. Barlow. New York: Avon Books, 1981.

Valéry, Paul. *The Art of Poetry.* Translated by Denise Folliot. Princeton, N.J.: Princeton Univ. Press, 1985.

Selected Writings. New York: New Directions, 1964.

Wasserstein, Wendy. *The Heidi Chronicles and Other Plays.* San Diego, Calif.: Harcourt Brace Jovanovich, 1990.

Wetzsteon, Ross. "Irene Fornes: The Elements of Style." *Village Voice* (April 29, 1986), pp. 42–5.

"Wally Shawn: The Holy Fool of the American Theater?" *Village Voice* (April 2, 1991), pp. 35–7.

Wilson, Edmund. *Axel's Castle.* New York: Scribner's, 1959.

INDEX

Index